GREAT
WRITING

Great
Britain

YOUR local
BOOKSHOP
SINCE 1982

1982

Waterstones

GRANTA

12 Addison Avenue, London W11 4QR | email editorial@granta.com
To subscribe go to www.granta.com, or call 845-267-3031 (toll-free 866-438-6150)
in the United States, 020 8955 7011 in the United Kingdom

ISSUE 119: SPRING 2012

EDITOR	John Freeman
DEPUTY EDITOR	Ellah Allfrey
ARTISTIC DIRECTOR	Michael Salu
ASSOCIATE EDITOR	Patrick Ryan
ONLINE EDITOR	Ted Hodgkinson
EDITORIAL ASSISTANT	Yuka Igarashi
PUBLICITY	Saskia Vogel
ASSISTANT DESIGNER	Daniela Silva
FINANCE	Geoffrey Gordon, Morgan Graver, Craig Nicholson
MARKETING AND SUBSCRIPTIONS	David Robinson
SALES DIRECTOR	Brigid Macleod
SALES MANAGER	Sharon Murphy
TO ADVERTISE CONTACT	Kate Rochester, katerochester@granta.com
IT MANAGER	Mark Williams
PRODUCTION ASSOCIATE	Sarah Wasley
PROOFS	Sarah Barlow, Katherine Fry, Juliette Mitchell, Jessica Rawlinson, Vimbai Shire
PUBLISHER	Sigrid Rausing
CONTRIBUTING EDITORS	Daniel Alarcón, Diana Athill, Peter Carey, Sophie Harrison, Isabel Hilton, Blake Morrison, John Ryle, Lucretia Stewart, Edmund White

This selection copyright © 2012 Granta Publications.

In the United States, Granta is published in association with Grove/Atlantic Inc., 841 Broadway, 4th Floor, New York, NY 10003, and distributed by PGW. All editorial queries should be addressed to the London office.

Granta, ISSN 173231, is published four times per year by Granta Publications, 12 Addison Avenue, London, W11 4QR.

The 2012 US annual subscription price is $48. Airfreight and mailing in the USA by agent named Air Business Ltd, c/o Worldnet Shipping Inc., 156–15, 146th Avenue, 2nd Floor, Jamaica, NY 11434, USA. Periodicals postage paid at Jamaica, NY 11431.

US POSTMASTER: Send address changes to Granta, PO Box 359, Congers, NY 10920-0359.

Subscription records are maintained at Granta Magazine, c/o Abacus Media, Bournehall House, Bournehall Road, Bushey WD23 3YG, UK.

Air Business is acting as our mailing agent.

Granta is printed and bound in Italy by Legoprint. This magazine is printed on paper that fulfils the criteria for 'Paper for permanent document' according to ISO 9706 and the American Library Standard ANSI/NIZO Z39.48-1992 and has been certified by the Forest Stewardship Council (FSC). Granta is indexed in the American Humanities Index.

ISBN 978-1-905881-56-7

CONTENTS

FICTION uncovered 2012

DISCOVER THE BEST OF BRITISH FICTION
SUMMER 2012

FICTION UNCOVERED FM
AT
FOYLES

Our radio station dedicated to British fiction
broadcasting live from Foyles on Charing Cross Road

FICTION UNCOVERED
AND THE
BOOK BARGE

Visit our floating bookshop on the canal
Leeds • Manchester • Oxford

live events, festival appearances and much more...

FICTION UNCOVERED 2012 TITLES ANNOUNCED 23 MAY 2012

Find out more at
fictionuncovered.co.uk

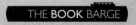

GRANTA

STEVENAGE

Gary Younge

In 1988 my mother took the bus to Stevenage town centre to do the weekly shop, came home and died in her sleep. She was forty-four; I was nineteen. Her passing was a matter of some civic note.

In the twenty years and more that she'd lived in the town my mother had been a nurse, schoolteacher, English teacher to Indian women, literacy teacher to adults, office bearer with the Stevenage West Indian Sports and Social Club and voluntary youth worker. She was deeply involved in the community. When she shopped she saw people she knew and when she saw people she knew she stopped and chatted. A single mother with three ravenous sons to feed on a tight budget, my mother had elevated bargain hunting to something of a science. She would team up with Mrs Provencal, a Ghanaian woman whose daughter was one of five black kids in my year at school. They worked the aisles of Sainsbury's and Tesco separately. Hovering around the breads and fruits on a Saturday afternoon until the goods were reduced to clear (stores didn't open on a Sunday back then), they would send word to each other of the price and ask how many loaves/buns/tomatoes were wanted. I know this because throughout my teens I was the messenger. Sprinting between stores with orders and prices through the drizzle and dusk like a human text message.

My mother's death made the front page of the *Stevenage Gazette*. For months afterwards former students and friends wrote touching letters to the paper in her memory. As news of the tragedy spread, a large number of people said how shocked they were, since they had seen her in the town centre just a few days before – as though anyone who goes shopping on Saturday could not possibly be dead by Sunday.

All of this meeting, greeting and shuttling, which – for my mother – were as integral to shopping as buying the groceries, did not happen by accident. Since the war, almost nothing about Stevenage had happened by accident. The new town was the product of two powerful forces: extensive planning and massive public investment. From the colour of the street signs to the layout of the town centre, everything was deliberate. As the first child of the New Towns Act, passed by the post-war Labour government, its conception was trumpeted with considerable fanfare. 'Stevenage will in a short time become world-famous,' said Lewis Silkin, the minister for Town and Country Planning, in 1946. 'People from all over the world will come to Stevenage to see how we, here in this country, are building for the new way of life.'

The same conditions responsible for bringing Stevenage New Town into existence – a state-led effort to rebuild the country – had brought my mother to Britain from Barbados. She arrived to work as a nurse in the NHS, which was founded two years after Stevenage was built. It was 1961, and she was eighteen and in possession of A levels in British Constitution, English Literature and European History and a British passport. The British government paid her fare so that she could work for the NHS and my mother paid them back once her training was complete and she had started earning. It was probably the only part of the transaction that did not involve a mutual deception. She thought she was coming to save money for a few years before returning 'home'. Instead she stayed for twenty-six years, raised a family and went back in a box (though she died suddenly, she had long insisted that she did not want to be buried in England). The government thought they were importing a worker, but a person came.

After training as a nurse, she reconnected with my father, a man she had known in Barbados and who had grown up in the same parish. They settled initially in Dulwich, south-east London, where my two older brothers were born. Then in the late sixties, after the wine company my father worked for relocated, they moved thirty miles north to Stevenage. My parents liked Stevenage for the same reason most people did – more space, good council housing, decent schools. The choice of house was more or less made for them by Nell Stilling, the woman who would become our neighbour and family friend. Most drew their curtains and looked askance at the prospect of a black family moving next door. Mrs Stilling, who read the *Mail* and adored the Queen, offered to warm the milk for my brother, who was then a baby. A couple of years later I was born and fifteen months after that my dad left.

While for my entire childhood Stevenage was the only place I really knew, it was not a place I would claim until I was much older. In *Gender and Nation*, Nira Yuval-Davis describes how Palestinian children in Lebanese refugee camps would call 'home' a village which may not have even existed for several decades but from which their parents were exiled. Stevenage was no refugee camp and my mother was no exile. Yet that sense of displacement, the rift between where you happen to be and where you understand you are from, was always familiar to me.

Until I was seventeen if anyone asked me where I was from I told them Barbados – a country I'd spent just six weeks in as a four-year-old. My mother was from elsewhere and proud of it. There was a flag of Barbados on our door and a map on our wall. The mantra was that when we walked into the house we were in Barbados.

My personal story certainly intensified these feelings of geographical ambivalence, but it didn't create them. Indeed, I think they were generally shared by my peers, regardless of their race and heritage. Beneath its concrete functionality, Stevenage may have hidden a number of idiosyncrasies; but for all that made it different, during the seventies and eighties being from Stevenage felt as though you weren't really from anywhere in particular. It was a place people passed on the train on their way up north or studied in town planning.

Otherwise it didn't feel obvious that anyone knew we were there. Our accent could best be described as 'not quite London' and no one could ever really place it on a map, not even another person from Stevenage if you met them elsewhere.

For most of my childhood the town did not have a football team. My friends were likely to support West Ham, Tottenham or Arsenal – the teams their parents had grown up with. The town's topography was completely unremarkable. When foreign exchange students came and asked what there was to see in town we would take them to London or Cambridge. To my knowledge only one of my friends' parents had actually gone to school in Stevenage.

For those raised amid natural beauty, Stevenage doubtless appeared hideous. During my first week as a student in Edinburgh I remember crossing George IV Bridge, looking to my left and seeing the upper ridge of Arthur's Seat over the Gothic masonry and wondering how such a thing – a huge hill in the middle of an old city – was possible. Then I looked to my right, saw the castle and realized that such imposing scenery was not just for school trips. People could actually live in it.

I've also always felt envious of people who feel a deep sense of affinity to where they live, whether it's beautiful or not. Liverpudlians, Glaswegians, Alabamians or Dubliners, whose sense of self is intimately connected to their sense of place. Stevenage could never quite provide that.

I don't think it's happenstance that for most of the last decade both of my brothers and I have lived outside the country (two of us in the US and one in Ireland) – there was little attachment to the soil to begin with and when it came to Stevenage there was precious little soil to attach yourself to.

But alongside the indifference to our immediate surroundings there was also the stubborn stain of the planners' Magic Marker. The town felt planned. It was colour-coded, with each neighbourhood assigned a specific shade so that you always knew where you were. In Bedwell, for example, where my mother had taught, all the street signs were blue; in Broadwater, where I grew up, they were brown. Designed to promote a sense of community, each area had its own smaller shopping centres with butchers, greengrocers, launderettes, newsagents and chip shops. The street names were also themed. One area paid tribute to great British women: Brontë Paths, Pankhurst Crescent, Eliot Road, Austen Paths, Siddons Road. Another was named for castles and stately homes: Blenheim Way, Balmoral Close, Ranworth Avenue, Petworth Close.

The town planners had given considerable thought to the traffic, too. The town was stitched together by almost a dozen roundabouts. Directions to my house from London were simple: exit the A1, go straight over six roundabouts and then turn right.

A lot of this worked. The way the town was built did make a sense of community possible. The local greengrocers and newsagents were run by my friends' dads; Mrs Stilling's son was the butcher. Mr Grix, who ran the hardware store, would cash Mum's cheques when there was more month left than money. And I don't remember seeing a single traffic jam, let alone a rush hour (although, since we didn't have a car, I can't say I was looking too hard).

So whatever sense of alienation we felt was environmental rather than social and had nothing to do with deprivation. As far as facilities were concerned it was a great place to grow up. It's just that we had no more reason to be there than anywhere else. The physical space we inhabited was shaped not by family ties, cultural affiliation or group identity but by some random, indifferent and entirely elusive force.

The town was literally built around us, with new developments perennially snacking on green space. By the age of eight, my eldest brother could legitimately look out from the bottom of our street and say: 'When I was growing up all this was fields.' It was only later that I would realize the obvious fact that those fields had once belonged to others. That the cows who used to graze at the very end of our street were part of some pre-municipal existence. Stevenage had at one stage been a quiet market town. In 1861 Charles Dickens described the high street as being 'like most other village streets: wide for its height, silent for its size, and drowsy in the dullest degree. The quietest little dwellings with the largest of window-shutters (to shut up nothing as if it were the Mint or the Bank of England . . .)'.

When Labour ordered the compulsory purchase of several thousand acres of land and started turfing people off their property after the war, there was considerable opposition. When Silkin came to town to explain his decision to dump 60,000 newcomers on their doorstep, he was roundly heckled. 'It's no good your jeering,' he told them. 'It's going to be done.' And done it was. One morning, in a final act of symbolic opposition, all the signposts to and from the town, as well as at the train station, were changed from Stevenage to Silkingrad.

In 1801 the population was 1,430; by 1901 it had almost trebled; by 2001 it had grown almost twentyfold to 79,724. In the end only the area around the Old Town high street remained unchanged. Within a generation, Stevenage's creation story had largely been expunged of these tales of imposition, resentment, displacement and conflict. Not, I think, because anyone thought we shouldn't know, but because few really cared.

My secondary school, Heathcote, was situated on the edge of Shephall Green. Every weekday, without ever knowing it, I walked through the only old hamlet in the New Town that had not been razed to the ground. Most of the Old Town did remain with Tudor-looking buildings, narrow alleyways and pubs aplenty. A huge flyover connected it to the New Town. As a teenager I went there to play chess and drink illegally with my mates. But I never had any sense, as I crossed over the dual carriageway, that I was a settler heading into indigenous territory. If I did then the racially charged order that I should 'go back to where I came from' would have been far easier to counter. We – the settlers – were all from somewhere else. And, at the outset at least, very few people wanted us there.

For better and for worse Stevenage came to exhibit most of the dreams, foibles, errors and successes of the post-war period. The brutality of war had made the political class utopian. The war's technological advances and social upheaval made it bold. Alongside a zeal for planning came a confidence that the state had not only a primary role in the rebuilding of the country but also a duty to shape the human environment. The town made no sense without government because, in its modern form, it would not exist without government. It was utilitarian to a fault, but the sting of ridicule recedes once one acknowledges both what it achieved and what it replaced. I remember seeing one of the final episodes of *Shine on Harvey Moon*, a TV series screened in the mid-eighties and set during the war. The family is huddled around a table in a cramped London flat when they get a letter telling them they've been accepted for a house in Stevenage. They're overjoyed. It's like they just got a green card or passed the Bar exam: it's a way in, out and up.

And as time went on there was plenty to be happy about. Stevenage boasted great amenities. A bowling alley, swimming pool, cinema, adventure playgrounds and youth clubs. In the mid-seventies a huge leisure centre with a theatre was completed. In the summer there were play schemes, where you could try table tennis, learn chess and do artwork, all funded by the local council. These became something of a family affair. My mother ran one in Shephalbury Park for several years, which my brothers and I attended as children. When we were old enough we worked in other play centres and then finally ran Shephalbury ourselves. As prizes for sports and good behaviour, we would hand out tokens for free admission to the bowling alley and the swimming pool, since all were council-run.

But primarily, particularly in light of the devastation to London's homes during and after the war, Stevenage's big draw was housing. In 2010 I came back to Stevenage to report on the general election. The town had become an electoral weathervane, voting for the winning side in every election since 1974. In 1979 it went from Labour to Tory, an event of particular importance because the MP at that time was Education Secretary Shirley Williams. In 1997 it went back to Labour, electing Barbara Follett, in many ways the personification of New Labour. In 2010, with the economy in collapse and public spending under scrutiny, the role of government was central to the debate. Stevenage in that context seemed the logical place to be. It voted Conservative.

I was surprised then, when interviewing people on my street where I'd grown up and others of my mother's generation, to discover how many professionals had been drawn in the sixties and seventies by the offer of good council housing with gardens front and back, three bedrooms and central heating. No one needed to tell you where the toilet was in any of the houses on our street because they were all in the same place. It was essentially the same house built over and over. The same was true elsewhere in town. But that degree of uniformity hadn't seemed to bother people back then, and social housing had yet to bear the stigma it holds now.

There was no sense of incongruity in Stevenage between being a young professional and living in social housing. That didn't make the town classless, but it certainly allowed for a diversity of aspiration and a population that ranged all the way from the fuck-ups to the foremen and from the uncivil to the civil servant. Among the fourteen or so families who lived on our row there was a policeman, a dinner lady, a contractor, a couple of painters and decorators, a couple of pensioners and an unemployed couple.

The predominance of council housing took both the shame and shine out of residency since there was nothing useful you could assume about anybody's status from where they lived, so long as they lived in Stevenage. There were poor people, us among them. But there were no 'no-go' areas. Stevenage was a working-class town, not as a euphemism for an area that was down-at-heel but in the sense that it was a town where people could find work. Combined with affordable housing, that was a great leveller. Throughout my junior-school years there were never more than three of us in my class who were on free dinners. People who lived there tended to work there. There was plenty to choose from: Kodak, Bowaters, Geo. W. King's – industry light and heavy, employment skilled and unskilled. Much of that work was deadly. The biggest employer in town was British Aerospace (BAe) which, among other things, made weapons. And while it did not quite reach the level of becoming a company town, it came close to feeling that way. The plant dominated the industrial area and absorbed school-leavers for apprenticeships. At one stage about an eighth of the town's workforce relied on it.

The residential mix and need for skilled labour made for good schools. The teachers were dedicated; the classes well resourced. It was all there if you wanted it. Growing up under a Bajan matriarchy that valued education above all else, my mother wanted it enough for all her children. There was never a time when I didn't think I had to go to university; there was never a time when I didn't think it was possible; and there was never anyone who suggested otherwise.

I recall one hot childhood summer, during lunch break at play scheme, sitting under a tree in Shephalbury Park talking with my brother and some friends about what we wanted to do when we grew up. Among us there were aspiring mechanics, models, footballers and hairdressers, all of whose pre-teen dreams were greeted with interest. My plans alone provoked screeches of derision: I said I wanted to go to university and be a doctor.

They laughed, in part because it was a square ambition for someone with a glamorous future to fantasize about. But also because it was so completely alien to any of our experiences. None of us at the time knew anyone who had been to university – apart from teachers, who, at that age, were an alien species anyway. I might as well have said I wanted to be Governor of the Bank of England, live underwater or become a centaur, since we didn't know anyone who had done those things either.

We worked hard and our mother sacrificed a great deal. But that would never have been sufficient by itself. Part of the answer as to how three black boys raised by a single mother made it to university does come down to government. Broke as we were, we never lived in an area that had been written off or went to schools that were written off, which means we were never written off. The county council gave stipends to the children of low-income families who stayed on until sixth form. All of us took free night classes at Stevenage College at O and A level. When I couldn't do all my options at school I did French there, falling asleep aged thirteen next to the heater after football practice, and being prodded by my nurturing teacher, Pierre. I went on to do A level with him. Most of the others in the college class were older folk with good French who wanted to keep it up so they could make good conversation with the locals on their holidays. It was not until I got to university where I studied to be a translator that I realized I'd learned pensioner French, with the words for things such as hip replacement and thermal underwear coming just a little too easily to me.

If the schools in Stevenage were good then education was, generally speaking, undervalued. Around 150 kids started my year in secondary school. It's my guess that around thirty stayed on after sixteen for sixth form, of whom around half went on to university. Many more could have done. Probably twice that number got decent O levels and could have easily pursued further education. But most didn't see the point. There was money to be made and the fruits of young adulthood to be tasted and to delay all that for more qualifications seemed pointless to them. Friends every bit as smart and smarter left at sixteen to work for the Gas Board, the railways and, of course, BAe. When I saw them again they would often lecture me about how my studying was a drain on their taxes. In the era of full grants and no tuition fees, other friends who wanted to go to university were discouraged from doing so by their parents. One friend's older brother, who worked at BAe, sat me down and calculated precisely, taking into account likely promotions, how much I would lose in wages if I was stupid enough to go to university. 'And that's not including overtime,' he added.

It was the eighties. Thatcher had our number; the *Sun* understood our impulses. Not greedy or venal necessarily – although Harry Enfield's 'Loadsamoney' character certainly struck a chord. But, in the wake of the ideological, electoral and organizational decline of the Labour Party, the labour movement and the Eastern bloc, the notion of public goods and the public good – the very concepts on which the town had been built – could not compete with the attractions of private materialism. The very creation of Stevenage New Town was underpinned by the notion that there was indeed such a thing as society, that it thrived through community and that government had a role in nurturing and sustaining both. Thatcherism was guided by the opposite.

The collapse of the political model that built Stevenage was not imposed against our will. Indeed, in many ways, the mood guiding its demise was far more consensual than that governing its invention. People rushed to it willingly and with open wallets. While it was a working-class town it was not particularly politically class-conscious and certainly not militant. Those who did not like Thatcher would talk, in broad terms, about her representing the rich. But that did not translate into any reflexive identification with trade union struggles or international solidarity campaigns.

During moments of patriotic fervour like the Falklands War, the royal wedding, the Queen's Jubilee or in the wake of an IRA attack, the town would rally dutifully to the flag. The devastation being wrought elsewhere, particularly up north and in the inner cities, felt like news from another country. Stevenage, during the early eighties, was doing fine – well, even. Those who weren't antagonistic towards the struggles of the miners, the GLC, teachers or the nurses, were, broadly speaking, ambivalent.

Outwardly, certainly, the biggest transformation came with the Housing Act in 1980. The legislation gave council tenants the right to buy their council house at a discount – the price depending on how long they'd been living in it – and forbade councils from spending the receipts until they had cleared their debts. In a town like Stevenage where most housing was originally of council stock, the effect was dramatic. With relatively little effort people immediately felt wealthier while the town – as an entity in itself – simultaneously became poorer.

People started to customize their homes with small front porches and paved garage ways.

House prices were soaring, and Stevenage became more of a commuter town. The boom meant more painting, more decorating, roofing and tiling – more reasons to leave school and make money. The building continued apace, but holistic planning was now a thing of the past. Big superstores started popping up on the outskirts of town, rendering the original pedestrianized shopping centre somewhat obsolete, since more people drove. Because people were less likely to get on the bus and go to town shopping, they were less likely to meet each other. Queensway was in the centre of town, but it was no longer a town centre in the way that it had been. If my mother had died in the same way ten years later, far fewer people would have seen her last hurrah in town.

When the housing market collapsed, house prices fell even as the porches remained. Some of my school friends had been through their first redundancy before their twenty-first birthday. As the council retreated from the housing market, so inequalities emerged between different parts of the town. With the council-housing stock depleted, the children of those who had bought were left to fend for themselves. Soon there were no-go areas. Gradually Stevenage gained a reputation for being a rough, even violent town. A few years back, while visiting Luton, I'd introduced myself to a couple of youngsters as someone from Stevenage. They sucked in hard as though I'd told them I'd grown up in the South Bronx.

Stevenage would have changed without Thatcherism. As young as my mother was when she died, Stevenage New Town was even younger and still developing. And it was not an island. Mr Grix, the local hardware store owner, could never have competed with B&Q; the end of the Cold War presented BAe with tough challenges and a town built with the traffic flow of 1946 in mind would always have had to re-evaluate its options. Thatcherism wasn't the only thing that happened to Stevenage, and some of what did happen was good. Central to the flowering of an organic identity, as opposed to one invented by the planners, was the emergence of a decent football team that finally made it to the league. Even that, however, would have been impossible without local government planning. In the seventies, the stadium had been bought by a private contractor who was so determined to use the land for something other than football that he dug the pitch up with JCB trucks and left it to rot. The council bought the land back, restored it, refurbished the stadium and the team went on to great things.

Queensway, once a hub, is now peppered with boarded-up shopfronts, charity stores, amusement arcades and loan shops. The bowling alley is now a car park; almost everything that was locally run has now been replaced by a chain, but the toilets are still free. The fountain and the clock tower are still standing, with the bronzed impression of Silkin somewhat tarnished with age. The years have not ravaged Stevenage but they have not been kind either. Mostly, though, it just feels empty – lacking the bustle of the social hub it once was.

In 2004, after thirty years of underperformance, my junior school 'rebranded' and changed its name. My secondary school, vamped up as a specialist engineering college, recently had its last intake and will close this year. In between the two schools is Shephalbury Park, where we used to spend summers at the play scheme. Portakabins now stand to one side as changing rooms for the footballers and cricketers who use the park. The pavilion has been burned down. You can walk across the still-paved floor, as though over a full-scale architect's floor plan, from the space where we played table tennis, to the arts room, and to the storage area where the balls, hoops and bats were kept. All that remains now are the concrete foundations; strong and grey, with small tufts of grass poking through the cracks. ∎

The Making of the English Landscape

It's too late now to start collecting football shirts,
bringing them back from trips abroad as souvenirs:
the sun-struck, God-given green and gold of Brazil;
Germany's bold, no-nonsense, trademark monochrome;
the loud red of 'emerging nation' South Korea;

then hanging them framed, arms folded across the chest
to show off the collars and cuffs and the piped sleeves
and the proud badges, shield-shaped, worn on the left breast,
embroidered with flags, mottos or mythical beasts.

So I'll turn instead to matters closer to home,
to these charters, maps and aerial photographs
of double ditches and heaped walls and lynchet banks,
of sheep trails still visible below city parks,
of drove roads contradicting four-lane motorways,
of sprawling farms underwritten by patchwork fields,
of capped wells, earthworks, middens and burial mounds,
the skeleton seen through the flesh, an embedded
watermarked view of when we were nothing and few.

And from outer space, this latest satellite image
taken just moments ago shows England at dusk,
its rivers cascading beyond its coast, the land
like a shipwreck's carcass raised on a sea-crane's hook,
nothing but keel, beams, spars, down to its bare bones.

WHEN YOU GROW INTO YOURSELF

Ross Raisin

A few drivers had slowed to look up at the side of the coach as it circled the roundabout. Along one stretch of its window, near the back, three pairs of white buttocks were pressed against the glass like a row of film-packed chicken breasts. As the coach lurched off the roundabout one of these pairs of buttocks briefly disappeared, before returning emphatically to its place alongside the others.

Inside the coach Tom sat alone beside his kitbag, looking across the aisle at the hysterical gurning faces of the three mooners. The middle one had dropped his trousers to his ankles, his cock bobbing stupidly with the motion of the vehicle as it overtook a caravan onto the dual carriageway. Tom turned away, embarrassed, glad that the short journey was nearly over.

The coach was on its way to a budget hotel on the outskirts of town, an away-match policy now insisted upon by the chairman in the aftermath of the opening weekend of the season. Tom had not been at the club then. He had signed a few weeks later, shortly after being let go by his boyhood club in a brief and tearful meeting with the new manager. The memory of that afternoon was still difficult to think about. All of the second-year apprentices lined up in the corridor among the new man's cardboard boxes and whiteboards; the office and its stale stink of the old manager's cigarettes. Tom had stood by the door as the manager perched on his desk, which was empty except for a scribbled piece of paper and a scratched glass case with a blue cap inside it.

'You're a good lad, Tommy. Your parents should be proud of you. No question you'll find a club. You're going to be some player, when you grow into yourself.'

Tom found out afterwards that he'd said the exact same thing to all of them, except the two he'd kept on. Eight lads he had progressed through all the youth levels with, all hoping now for another club to phone them as they thumbed through the jobs pages or took on work at the recruitment agency, the shopping centre, the multiplex, waiting to grow into themselves. Unlike most of them, though, Tom did find a club. A small town down south, near the coast. The chairman phoned up himself, one morning, and arranged for him to stay in a hotel for the night so that he could come down and talk to them.

'Who?' his sister had said when he told his family. 'League what?'

'Two. They came up from the Blue Square last year. Chairman says they've got some money behind them.'

His sister told him well done and then went upstairs to ring her friends and tell them the news.

The three backsides had returned to their seats. They were still laughing. One of them, scanning round to see if anybody was still watching them, caught Tom's eye, and Tom gave him a dumb grin before turning to look out of the window. Cars moved past them in the other lane. Out of some, the blue-and-yellow scarf of that day's opposition flapped and spanked against back windows, and one or two drivers honked their horns as they overtook the coach.

The match had begun promisingly. It was his first start for the team, and the sick cramping feeling of the changing room soon left him as he became quickly involved in the game. In one early muscular exchange, as possession swapped repeatedly from one side to the other, the ball spilled out to him on the wing and he ran instantly at the fullback, who, stumbling, tripped, ballooning the ball out over their falling bodies for a corner. A short way into the half, however, a bungle between the two central defenders – who were sat now in the seats in front of Tom watching *Total Wipeout* on a laptop – resulted in a goal for the home side. After that, the confidence went from the team. They lost 3–1. In the miserable sweaty fug of the changing room afterwards the manager called them a bunch of soft fucking faggots, and when one of the younger players giggled, the manager stepped forwards and kicked him in the leg.

The coach had left the dual carriageway and was now moving slowly down a superstore-lined arterial road, coming to a halt at traffic lights. A group of home supporters stood outside a pub, smoking. It took a moment for any of them to notice the coach, and when one of them did he seemed unsure what to do, watching it anxiously until a couple of the others followed his stare and started immediately into a frenzy of hand gestures. At his old club, the coach had tinted windows – even the reserve-team coach. In this league, though, the supporters were always in your face. They came up to you in the street and at the supermarket, and inside the small, tight, windswept grounds where they stood grimacing in huddles along the terracing, individual faces and voices were already recognizable to him. The lights changed, and he gave a final glance at the group, rhythmically fist-pumping now in an ecstasy of abuse as the coach began to pull away in the direction of the hotel.

He was rooming with Chris Balbriggan – a situation Balbriggan seemed none too happy with, judging by the way he threw his bag onto the bed by the window, turned the television on too loud and pounded gruntingly at the window for a couple of minutes before accepting finally that it was not designed to open. He stayed there staring out of it instead, occasionally giving a small shake of his head, at his misfortune, or at the flat-roofed view of the neighbouring retail estate. Balbriggan, Yates and Frank Foley, the goalkeeper, were no longer allowed to stay with one another, in any combination, and had all been paired with younger or newer members of the squad.

Although they were banned from room-sharing, the manager did not seem to mind those three keeping company on the nights out after matches. In fact, they were the players that the manager himself kept to, and they formed a boisterous circle near the bar counter of the first place the team went into, while the other players piled into a large sticky red booth or went in pairs around the floor jokingly strong-arming their way into groups of girls.

There was nowhere left to sit in the booth so Tom stood on the outside with the other young players – most of whom had come through the youth team and stuck together – smiling and gravely trying to hear what was being said above the music. Sat immediately below him, Gavin Easter, the right back, was telling a story. Tom kept his eyes on the top of his head, trying, in case anybody should glance at him, to look coolly amused. He could see the raw greased scalp through Easter's stiff clumping hair. He couldn't hear a word. When the story was finished, and the others laughed, Easter leaned back, obviously unaware of Tom stood right behind him because when his shoulder touched Tom's thigh he twisted to look up, and smiled. In a voice that was quiet enough it was probably meant just for him, he said: 'Christ, Tom, if I'd got that close to their lad today maybe we wouldn't have got thumped so badly.' In that moment, Tom felt so grateful that he was almost moved to grip him by the shoulder and say something funny in reply.

He went to the toilet instead. On his way back, in order to avoid being bought a drink, he moved to the bar to buy one for himself. He did not notice, until he got served, that he was wedged up against the back of Frank Foley. Foley was talking to a tall girl with smooth pale shoulders, stood beside him, and each time he leaned in to speak to her his large backside butted against Tom's waist.

The girl was frowning.

'What?'

There was another press of the backside and she nodded, looking out at the room briefly, before turning back to Foley.

'Sorry, love, I've never heard of you.'

She moved to collect three tall glasses of dark liquid and jostled her way out from the bar. Foley stayed where he was, with one arm rested on the counter, looking at his pint. When Tom got out from the bar he was still there, unmoving, the same expression on his face as 2,000 other people had already seen three times earlier that day.

Balbriggan did not come back to the room all night, as far as Tom was aware. Tom knew that Balbriggan had returned to the hotel from the nightclub they'd ended up at because he was among the mob in the cafe-bar singing and wrestling and drinking from the bottle of rum that somebody had taken from behind the mangled bar shutters. Tom stayed for about half an hour before going up to bed. He fell asleep immediately, and deeply, before waking just after four with a stiffness in both legs and his face damp with sweat. From the flat glare of a security light outside the window he could see the kitbag still on top of the other bed. He stared at it for a while as he thought back on the day, the match, the night – and a familiar unease came over him that made him close his eyes. His eyelids felt heavy, gummy with perspiration. He became aware of a faint sobbing noise out in the corridor. He kept his eyes closed, trying to shut it out – the noise, the uneasy feeling, the security light.

What got him out of bed in the end was not so much care or curiosity but the creeping anxious thought that if he stayed there listening for much longer then he might begin to cry himself.

He saw immediately where the noise was coming from. At the end of the corridor, in a leggy heap against the wall, beside a fire extinguisher, a young girl was slumped forward with her forehead resting against her knee. He moved towards her. There was the smell of vomit, and a dark tidemark on her shin and calf where it had clung and spiralled down her leg like a chocolate fountain. She was still sobbing quietly but did not look up at him as he kneeled in front of her. She did not respond even as he positioned one arm under her armpits, the other under the tacky back of one knee, then the other, and lifted her up. In the brightness of the corridor lighting, with her eye make-up bleeding and a small pink rash on one of her temples, she looked to him very young, younger even than his sister.

'It's OK,' he whispered. 'It's OK.'

He carried her into the room and kicked Balbriggan's bag off the bed before laying her down and gently arranging the covers over her.

She was still asleep in the exact same position when Balbriggan came into the room when it was light outside. He leaned over Tom's bed gigglingly and slapped him on the cheeks a few times until he was fully awake. As Balbriggan left the room, looking at the girl and smirking, an unstoppable sensation of pride flared briefly inside Tom, that turned almost immediately to guilt and stayed with him as he got up, showered and woke the girl – who moved silently into the bathroom to wash her face and leg before letting herself out into the corridor.

When he got to the ground floor to join the squad, she was nowhere to be seen. He didn't ask after her, and he didn't say anything about what had happened to any of the others. He kept to himself – as they filed out of the hotel to the mournful sound of lobby music and the tired, unhappy glances of reception staff – noticing, as he went through the doors, the milky sap in the yucca plant, bent and lolling next to the entrance where the two central defenders had struggled about on top of each other the night before.

The following Saturday he was on the bench. Late in the match, with the team 2–0 down, the manager sent him on, and in his eagerness to show his worth, Tom raced into a tackle on the fullback that left him with a badly bruised foot. The injury kept him out of the next two matches. By the time the foot had healed, the manager – with the team in the relegation zone two months into the season – had brought in three loan players, one of them an out-and-out right-winger, the same side as Tom. On the afternoon of Tom's return to training, the manager approached him during the warm-down to say that he would not be in the next away-match squad.

He spent the evening of the match in his digs, occasionally checking the score on his laptop. He watched television, spoke briefly on the phone to his family and ate a takeaway, a pizza. His dad wanted to come down and help him find a flat of his own to rent. It was getting silly now, his dad said. When Tom signed, the chairman told them that the club would help with finding a place for him, and in the meantime the chairman had one or two small flats of his own that new players could stay in until they got fixed up. As yet, nobody had spoken to him about moving and, as he told his dad on the phone, this didn't feel like the right time to go to the manager asking for help. His dad came down the following week. He had arranged a couple of days off work. They went for a drink, and a meal, and the next day found a studio flat in a new apartment block near the town centre where, they agreed, he would be more in the thick of things. He was proud of him, his dad said. He was doing well, adjusting, considering his age. They went to a match together, which ended in the first victory of the season. They sat in the main stand. Tom didn't tell him that he had bought their tickets. His dad said that the way this manager liked to play didn't suit his game; it was big-man hoofball and he would need to be patient, roll his sleeves up.

After his dad left, and until the new place was ready, he carried on as before: driving to the training ground in the morning, returning to his digs in the late afternoon. A few times after training and the canteen he went with the other players to the pub across the road where they filled the hours with pool and drinking games and the afternoon races; or sometimes he would drive the short distance to the coast, to one or another of the small resorts there, and walk along the seafronts and beaches. On one of these afternoons there were three boys of about his own age sitting on a bench along a promenade, who stopped their conversation to look up at him as he walked past. When he was a short way further on one of them shouted something, but it got lost in the wind and the movement of the ocean.

Following an especially cheerless defeat the manager called them all in for training the next morning, even though this would normally be a rest day. He was in an unusually threatening mood. In bitter silence they strained and hobbled for lap after lap around the pitches until he was done with them. As the squad began dragging back to the changing rooms, Tom asked the reserve goalkeeper, Hoyle, if he fancied staying behind to practise a few crosses. It wasn't to impress the manager – even though that was of course what the other players would think – but because of the guilty, lonely feeling he had been left with since his dad left. Be patient. Roll your sleeves up. Besides which, the manager always strode away immediately on calling an end to the session, still in his tracksuit, to go and see to his van-hire company.

They practised crossing and catching together for about half an hour, until Hoyle said he was going in. Tom told him he might stay out a bit longer, practise a few drills. Hoyle laughed. 'You're not in the Premiership now, mate. That lot will be in the pub in ten minutes.'

He spaced out half a dozen cones along the right-hand side of the pitch and emptied a bag of balls by the cone furthest from the goal. Then he repeated a shuttle: dribbling around each cone until he reached the dead-ball line, looked up and swung a cross in, aiming each time for the same spot at the near post. He did this until all of the balls were scattered over the neighbouring pitch, where the groundsman had been driving up and down, mowing the grass.

This groundsman now got off his mower and started to jog about, fetching and kicking the balls back to him. Tom, embarrassed, ran to collect the balls himself, but as he got closer he saw that the groundsman was in fact enjoying himself, smiling, and kicking each ball with deliberate aim towards the goal. He was still at it when Tom reached the join of the two pitches, where he stood and watched him kick the rest of the balls. When they were all returned, many of them into the net, the man looked up at him.

'Don't suppose you want to try a few penalties against me, do you?'

He was the younger of the two groundsmen, probably in his early twenties – the older one was in charge of the stadium pitch – and as Tom fired balls at him from the penalty spot he began to wonder if he had been a footballer himself. He was agile, even in his heavy boots and canvas trousers, gleefully diving and saving three of the penalties with the leathery palms of his gardening gloves. Maybe he had been with the club's youth team; one of those who didn't make the cut. When the balls were finished, Tom walked towards him.

'You're good, you know.'

The man was sweating, and wiped a long muddy smear over his broad forehead with the back of a glove. 'Obviously not been taking tips off you lot then, have I?'

He grinned, then started walking back to his mower, as Tom collected the balls and the cones and went to change.

The other players, including Hoyle, had all left, so he took his time showering and changing, enjoying the quiet echo of his studs on the concrete floor and the still-steamy warmth of the shower room, smiling occasionally at the thought of that impromptu penalty session. Afterwards, as he gathered his things, he stared ahead at the pool of shower water struggling around the drain. The thought of driving, of empty windswept beaches, of his bare room in the chairman's flat – his kitbag suddenly felt like a heavy weight in his hand and he sat down, watching as the last of the water eddied and choked down the hole.

He came out onto the pitches and listened for the sound of the mower, but all he could hear was the noise of cars in the distance beyond the fencing and scrubland. On the other side of the four pitches from the road was the small graffitied outbuilding where the groundskeeping equipment was kept, and he made towards this now, trying to ignore the exposed, self-conscious sensation as he walked across the empty expanse of reeking cut grass.

He could see the man through the doorway, carefully pouring the last of one pot of white paint into another on top of a trestle table. Before Tom reached the building, he looked round in surprise and, Tom thought, a little amusement.

'What, more penalties?'

The man looked down again and shook the last of the paint into the pot. Tom stood in the doorway. He knew he should say something but he didn't know what that should be. The man did not seem bothered that he was standing there in his doorway watching him work. On the walls, among mounted rakes and shelves of canisters and paint and sprinklers, there were old team posters and a long dirty club scarf that had been nailed up, flecked with paint. Somehow the sight of these things filled Tom with a faint sadness. He watched the man press lids onto the paint pots and move towards the dustbin by the door with the empty pot.

He was about to open the dustbin when Tom reached forward nervously to clasp him on the arm. The man looked at him. Tom let his hand fall to his side and looked down – ashamed, unsure what to say – at the paint pot still in the man's hand, his heavy boots, and his own trainers, now stained with green. He was conscious of how clean he was this close up to the man's work clothes, marked with mud, grass, paint. Tom dared not look up. He listened to the dim thrum of the road. After a few seconds the man turned and Tom watched his back as he moved away, hearing then the unbearable clunk of the paint pot being put down onto the table.

Tom turned to look out of the doorway at the wide abandoned field and he felt the warmth of the man against him. The slow, gradual press of his hands on Tom's sides. Tom stepped forward, pulling himself gently away. Then he turned and looked right at him, at his large doleful face, and he was filled with a sudden glorious sense of risk as the man stood there, waiting for him.

The man was in some pain at first. Tom stopped, not knowing what to do. This had happened the other time, a couple of years ago – neither of them then had been sure how to go on and so they hadn't, trying instead other things, frustrated.

After a moment though, of calmly guiding Tom's hand and then moving it aside, the man indicated for him to continue.

Later, he would remember the smell of paint, and petrol, in the man's hair; the grass cuttings caught there, gradually working themselves loose.

There was no training the next morning because of the weekend's match, so he spent the day moving into his new flat. There was not a lot to move. By midday, he had driven all of his things over from the other place and put them in: his clothes, his stereo, his family's old pots and pans, his posters of his boyhood club. He spent the afternoon arranging these things, with a growing sick jittery sense of how permanent it felt. The thought of the future filled him with anxiety as he moved about the small clean flat and folded his clothes into the wardrobe, sorted the television reception, tacked his posters onto the bedroom walls, then removed them and put them up in the corridor.

He needed to phone his dad and tell him he was in, but he couldn't.

On the afternoon of Saturday's match he went to the players' bar with the other uninvolved members of the first-team squad. He was the only player to watch the match. He stepped out of the bar into the tiny walled-off area at the top of the main stand and sat drinking alone, following absently as the team laboured to a one-all draw, the muffled noise through the glass behind him of Chris Yates and Frank Foley arguing, on and off, all through the match.

He had forgotten to check his route from the flat before he left and got lost around the edge of town, arriving at the training ground over half an hour late. The squad had already begun a keep-ball routine when the manager, his arms folded, feet planted apart, saw him running towards them.

'Three full circuits, dickhead. Go.'

He started immediately into a fast pace, running in the other direction from the outbuilding, and by the time he had been going only a few minutes, and he heard distantly behind him the sound of the mower starting up, his breath was already coming thickly and his heart thumping. He felt his legs and his chest tighten as he ran faster still – without caring how it would look to the manager and the players – not allowing himself to look round until he had reached the turn at the road side of the pitches.

He saw the small figure on top of the mower as it moved slowly down the side of the furthest pitch and, even from that distance, he knew that it was the other groundsman.

He completed the three circuits and rejoined the others, careful to keep his head down and join fiercely into the training routine, in case any of them might look at his face.

He trained on each of the following days with an intensity that caused him, by the end of the week, to be the object of frequent bruising challenges, all of which went overlooked by the manager and his assistant, surprised and pleased as they were at the sudden unexpected competitiveness brought about by their coaching. His relations with the other players were not helped either by his insistence on staying behind after the session to train alone, sprinting and sweating, watching, worrying, constantly wondering why – had the two groundsmen swapped roles, or was it something else? The sour smell of the cut grass, as he limped cramping back to the changing rooms, was almost overpowering.

After two weeks of furious training the manager called him into his office.

'Son, this is what I'd wanted to see when I signed you.'

He was being put back in the first-team squad, the manager told him smugly.

On Tuesday night he was on the bench for a home match. He spent all of it warming up along the touchline, running up and down the side of the pitch, trying to ignore the occasional shouts from the bored, unhappy supporters in the main stand.

Even as the match came towards the end of injury time, and he had not been brought on, he continued to stretch and pace along the tidy lush fringe until, as one fan had already pointed out to him, he was more tired than he had been at the end of the two matches he'd played.

And then, one morning later that week during a chest-control routine, there he was – leaving the outbuilding as though that was where he had been this whole time. Tom tried not to look. He concentrated on the drills, sprinting, jumping, heading, attempting to distract himself from the hollow racing sensation in his stomach that grew each time there was an interval of quiet from the steady hum of the mower. At the end of the session he came in with the others. He showered, turning the knob to its coldest until he was nearly unable to breathe.

The next day he continued to look away. Only during the runs, when they jogged in a long column, would he allow himself to watch him. And it was at these times that he would see him looking, as if at the whole squad, from where he sat on the mower or rolled crisp, shocking-white lines onto the grass.

The rest of the squad had showered and changed, but Tom stayed sitting in his towel on the splintered bench until they had all left. Even though he had stopped training alone, nobody waited for him any more or asked if he was coming to the canteen or the pub. He sat there for some time before he put his clothes on, then left the room, stepped into the cold prefab corridor, and began walking to the car park.

He got into his car, which was parked to one side where the gravel surface dipped slightly towards nettle bushes and a low dead tree, and waited.

The man was one of the last to leave. The assistant manager, the physio, some of the players and the canteen staff had all got into their cars and driven off while Tom sat there.

He felt his blood throbbing against the headrest as he observed him in his rear-view mirror, coming up the path, calmly approaching the blue car parked on its own in the middle of the car park. He got in and – Tom could just make out his movements through the windscreen – adjusted his radio or something on the dashboard for a moment before starting the engine and slowly pulling away.

The team won another match, away, resoundingly. Tom did not play. His dad called him afterwards and said that he wanted to come down and see him, or for Tom to come and spend a few days at home. Tom lied and told him that neither would be possible, because the manager was making them do extra, and longer, training sessions. His dad told him again to be patient and keep his sleeves rolled up, that his chance would come, eventually.

One week on from the reappearance of the groundsman, Tom was sitting in the canteen, surrounded by the smell of deodorant and soft exhausted food, at the long central table around which the squad were athletically devouring jacket potatoes, baked beans, chips, chilli con carnes. He was on the bench at one end of the table, facing away from the entrance, and so did not at first see the groundsman coming in. Only when he had come past and stood at the hot grubby glass of the display cabinet did Tom spot him. He was waiting for the server to come back through from the kitchen. Tom watched the back of his head anxiously as he looked down at the cracked empty dishes and the remaining jacket potatoes. Only when he took his plate of potato and beans and walked, without looking over, to an empty table on the other side of the room did Tom notice Balbriggan, sat opposite him, following the man's movement. Tom went still with fear when he saw the small smile on Balbriggan's face as he nudged Foley on the arm, nodding in the direction of the groundsman.

Foley looked around, baffled, not sure what he was supposed to be seeing.

'You know what he is, that guy?' Balbriggan was staring across the room, his small stupid eyes proud, gleeful.

'Who?'

'Him – the new groundsman.'

Tom looked over now, too, to where the man sat by a window eating slowly and alone, his bright immaculate pitches stretching away through the window beyond him.

Foley frowned briefly, confused, as Balbriggan whispered into his ear, before turning back to what was left of his chilli con carne.

Tom sat in his car with the radio on low as the other vehicles departed one by one until only a few remained.

Balbriggan had continued talking to Foley for some time after they turned their attention away from the groundsman. He complained about the grass, that it was too long, that it should be a fucking rugby pitch. Tom had sat there listening to them as anger, and pity, raged inside him, making him want to stand up and damage something, to damage Balbriggan, to pick up his plate and smash it on the top of Balbriggan's dense tanned head. He stayed there with his meal half finished until those two and a few of the other players had left the canteen. The man must have been aware of him. He wondered if he was aware too of what the players said about him. Tom looked across only once. He was still eating, his head bent towards his food; the wide, open face difficult to read. Tom had felt again that same faint sadness as when he'd watched him press in paint-pot lids on the table in front of the old club scarf. He stood up, walked over to put his tray onto the stacking tower by the door and left.

The manager was leaning on his sunroof, talking into his phone. Tom could not fully hear what he was saying but he made out 'board' and 'spastic' before the manager flipped the phone shut and got into his car to leave. When the sound of the engine had died down the lane and the car park was again in silence, Tom got out. Quickly, looking around him, he walked towards the blue car. He stopped for a few seconds in front of it, looking through the windscreen at the few scattered CDs and payslip envelope on the mucky passenger seat, before stepping forward and pulling out one of the windscreen wipers. He checked over his shoulder, then placed a piece of paper onto the glass and let the wiper retract to pin it in place. Only one word had been written on it, in large letters, slightly crumpled now under the pressure of the wiper. Faggot. Tom stared at it for a moment, then turned, walked unsteadily back to his car, started the engine and drove away. ■

SILT

Robert Macfarlane

Half a mile offshore, walking on silver water, we found a curved path that extended gracefully and without apparent end to our north and south. It was a shallow tidal channel and the water it held caught and pooled the sun, such that its route existed principally as flux; a phenomenon of light and of currents. Its bright line curved away from us: an ogee or line of beauty whose origin we could not explain and whose invitation to follow we could not disobey, so we walked it northwards, along that glowing track made neither of water nor of land, which led us further and still further out to sea.

If you consult a large-scale map of the Essex coastline between the River Crouch and the River Thames, you will see a footpath – its route marked with a stitch-line of crosses and dashes – leaving the land at a place called Wakering Stairs and then heading due east, straight out to sea. Several hundred yards offshore, it curls north-east and runs in this direction for around three miles, still offshore, before rolling back to make landfall at Fisherman's Head, the uppermost tip of a large, low-lying and little-known marshy island called Foulness.

This is the Broomway, allegedly 'the deadliest' path in Britain and certainly the unearthliest path I have ever walked. The Broomway is thought to have killed more than a hundred people over the centuries; it seems likely that there were other victims whose fates went unrecorded. Sixty-six of its dead are buried in the little Foulness churchyard; the bodies of the other known dead were not recovered. If the Broomway hadn't existed, Wilkie Collins might have had to invent it. Edwardian newspapers, alert to its reputation, rechristened it 'The Doomway'. Even the Ordnance Survey map registers, in its sober fashion, the

gothic atmosphere of the path. Printed in large pink lettering on the
1:25,000 map of that stretch of coast is the following message:

WARNING

PUBLIC RIGHTS OF WAY ACROSS MAPLIN SANDS

CAN BE DANGEROUS. SEEK LOCAL GUIDANCE.

The Broomway is the less notorious of Britain's two great
offshore footpaths, the other being the route that crosses the sands
of Morecambe Bay from Hest Bank to Kents Bank by way of Priest
Skear. As at Morecambe Bay, the Broomway traverses vast sand and
mud flats that stretch almost unsloped for miles. When the tide goes
out at Morecambe and Foulness, it goes out a great distance, revealing
shires of sand packed hard enough to support the weight of a walker.
When the tide comes back in, though, it comes fast – galloping over
the sands at speeds quicker than a human can run. Disorientation is
a danger as well as inundation: in mist, rain or fog, it is easy to lose
direction in such self-similar terrain, with shining sand extending in
all directions. Nor are all of the surfaces that you encounter reliable:
there is mud that can trap you and quicksand that can swallow you.
Morecambe is infamously treacherous, its worst tragedy being the
death in February 2004 of at least twenty-one Chinese cockle-pickers,
illegal immigrants who were inexperienced in the lore of the estuary
and insufficiently aware of the danger of the tides, but who had been
sent by their gangmaster far out onto the sands to harvest cockles.

Unlike the Morecambe Bay path, whose route fluctuates and
whose walking therefore requires both improvisation and vigilance,
the route of the Broomway seems to have been broadly consistent
since at least 1419 (when it is referred to in a manorial record).
Conceptually, both the Morecambe crossing and the Broomway are
close to paradox. They are rights of way and as such are inscribed on
maps and in law, but they are also swept clean of the trace of passage
twice daily by the tides. What do you call a path that is no path? A
riddle? A sequence of compass bearings? A death trap?

The geology and archaeology of the Broomway are disputed and shifting. Various theories have been proposed to explain its existence, including that it sits on top of a durable reef of chalk. Certainly, it takes its name from the four hundred or so 'brooms' that were formerly placed at intervals of between thirty and sixty yards on either side of the track, thereby indicating the safe passage on the hard sand that lay between them.

Until 1932, the Broomway was the only means of getting to and from Foulness save by boat, for the island was isolated from the mainland by uncrossable creeks and stretches of mud known as the Black Grounds. For centuries, hazel wattles were bound and laid as floating causeways to enable safe passage over the Black Grounds and onto the weight-bearing sands. These causeways were analogous in technology and principle to the Sweet Track in Somerset.* At some point the wattles were replaced with jetties of rubble. During the eighteenth and nineteenth centuries, coach drivers would muster in the tavern at Wakering and drink while waiting for the tides to be right for the ride to Foulness. Several of them died on the job, befuddled by weather, or alcohol, or both. In the aftermath of the North Sea Storm of 1953, when floodwaters killed hundreds of people along the English east coast, the Broomway was the only reliable means of access to Foulness: army vehicles raced back and forth along its firm sand, evacuating the dead and injured. The island is currently owned by the Ministry of Defence, which purchased it during the First World War for 'research purposes'

---

* The wooden road laid across the spongy Somerset levels during the early Neolithic, to permit passage between areas of higher, drier ground: the hills of the Mendips and the hummocks of Glastonbury. Precise pollen dating allows us to know that at Shapwick, near Westhay (place names which sound as if they should come from Shetland, not Somerset), in the spring of 3806 BC, rods of alder, hazel, holly, oak, ash and lime were bound and laid in a track, like a slung walkway, across the levels, along which Neolithic walkers bounced and floated as they traversed the bogs.

and which continues to conduct artillery-firing tests out over the sands.

I have for years wanted to walk the Broomway, but have been deterred from doing so by its reputation. Then a friend put me in contact with a man called Patrick Arnold, who had been born and raised on Foulness, and who knew the Broomway better than anyone living. Patrick kindly offered to accompany me along it, and we agreed to walk the path together on a Sunday, when the Ministry of Defence would not be firing, and when the tide times were right.

The Monday before that Sunday, a letter arrived. I recognized Patrick's handwriting on the envelope. 'With sadness,' the letter began stiffly, 'I must withdraw my offer to guide you along the "most dangerous road in England".' I felt a rush of disappointment. Patrick went on to explain that his elderly mother, for whom he cared, was too frail for him to leave her 'for many hours without being exceedingly anxious about her welfare'. However, he continued, and here my heart rose – he thought I might 'navigate the Broomway alone, without suffering any mischief'.

Along with the letter, Patrick had sent the following documents: a hand-drawn map of the coastline between Wakering Stairs and Foulness showing the route of the Broomway and its tributary causeways; a numbered list of observations concerning appropriate clothing to wear on the Broomway; and some points of advice as to how best to avoid dying on it.

Patrick owed his life to the Broomway. 'Let me tell you,' he explained to me the first time we spoke. 'There was a man called Mr William Harvey, and one day in 1857 he set out with a coach and horses to cross the Broomway. Well, he never arrived, and so they went looking for him. Of the horses no trace was found. The coach was discovered upside down in the sands, and there was William's drowned body lying dead on the flats.

'Well, after she'd done with her grieving, William Harvey's widow went on to marry a Mr Lily, and of that congress was born my great-grandfather. So while the accident was Mrs Harvey's great loss – and indeed also Mr Harvey's – it was eventually my great gain. In this way, do you see, I am grateful to the Broomway, and so I have devoted myself to walking and researching it.'

Patrick spoke with precision, and with faint hints of Victoriana. He had worked onshore as a form-maker and carpenter until his retirement, but he knew the sea well and held the speed record for rowing single-handedly from London to Ostend. He told me stories about the Essex coast: about the great fleets of collier-tugs that would assemble in the mouth of the Thames; about the dangers of easterlies blowing big ships onto the lee shore; and most often about the Broomway, of which he spoke respectfully but fondly as 'an old friend'.

Patrick had read almost every available account of walking the Broomway, and he relished the grisly melodrama of its past. Whenever we spoke he would have fresh tales for me, dredged from Broomway lore: a nineteenth-century coroner's deposition of the difficulty of identifying bodies once the crabs had been to work on faces and fingers, say; or a survivor who had written in a letter to a friend of the 'sheer panic' that he experienced as the rain fell around him and he wandered the sands in search of the right route.

'He was convinced he was walking towards the Mouse Lightship,' said Patrick, 'but, in fact, he was walking out to sea, towards his death, and he was saved only by the accident of stumbling into a fish kettle – copper-nailed so as not to rust – which he knew had to have its closed point facing out to sea, and its open mouth gaping perpendicular to the shore, such that fish would become trapped in it during the retreat of the tide. This gave him the orientation he needed, and he made it safely back along the path. He was a lucky man.'

Until hand-held compasses became available to walkers, the safest way of walking the Broomway in bad conditions, when it was impossible to see from broom to broom, was with stone and thread. Walkers carried a 200-foot length of linen thread, with one end tied to a small stone. They would place the stone next to a broom and then walk away in what they believed to be the right direction, unspooling the thread as they went, until they could see the next broom. If they went astray, they could trace the thread back to the stone and try again. If they went the right way, they hauled in the stone and repeated the action. It was slow and painstaking work, but in this manner people could notionally walk the Broomway in safety, whatever the weather.

'It's a weird world out there on the flats,' Patrick said. 'Nothing looks the same as normal. Gulls can seem as big as eagles. Scale and distance change. It's very easy to lose your bearings, especially at dusk or dark. Then it's the lights on the Kent shore that often do it. People think they're walking back to the Essex coast, when in fact they're walking across towards Kent and so out into the tide. The mud's the thing to watch, too; step in the wrong places, and it'll bog you down and suck you in, ready for the tide to get you.'

Two days before I left to walk the Broomway, my Alaskan friend James helpfully recommended that I take a small sharp hatchet with me. 'That way, if you get stuck in the mud with the tide coming in, you can cut your legs off at the ankles and escape.'

Patrick had a final warning. 'The Broomway will be there another day, but if you try to walk it in mist, you may not be. So if it's misty when you arrive at Wakering Stairs, turn round and go home.'

It was misty when I arrived at Wakering Stairs early on a Sunday morning, and the air was white. It wasn't a haar, a proper North Sea mist that blanked out the world. More of a dense sea haze. But visibility was poor enough that the foghorns were sounding, great bovine reverbs drifting up and down the coast. I stood on the sea wall, looking out into the mist, feeling the foghorns vibrating in my chest, and wondering if I could imaginatively recategorize the weather conditions such that I could disregard Patrick's final warning. I felt slightly sick with anxiety, but eager to walk.

With me, also nervous, was my old friend David, whom I had

convinced to join me on the path. David is a former scholar of Renaissance literature, turned antiquarian book dealer, turned barrister, turned tax lawyer. He is probably the only Marxist tax lawyer in London, possibly in the world. He likes wearing breeches, likes walking barefoot, and hopes daily for the downfall of capitalism. He is six foot seven, very thin, very clever, and has little interest in people who take it upon themselves to comment without invitation on his height and spindliness. We have covered a lot of miles together.

The air at Wakering Stairs was warm and close; thick like gel in the nose and mouth. The tide had recently turned, and just offshore the exposed Black Grounds were steaming: a brown mudscape of canyons and buttresses, turgid and gleaming, through which silver streams riddled. Sandpipers and oystercatchers strutted in search of breakfast. The surfaces of my body felt spongy, absorbent. The creeks and channels bubbled and glistened. Two big black-backed gulls pottered the tideline, monitoring us with lackadaisical, violent eyes.

Where the road met the sea wall, there was a heavy metal STOP barrier, tagged with a blue graffiti scrawl. A red firing flag drooped at the foot of a tall flagpole. Beyond the stop barrier was a bank of signs in waspy yellow-and-black type and imperative grammar, detailing by-laws, tautologically identifying themselves as warnings, indemnifying the MoD against drownings, explosions and mud deaths, offering caveats to the walker, and grudgingly admitting that this was, indeed, the beginning of a public right of way:

WARNING: THE BROOMWAY IS UNMARKED
AND VERY HAZARDOUS TO PEDESTRIANS.

WARNING: DO NOT APPROACH OR TOUCH ANY OBJECT
AS IT MAY EXPLODE AND KILL YOU.

Away from the sea wall ran the causeway, perhaps five yards wide, formed of brick rubble and grey hard core. It headed out to sea over the mud, before disappearing into water and mist. Poles had been driven into the mud to either side of the path, six feet tall, marking out its curling line. There were a few tussocks of eelgrass. The water's surface was sheened with greys and silvers, like the patina on old mirror glass. Otherwise, the causeway appeared to lead into a textureless world of white.

Three oystercatchers flew overhead with quick-flick wingstrokes, piping as they passed. We climbed the ramp to the summit of the sea wall, stepped over a scatter of beer cans and walked down towards the start of the causeway. I stooped to gather a handful of white cockleshells from among the shore rocks. I subdued the alarm my brain was raising at the idea of walking out to sea fully clothed, as only suicides do.

We walked along the rubble and sea-cracked hardstanding, out along the causeway and over the mud. A man with his dog paused on the sea wall to watch us go. Here and there we had to wait for the tide to recede, revealing more of the path before us. I peered over the edge of the causeway as if off a pier, though the water to either side was only a few inches deep. A goby in a pool wriggled its aspic body deeper into the sand.

After three hundred yards the causeway ended for real, dipping beneath the sand like a river passing underground. Further out, a shallow sheen of water lay on top of the sand, stretching away. The diffused light made depth perception impossible, so that it seemed as if we were simply going to walk onwards into ocean. We stopped at the end of the causeway, looking out across the pathless future.

'I think there's a sun somewhere up there, burning all this off,' said David brightly. 'I think we'll be in sunshine by the end of the day.'

It seemed hard to believe. But it was true that the light had sharpened slightly in the twenty minutes it had taken us to walk to the end of the causeway. I glanced back at the sea wall, but it was barely visible now through the haze. A scorching band of low white light seaward; a thin magnesium burn line.

I could hear the pop and bubble of the revealed sand, beautifully ridged, its lines broken by millions of casts, noodly messes of black silt that had been squeezed up by ragworms and razor shells. The squid-ink colour of the casts they left was a reminder that just below the hard sand was the mud. I took off my shoes and placed them on a stand of eelgrass. For some reason I couldn't overcome my sense of tides as volatile rather than fixed, capricious rather than regulated. What if the tides disobeyed the moon, on this day of all days?

'I'm worried that if we don't make it back in time, the tide will float off with my shoes,' I said to David.

'If we don't make it back in time, the tide will float off with your body,' he replied.

We stepped off the causeway. The water was warm on the skin, puddling to ankle depth. Underfoot I could feel the brain-like corrugations of the hard sand, so firmly packed that there was no give under the pressure of my step. Beyond us extended the sheer mirror plane of the water, disrupted only here and there by shallow humps of sand and green slews of weed.

We walked on out over the mirror. I could hear the man whistling to his dog now far away on the sea wall. Otherwise, there was nothing except bronze sand and mercury water, and so we continued through the lustrous air, out onto the flats and back into the Mesolithic.

In 1931 a trawler called the *Colinda* was night-fishing around twenty-five miles off the Norfolk coast, in the southern North Sea. When the men pulled in their nets and began to sort the fish from the flotsam and rubble that had also been trapped, one of the men found, part embedded in a hunk of peat, a curious object: sharp and shapely, clearly an artefact, and about twenty centimetres long. The man handed it to the trawler captain, Pilgrim Lockwood. Lockwood passed it to the owner of the *Colinda*, who passed it to a friend and in this roundabout way the object at last reached an archaeologist called Muir Evans who was able to identify it as a harpoon point, made from antler and with barbs carved on one side.

The Colinda Point, as it is now known, was one of the first archaeological clues to the existence of a vast, lost and once-inhabited landscape: a Mesolithic Atlantis that lies under the southern half of what is now the North Sea. Even to conceive the possibility of such a landscape's existence – unaided by the technology that assists contemporary archaeologists – was in the 1930s an audacious thought experiment. To imagine much of the North Sea drained away? To imagine what is now seabed as dry land? To imagine what is now the east coast of England as continuous with what is now the north-west coast of Germany and Holland? To imagine a Mesolithic culture existing in this vanished world?

The drowned land that the Colinda Point – dated to between 10,000 and 4000 BC – helped bring back to light is now known as Doggerland, and thanks to the collaborative work of a remarkable group of archaeologists, geologists, palaeobotanists and Dutch and East Anglian fishermen, our knowledge of the region is extensive.

Around 12,000 years ago, during the most recent glaciation, so much water was locked up in the ice caps and glaciers that the sea levels around Britain were up to four hundred feet lower than they are today. Doggerland, then exposed, would have been harsh tundra. But as global temperatures rose, melting ice sent freshwater rivers spinning through that tundra, irrigating and fertilizing it, such that it developed into a habitable, even hospitable, terrain. We know that there were trout in the rivers of Doggerland, wild boar and deer in its oak and ash woods, and that stinging nettles grew among its grasses. Using seismic-survey data of the seabed acquired from an oil company, archaeologists have been able to back-map an area of Doggerland around the size of Wales. Like early colonists, researchers have christened the features of this rediscovered world. The Spines is an area of steep dunes, probably running down to a river which, at its peak flow, was almost as big as the Rhine is today. The river has been named the Shotton River in honour of the Birmingham geologist Fred Shotton (who, among other distinctions, was dropped behind enemy lines to analyse the geology of the Normandy beachheads before the D-Day landings). Dogger Bank – a name familiar from the Shipping Forecast – is an upland area of plateau in north Doggerland, and the Outer Silver Pit is a giant basin flanked by two huge sandbanks, almost sixty miles long.

As temperatures increased further and more land ice melted, Doggerland was gradually inundated. Dogger Bank would have survived as a large island, before it too disappeared around 5000 BC, and the flooding of Doggerland was complete. The creep of the sea level across the land – up to one or two metres per century – would have been noticeable in a generation, but is unlikely to have taken people by surprise. As such, the Mesolithic retreat from Doggerland represents one of the earliest sustained human responses to climate change. Considering Doggerland now, it is hard not to think forwards as well as backwards. To those living on the vulnerable east coast of England, drowned Doggerland offers a glimpse of the future. Around the coasts of Norfolk and Suffolk, the land is being bitten back by the ocean. Graveyards are shedding their dead and their headstones into the sea. Dwellings that were once miles inland are now cliff-edge, and on the point of abandonment. Eccles Church on the Norfolk coast vanished into the sea in 1895. Anti-aircraft batteries and pillboxes built on cliffs in 1940 are now slumped on beaches or sunk offshore. Roads end in mid-air. Footpaths that once ran along the coast have crumbled. Consulting historical maps of East Anglia, you realize that substantial areas of the region have already joined Doggerland: coastlines have become ghostlines. In places such as these the undertow of the past is strong – liable to take your legs from you and pull you down without warning.

At Dunwich, an entire town was swallowed by the sea over several centuries. Nothing of it is now left, though late-nineteenth-century photographs exist of its last towers standing crooked on the beach. Historical data about Dunwich is sufficiently profuse that maps have been made of the former outline of streets, buildings and churches, and their positions relative to the current shore. In this way, swimming off the shingle beach, you can float over invisible streets and buildings: the further out you go, the further back in history you've reached. Once, unaware of the ebb tide that was ripping round the coast, I crunched over the shingle and swam to around 1842 before I realized that I was being pulled rapidly out to sea, and struck out in panic for the present day.

It is likely that, thousands of years in the future, when the temperature cycles have turned again and the world's water is once more locked up in ice, Doggerland will be re-exposed; filled this time with the wreckage of an Anthropocene culture – a vast junkyard of beached derricks and stranded sea forts, botched pipes and wiring, the concrete caltrops of anti-tank defences, fleets of grounded and upended boats and the spoil heaps of former houses.

Out and on we walked, barefoot over and into the mirror-world. I glanced back at the coast. The air was grainy and flickering, like an old newsreel. The sea wall had hazed out to a thin black strip. Structures of unknown purpose – a white-beamed gantry, a low-slung barracks – showed on the shoreline. Every few hundred yards, I dropped a white cockleshell. The light had modified again, from nacreous to granular to dense. Sound travelled oddly. The muted pop-popping of gunfire was smudgy, but the call of a cuckoo from somewhere on the treeless shore rang sharply to us. A pale sun glared through the mist, its white eye multiplying in pools and ripples.

The miniature sandscapes of ridge and valley pressed into the soles of my feet, and for days after the walk I would feel a memory of that pressure and pattern. The ripple-line of the ridges was recapitulated wherever I looked: in small bivalves between whose parted shells poked frilled lips, and in serpentine channels, apparent because they caught and returned the light differently to the shallower water. All these forms possessed the S-shaped double bend that William Hogarth in 1753 christened the 'ogee', exquisite in its functionless and repetitive elegance; a line that drew the eye onwards.

With so few orientation points and so many beckoning paths, we were finding it hard to stay on course. I was experiencing a powerful desire to walk straight out to sea and explore the greater freedoms of this empty tidal world. But we were both still anxious about straying far from the notional path of the Broomway and encountering the black muds or the quicksands.

Patrick's directions said that we should reach something called the Maypole, a sunken telegraph pole with crosspieces that marked the south-eastern edge of a tidal channel called Havengore Creek. But we were not paying sufficient attention to our pacings and distances. We became confused by other spars, sticking up from the mud here and there: relics of wrecks, perhaps, or more likely the mark points of former channels long since silted up by the shifting sands. At last we reached what was surely the Maypole. It looked like the final yards of a galleon's topmast, the body of the ship long since buried in those deep sands. At its base, currents had carved deep warm basins of water in which we wallowed our feet, sending shrimps scurrying. We took an onwards bearing and continued over the silver shield of the water.

My thoughts were beginning to move unusually, worked upon and changed by the mind-altering surfaces of this offshore world and by the elation that arose from walking securely on water. Out there, nothing could be only itself. The eye's vision fed on false colour values. Similes, metaphors and illusions bred. Ideas of opposition felt outflanked, melted away. Gull-eagles dipped and glided in the outer reaches of the mist. The sand served as the water's tain: 'tain', from the French for 'tin', being the lustreless backing of a mirror which makes reflection possible but limits the onward gaze, disallowing the view of a concept or idea beyond that point.

Walking always with us were our reflections, our attentive ghost selves. For the water acted as a mirror line, such that we both appeared joined at the ankles with our doubles, me more than twelve feet tall and David a foot taller still. If anyone had been able to look out from the shore, through the mist, they would have seen two giant walkers striding over the sea.

Several years ago the sculptor Antony Gormley buried a full-size iron cast of his own body upside down in the ground of Cambridge's Archaeological Research Institute. Only the undersides of the iron man's feet show on the surface. Two days before coming to walk the

Broomway I had slipped off my shoes and socks and stood barefoot in the rusty prints, sole to sole with that buried body. Now that act of doubling had itself been unexpectedly repeated out here on the sands. Everywhere I looked were pivot points and fulcrums, symmetries and proliferations: the thorax points of a winged world. Sand mimicked water, water mimicked sand and the air duplicated the textures of both. Hinged cuckoo calls; razor shells and cockleshells; our own reflections; a profusion of suns; the glide of transparent over solid. When I think back to the outer miles of that walk, I now recall a strong disorder of perception that caused illusions of the spirit as well as of the eye. I recall thought becoming sensational; the substance of landscape so influencing mind that mind's own substance was altered.

You enter the mirror-world by a causeway and you leave it by one. From Asplin Head, a rubble jetty as wide as a farm track reaches out over the Black Grounds, offering safe passage to shore. As we approached the jetty's outermost point, the sand began to give way underfoot and we broke through into sucking black mud. It was like striking oil – the glittering rich ooze gouting up around our feet. We slurped onwards to the causeway, the rubble of which had been colonized by a lurid green weed.

I walked alongside the causeway rather than on it, finding that if I kept moving over the mud I didn't sink. I passed through miniature cactus forests of samphire and between torn chunks of ferroconcrete. The surface of the mud, a gritty curded paste, was intricately marked with the filigree of worm tracks and crab scrabbles. In the centre of the causeway, where the mud had dried and cracked into star patterns, there were many wader footprints – sandpipers, oystercatchers and gulls. The slithery clay offered pleasure to the foot, and mud curled between my toes with each step, oily as butter. By the time we reached the sea wall, David and I both wore diving boots of clay. We washed them off in a puddle, and stepped up onto a boat ramp. We had made landfall.

We sat on the out-slope of the sea wall, eating sandwiches and talking. David took a photograph of the MoD sign that read:

PHOTOGRAPHY IS PROHIBITED. The sun was fully out now, and barely a wisp of the early-day mist survived. The clay dried fast on my legs, crisping the hairs and tightening my skin so that I felt kiln-fired – a mud-man. To my joy, three avocets rose from the salt marsh and flew screeching in circles above us, before rocketing back down into the sea lavender. I thought of the curlew I had seen in numbers out on this coast earlier in the year, their curved beaks and heavy bodies distinctive in flight, and about how the paths of birds and animals were really the oldest ways of them all: aerial migration routes – bringing geese to this shore from Siberia, peregrines from Scandinavia – scored invisibly into the sky over millennia and signed by magnetic forces. Staggering recent research into avian navigation has revealed that, by means of retinal proteins called cryptochromes, birds can actually *see* magnetic fields. Magnetic-force structures are visible as darker or lighter forms, which are superimposed on the conventionally visible landscape, and so help to guide the birds to their destinations.

Beyond the causeway's end, the shining sands stretched to a horizon line. One of Foulness's farmers, John Burroughs, has spoken wistfully of coming out onto the sands in late autumn to hunt wigeon: he brings a board to use as a shooting stick and, leaning against it, feels that he 'could be on the far side of the moon'. That felt exactly right: the walk out to sea as a soft lunacy, a passage beyond this world.

In his weird way book of 1909, *Afoot in England*, W.H. Hudson described being on the Norfolk coast under similar conditions to the ones David and I had experienced that morning on the Broomway. The tide was low and Hudson was far out on the blond sands watching herring gulls, when a 'soft bluish silvery sea-haze' began to build that caused sky, water and land to become 'blended and interfused', producing a 'new country' that was 'neither earth nor sea'. The haze also magnified the gulls until they seem no longer 'familiar birds', but 'twice as big as gulls, and . . . of a dazzling whiteness and of no definite shape'. Hudson's prose registers the experience as mystical: a metaphysical hallucination brought about by material illusion. The gulls temporarily appear to him as ghost-gulls or spirit-birds that merely 'lived in or were passing through the world', presences made briefly visible by the haze. Then, in a brilliant reversal, he imagines that he himself – 'standing far out on the sparkling sands, with the sparkling sea on one side' – is also dematerialized, 'a formless shining white being standing by the sea, and then perhaps as a winged shadow floating in the haze'. 'That', concludes Hudson, 'was the effect on my mind: this natural world was changed to a supernatural.'

Felt pressure, sensed texture and perceived space can work upon the body and so too upon the mind, altering the textures and inclinations of thought. The American farmer and writer Wendell Berry suggests this in a fine essay called 'The Rise', in which he describes setting float in a canoe on a river in spate. 'No matter how deliberately we moved from the shore into the sudden violence of a river on the rise,' writes Berry, 'there would . . . be several uneasy minutes of transition. The river is another world, which means that one's senses and reflexes must begin to live another life.'

We lack – we need – a term for those places where one experiences a 'transition' from a known landscape onto John's 'far side of the moon', into Hudson's 'new country', into Berry's 'another world': somewhere we feel and think differently. I have for some time now been imagining such transitions as border crossings. These borders do not correspond to national boundaries, and papers and documents are unrequired at them. Their traverse is generally unbiddable, and no reliable map exists of their routes and lines. They exist even in familiar landscapes: there when you cross a certain watershed, mountain pass, treeline or snowline, or enter rain, storm or mist, or pass from boulder clay onto sand, or chalk onto greenstone. Such moments are rites of passage that reconfigure local geographies, leaving known places suddenly outlandish or quickened, revealing continents within countries.

What might we call such incidents and instances – or, rather, how to name the lands that are found beyond these frontiers? 'Xenotopias', perhaps, meaning 'foreign places' or 'out-of-place places', a term to complement our utopias and our dystopias. Martin Martin, the traveller and writer who in the 1690s set sail to explore the Scottish seaboard, knew that one does not need to displace oneself vastly within space to find difference. 'It is a piece of weakness and folly merely to value things because of their distance from the place where we are born,' he wrote in 1697, 'thus men have travelled far enough in the search of foreign plants and animals, and yet continue strangers to those produced in their own natural climate.' So did Henry David Thoreau: 'An absolutely new prospect is a great happiness, and I can still get this any afternoon. Two or three hours' walking will carry me to as strange a country as I expect ever to see. A single farmhouse which I had not seen before is sometimes as good as the dominions of the King of Dahomey.'

The American writer William Fox has spent his career exploring what he calls 'cognitive dissonance in isotropic spaces', which might be more plainly translated as 'how we get easily lost in spaces that appear much the same in all directions'. Fox's thesis is that we are unable to orient ourselves in self-similar landscapes because we evolved in the dense, close-hand environments of jungle and savannah. In repetitive, data-depleted landscapes with few sight markers 'our natural navigation abilities begin to fail catastrophically'. Fox visited the Antarctic, the American deserts and volcanic calderas in the Pacific to explore such monotone spaces – but David and I had stumbled into one a few hundred yards off the Essex coast.

We walked back along the causeway to the point where the invisible Broomway began, and there we turned into the wind and returned along the route by which we had come. With the sun now fully out, each sand ridge carried its own line of light, running along its summit like an inlaid wire, and in each pool burned a tiny version of the sun, a bright borehole to the earth's white core. Our shadows were with us now as well as our reflections: the two of us had been four on the way out to the island, and we were six on our return.

Perhaps halfway back to the Maypole, emboldened by the day,

we could no longer resist the temptation to explore further across the sand flats, and so we turned perpendicular to the line of the land and began walking straight out to sea, leaving the imagined safety of the Broomway behind us.

We did not know where the sand would quicken to mud, and yet somehow it never felt dangerous or rash. The tide was out and the moon would hold it out, and we had two hours in which to discover this vast revealed world: no more than two hours, surely, but surely also no less. The serenity of the space through which we were moving calmed me to the point of invulnerability, and thus we walked on. A mile out, the white mist still hovered, and in the haze I started to perceive impossible forms and shapes: a fleet of Viking longboats with high lug-rigged square sails; a squadron of feluccas, dhows and sgoths; cityscapes (the skyline of Istanbul, the profile of the Houses of Parliament). When I looked back, the coastline was all but imperceptible, and it was apparent that our footprints had been erased behind us, and so we splashed tracelessly on out to the tidal limit. It felt at that moment wholly true that a horizon might exert as potent a pull upon the mind as a mountain's summit.

Eventually, reluctantly, nearly two miles offshore, with the tide approaching its turn and our worries at last starting to rise through our calm – black mud through sand – we began a long slow arc back towards the coastline and the path of the Broomway, away from the outermost point. There was the return of bearings, the approach to land, a settling to recognizability. As we returned to shore, we laid plans to walk the Broomway again, later in the year, but this time at night.

Mud-caked and silly with the sun and the miles, a pair of Mesolithic tramps, we left the sand where it met the causeway near Wakering Stairs. There at the causeway's frayed end, on the brink of the Black Grounds, were the marker poles, and there – perched on the top of their stand of eelgrass – were my faithful trainers. I put them on and we walked out of Doggerland, or whichever country it was that we had discovered that day, off the mirror and onto the sea wall. For days afterwards I felt calm, level, shining, sand-flat. ∎

GRANTA

THE CELT

Mario Vargas Llosa

TRANSLATED FROM THE SPANISH BY EDITH GROSSMAN

Pentonville Prison, 1916

When they opened the door to his cell, the street noise that the stone walls had muffled came in along with the stream of light and a blast of wind. Roger woke in alarm. Blinking, still confused, struggling to calm down, he saw the silhouette of the sheriff leaning in the doorway, his flabby face, with its blond moustache and reproachful little eyes, contemplating him with a dislike the jailer had never tried to hide. This was someone who would suffer if the British government granted his request for clemency.

'Visitor,' muttered the sheriff, not taking his eyes off the prisoner.

He stood, rubbing his arms. How long had he slept? Not knowing the time was one of the torments of Pentonville. In Brixton Prison and the Tower of London he had heard the bells that marked the half-hour and the hour; here, thick walls kept the clamour of the church bells along the Caledonian Road and the noise of Islington Market from reaching the prison interior, and the guards posted at the door strictly obeyed the order not to speak to him. The sheriff put handcuffs on the prisoner and indicated that he should follow him. Was his lawyer bringing good news? Had the Cabinet met and reached a decision? Perhaps the sheriff's gaze was more filled than ever with the anger Roger inspired in him because his sentence had been commuted. They walked down the long passageway of red brick blackened by grime, past the metal doors of the cells and the discoloured walls where every twenty or twenty-five paces a high barred window allowed him to glimpse a small piece of grey sky.

When Roger entered the narrow visitors' room, his heart sank. Waiting for him was not his attorney, Maître George Gavan

Duffy, but one of his assistants, a blond, sickly-looking young man with prominent cheekbones who dressed like a fop and whom he had seen during the four days of his trial, carrying and fetching papers for the defence lawyers. Why, instead of coming in person, had Gavan Duffy sent one of his clerks?

The young man looked at him with anger and disgust in his eyes. What was wrong with this imbecile? He looks at me as if I were vermin, thought Roger.

'Any news?'

The young man shook his head.

'Regarding the petition for pardon, not yet,' he murmured drily, grimacing in a way that made him look even sicklier. 'It's necessary to wait for the Council of Ministers to meet.' The presence of the sheriff and another guard in the small room irritated Roger. Though they remained silent and motionless, he knew they were listening to everything. The idea oppressed his chest and made it difficult for him to breathe. 'But considering recent events,' the young man added, blinking rapidly and opening and closing his mouth in an exaggerated way, 'everything is more difficult now.'

'Outside news doesn't reach Pentonville. What happened?' What if the German admiralty had finally decided to attack Great Britain from the Irish coast? What if the dreamed-of invasion had taken place and the Kaiser's cannon were avenging at this very moment the Irish patriots shot by the English in the Easter Rising? If the war had taken that direction, his plans would be realized in spite of everything.

'Now it has become difficult, perhaps impossible, to succeed,' the clerk repeated. He was pale, containing his indignation, and Roger detected his skull beneath the whitish skin of his complexion. He sensed that behind him the sheriff was smiling.

'What are you talking about? Mr Gavan Duffy was optimistic about the petition. What happened to make him change his mind?'

'Your diaries,' the young man hissed. He had lowered his voice and it was difficult for Roger to hear him. 'Scotland Yard found them in your house on Ebury Street.'

He paused for a long time, waiting for Roger to say something. But since he had fallen mute, the clerk gave free rein to his indignation.

'My good man, how could you be so stupid?' He spoke slowly, making his rage more obvious. 'How could you, my good man, put such things on paper? And if you did, how could you not take the basic precaution of destroying those diaries before embarking on a conspiracy against the British Empire?

'Portions of those diaries are circulating everywhere now,' the clerk added, calmer, though his disgust persisted, not looking at Roger. 'In the Admiralty, the minister's spokesman, Captain Reginald Hall himself, has given copies to dozens of reporters. They're all over London. In Parliament, the House of Lords, Liberal and Conservative clubs, editorial offices, churches. It's the only topic of conversation in the city.'

Roger did not say anything. He did not move. Once again he had the strange sensation that had taken hold of him many times in recent months, ever since that grey, rainy April morning in 1916 when, numb with cold, he was arrested in the ruins of McKenna's Fort, in the south of Ireland: this did not have to do with him, they were talking about someone else, these things were happening to someone else.

'I know your private life is not my business, or Mr Gavan Duffy's, or anyone's,' added the young clerk, making an effort to lower the fury that saturated his voice. 'This is a strictly professional matter. Mr Gavan Duffy wanted to bring you up to date regarding the situation. And to prepare you. The request for clemency may be compromised. This morning there are already protests in some newspapers, confidences betrayed, rumours regarding the content of your diaries. The favourable public response to the petition might be affected. Merely a supposition, of course. Mr Gavan Duffy will keep you informed. Do you wish me to give him a message?'

With an almost imperceptible movement of his head, the prisoner refused. He turned immediately afterwards, facing the door of the visitors' room. The sheriff signalled the guard, who unbolted and opened the door. The return to his cell seemed interminable. During his passage down the long hall with the rock-like walls of blackened red brick, Roger had the feeling that at any moment he might trip and fall face down on those damp stones and not get up again. When he reached the metal door of his cell, he remembered: on the day they brought him to Pentonville, the sheriff had told him that, without exception, all the prisoners who occupied this cell had ended up on the gallows.

'Could I bathe today?' he asked before he went in.

The fat jailer shook his head, looking into his eyes with the same repugnance Roger had detected in the clerk's gaze.

'You cannot bathe until the day of your execution,' said the sheriff, relishing each word. 'And, on that day, only if it's your final wish. Others, instead of a bath, prefer a good meal. A bad business for Mr Ellis, because then, when they feel the noose, they shit themselves. And leave the place like a pigsty. Mr Ellis is the hangman.'

Regarding his birth on 1 September 1864, in Doyle's Cottage, Lawson Terrace, in Sandycove, a Dublin suburb, he remembered nothing, of course. Even though he always knew he had first seen the light of day in the capital of Ireland, for much of his life he took for granted what his father, Captain Roger Casement, who had served for eight years with distinction in the Third Regiment of Light Dragoons in India, had inculcated in him: his true birthplace was County Antrim, in the heart of Ulster, the Protestant and pro-British Ireland where the Casement line had been established since the eighteenth century.

Roger was brought up and educated as an Anglican in the Church of Ireland, as were his sister and brothers, Agnes (Nina), Charles and Tom – all three older than he – but since earliest childhood he had intuited that in matters of religion not everything in his family was as harmonious as in other areas. Even for a very young child it was impossible not to notice that his mother, when she was with her sisters and Scots cousins, behaved in a way that seemed to hide something.

He would discover what it was when he was an adolescent: even though Anne Jephson had apparently converted to Protestantism in order to marry his father, behind her husband's back she continued to be a Catholic ('Papist', Captain Casement would have said), going to confession, hearing Mass and taking Communion, and, in the most jealously guarded of secrets, he himself had been baptized a Catholic at the age of four, during a holiday he and his siblings took with their mother to Rhyl, in the north of Wales, to visit their maternal aunts and uncles.

During those years in Dublin, or the times they spent in London and Jersey, Roger had absolutely no interest in religion, though during the Sunday ceremony he would pray, sing and follow the service with respect in order not to displease his father. His mother had given him piano lessons and he had a clear, tuneful voice for which he was applauded at family gatherings when he sang old Irish ballads. What really interested him at that time were the stories Captain Casement, when he was in a good humour, recounted to him and his brothers and sister. Stories about India and Afghanistan, especially his battles with Afghans and Sikhs. Those exotic names and landscapes, those travels crossing forests and mountains that concealed treasures, wild beasts, predatory animals, ancient peoples with strange customs and savage gods, fired his imagination. At times the other children were bored by the stories, but young Roger could have spent hours, even days, listening to his father's adventures along the remote frontiers of the Empire.

Though he admired his father, the parent Roger really loved was his mother, a slender woman who seemed to float instead of walk, who had light eyes and hair, whose extremely soft hands when they tousled his curls or caressed his body at bath time filled him with happiness. One of the first things he would learn – at the age of five or six – was that he could run into his mother's arms only when the captain was not nearby. His father, true to the Puritan tradition of his family, did not believe in coddling children, since this made them soft in the struggle to survive. In his father's presence, Roger kept his distance from the pale, delicate Anne Jephson. But when the captain went out to meet friends at his club or take a walk, the boy would run to her and she would cover him with kisses and caresses. At times Nina, Charles and Tom protested: 'You love Roger more than us.' Their mother assured them she did not, she loved them all the same, except Roger was very little and needed more attention and affection than the older ones.

When his mother died, in 1873, Roger was nine years old. He had learned to swim and won all the races with children his age and even older. Unlike Nina, Charles and Tom, who shed many tears during the wake and burial of Anne Jephson, Roger did not cry even once. During those gloomy days, the Casement household was transformed into a funeral chapel filled with people dressed in mourning who spoke in low voices and embraced Captain Casement and the four children with contrite faces, pronouncing words of condolence. For many days he couldn't say a word, as if he had fallen mute. He responded to questions with movements of his head, or gestures, and remained serious, his head lowered and his gaze lost, even at night in the darkened room, unable to sleep. From then on and for the rest of his life, from time to time in dreams the figure of Anne Jephson would come to visit him with that inviting smile, opening her arms where he would huddle, feeling protected and happy with those slim fingers on his head, his back, his cheeks, a sensation that seemed to defend him against the evils of the world.

His brothers and sister were soon consoled. And Roger too, apparently. Because even though he recovered his speech, this was a subject he never mentioned.

The one who was not consoled and never became himself again was Captain Roger Casement. Since he wasn't effusive and young Roger and the other children had never seen him showering their mother with gallantries, the four of them were surprised at the cataclysm his wife's disappearance meant for their father. Always so meticulous, he dressed carelessly now, he let his beard grow, scowled, his eyes filled with resentment as if his children were to blame for his being a widower. Shortly after Anne's death, he decided to leave Dublin and sent the four children to Ulster, to Magherintemple House, the family estate, where from then on their paternal great-uncle, John Casement, and his wife Charlotte, would take charge of their upbringing. Their father, as if wanting to have nothing to do with them, went to live thirty miles away, at the Adair Arms Hotel in Ballymena where, as Great-Uncle John let slip occasionally, Captain Casement, 'half mad with grief and loneliness', dedicated his days and his nights to spiritualism, attempting to communicate with his dead wife through mediums, cards and crystal balls.

From then on Roger rarely saw his father and never again heard him tell those stories about India and Afghanistan. Captain Roger Casement died of tuberculosis in 1876, three years after his wife. Roger had just turned twelve.

When Roger was fifteen, Great-Uncle John Casement advised him to abandon his studies and look for work, since he and his brothers and sister had no income to live on. He happily accepted the advice. By mutual agreement they decided Roger would go to Liverpool where there were more possibilities for work than in Northern Ireland, and live with his aunt and her husband, Grace and Edward Bannister. In fact, shortly after arriving at the Bannisters', Uncle Edward obtained a position for him in the same company where he himself had worked for so many years. Roger began as an apprentice in the shipping company soon after his fifteenth birthday. He looked older. He was very tall and slim, with deep grey eyes, curly black hair, very light skin, even teeth, and he was temperate, discreet, neat, amiable and obliging. He spoke English with an Irish accent, the cause of jokes among his cousins.

He was a serious boy, tenacious and laconic, not very well prepared intellectually but hard-working. He took his duties in the Department of Administration and Accounting very seriously, determined to learn. At first, his tasks were those of a messenger. He fetched and carried documents from one office to another and went to the port to take care of formalities regarding ships, customs and warehouses. In the four years he worked at Elder Dempster Lines, Roger did not become intimate with anyone due to his retiring manner and austere habits: opposed to carousing, he practically did not drink and was never seen frequenting the bars and brothels in the port. He did, however, become an inveterate smoker. His passion for Africa and his commitment to doing well in the company led him to read carefully and fill with notes the pamphlets and publications dealing with maritime trade between the British Empire and West Africa that made the rounds of the offices. Then he would repeat with conviction the ideas that permeated those texts. Bringing European products to Africa and importing the raw materials that African soil produced was, more than a commercial operation, an enterprise in favour of the progress of peoples caught in pre-history, sunk in cannibalism and the slave trade. Commerce brought religion, morality, law, the values of a modern, educated, free and democratic Europe, progress that would eventually transform tribal unfortunates into men and women of our time. In this enterprise, the British Empire was in the vanguard of Europe, and one had to feel proud of being part of it and the work accomplished at Elder Dempster Lines. His office colleagues exchanged mocking looks and wondered whether young Roger Casement was a fool or a smart alec, whether he believed that nonsense or declaimed it in order to look good to his superiors.

He made three trips to West Africa on the SS *Bounny* and the experience filled him with so much enthusiasm that after the third voyage he gave up his job and announced to his siblings, aunt, uncle and cousins that he had decided to live and work in Africa. He did this in an exalted way and, as his Uncle Edward said to him, like those crusaders in the Middle Ages who left for the East to liberate Jerusalem. The family went to the port to see him off, and his cousin Gee and sister Nina shed some tears. Roger was twenty years old.

Pentonville Prison, 1916

'Visitor,' muttered the sheriff, looking at him with contempt in his eyes and voice. While Roger stood and dusted off his prisoner's uniform with his hands, he added sarcastically: 'You're in the papers again today, Mr Casement. Not for being a traitor to your country –'

'My country is Ireland,' Roger interrupted.

'– but because of your perversions.' The sheriff made a clucking noise with his tongue as if he were going to spit. 'A traitor and pervert at the same time. What garbage! It will be a pleasure to see you dancing at the end of a rope, ex-Sir Roger.'

'The Cabinet turned down the petition for clemency?'

'Not yet,' the sheriff hesitated before answering. 'But it will. And so will His Majesty the King, of course.'

'I won't petition him for clemency. He's your king, not mine.'

'Ireland is British,' muttered the sheriff. 'Now more than ever after crushing that cowardly Easter Week Rising in Dublin. A stab in the back of a country at war. I wouldn't have shot your leaders, I would've hanged them.'

He fell silent because they had reached the visitors' room.

It wasn't Father Carey, the Catholic chaplain at Pentonville Prison, who had come to see him, but Gertrude, Gee, his cousin. She embraced him tightly and Roger felt her trembling in his arms. He thought of a little bird numb with cold. Gee had aged since his imprisonment and trial. The clear light of her eyes had gone out and there were wrinkles on her face, neck and hands. She dressed in dark, worn clothing.

'I must stink like all the rubbish in the world,' Roger joked, pointing at his coarse blue uniform. 'They took away my right to bathe. They'll give it back only once, if I'm executed.'

'You won't be, the Council of Ministers will grant clemency,' Gertrude asserted, nodding to give more force to her words. 'President Wilson will intercede with the British government on your behalf, Roger. He's promised to send a telegram. They'll grant it, there won't be an execution, believe me.'

The way she said this was so strained, her voice broke so much, that Roger felt sorry for her, for all his friends who, like Gee, suffered these days from the same anguish and uncertainty. He wanted to ask about the attacks in the papers the jailer had mentioned but controlled himself. The president of the United States would intercede for him? If he did, his action would have an effect. There was still a possibility the Cabinet would commute his sentence.

There was no place to sit, and Roger and Gertrude remained standing, very close together, their backs to the sheriff and the guard. The four presences transformed the small visitors' room into a claustrophobic place.

'No one believes the vile things they're publishing about you,' said Gertrude, lowering her voice to a whisper, as if the two men standing there might hear her. 'Every decent person is indignant that the government is using this kind of slander to weaken the manifesto so many important people have signed in your favour, Roger.'

Her voice broke, as if she were going to sob. Roger embraced her again.

'You know that everything I've done has been for Ireland, don't you? For a noble, generous cause. Isn't that true, Gee?'

She had started to sob, very quietly, her face pressed against his chest.

'We're doing everything, everything to help you, Roger,' said Gee, becoming very serious again. Her voice had aged too; firm and pleasant once, it now was hesitant and cracked. 'We who love you, and there are many of us. Moving heaven and earth. Writing letters, visiting politicians, officials, diplomats. Explaining, pleading. Knocking at every door.'

'Ten minutes,' decreed the sheriff. 'Time to say goodbye.'

Central Africa, 1903

The journey of the British consul, Roger Casement, up the Congo River, which began on 5 June 1903 and would change his life forever, had been scheduled to begin the previous year. He had been suggesting this expedition to the Foreign Office since 1900 when, after serving in Old Calabar (Nigeria), Lourenço Marques (Maputo) and São Paulo de Luanda (Angola), he officially took up residence as Consul of Great Britain in Boma – a misbegotten village – claiming that the best way to prepare a report on the situation of the natives in the Congo Free State was to leave this remote capital for the forests and tribes of the Middle and Upper Congo. That was where the exploitation was occurring that he had been reporting to the Ministry of Foreign Relations since his arrival in these territories. Finally, after weighing those reasons of state that never failed to turn the consul's stomach, even though he understood them – Great Britain was an ally of Belgium and did not want to push her into Germany's arms – the Foreign Office authorized him to undertake the journey to the villages, stations, missions, posts, encampments and factories where the extraction of rubber took place, the black gold avidly coveted now all over the world for tyres and bumpers on trucks and cars and a thousand other industrial and household uses. He had to verify on the ground how much truth was in the denunciations of atrocities committed against natives in the Congo of His Majesty Leopold II, King of the Belgians, made by the Aborigines' Protection Society in London and some Baptist churches and Catholic missions in Europe and the United States.

He prepared for the journey with his customary meticulousness and an enthusiasm he hid from Belgian functionaries and the colonists and merchants of Boma. Now, with a thorough knowledge of the subject, he would be able to argue to his superiors that the Empire, faithful to its tradition of justice and fair play, should lead an international campaign to put an end to this ignominy.

But then, in the middle of 1902, he had his third attack of malaria, one even worse than the previous two; he had suffered from the disease ever since he had come to Africa in 1884, just when he had realized his life's desire: to be part of an expedition headed by the most famous adventurer on African soil, Henry Morton Stanley. To serve at the pleasure of the explorer who, in a legendary trek of close to three years between 1874 and 1877, had crossed Africa from east to west, following the course of the Congo River from its source to its mouth in the Atlantic! To accompany the hero who found the missing Dr Livingstone! That was when he suffered his first attack, as if the gods wanted to extinguish his exaltation. But this was nothing compared to the second three years later – 1887 – and above all, this third attack, in 1902, when for the first time he thought he would die. The symptoms were the same that dawn in the middle of 1902 when, his travelling bag already packed with maps, compass, pencils and notebooks, he felt himself trembling with cold as he opened his eyes in the bedroom on the top floor of his house in Boma, in the colonists' district. He moved aside the mosquito netting and saw through the windows, without glass or curtains but with metal screens to keep out insects and riddled now by a downpour, the muddy waters of the great river and the outline of islands covered with vegetation. He couldn't stand. His legs collapsed under him, as if they were made of rags. John, his bulldog, was frightened and began to jump and bark. He let himself fall back into bed. His body was burning and the cold penetrated his bones. He shouted for Charlie and Mawuku, the Congolese steward and cook who slept on the lower floor, but no one answered. They must have gone out and, caught by the storm, run to take shelter under a baobab tree until it abated. Malaria again? The consul cursed. Just on the eve of the expedition? He would have diarrhoea and haemorrhages, and a debilitated state that would oblige him to stay in bed for days, weeks, dazed and shivering.

For three weeks Roger was devastated by fevers and fits of shivering. He lost a stone, and on the first day he could stand, he took a few steps and fell to the floor exhausted, in a state of weakness he did not recall having felt before. He telegraphed the Foreign Office that the state of his health obliged him to postpone the expedition. And since the rains made the forests and river impassable then, the expedition to the interior of the Congo Free State had to wait a few more months that would turn into a year. Another year, recovering very slowly from the fevers and trying to regain the weight he had lost, picking up the tennis racket again, swimming, playing bridge or chess to pass the long nights in Boma, while he resumed his tedious consular tasks: making note of the ships that arrived and departed, the goods the merchant ships of Antwerp unloaded – rifles, munitions, chicote whips, wine, holy pictures, crucifixes, coloured glass beads – and the ones they carried to Europe, the immense stacks of rubber, ivory and animal skins.

The apparent reason for the 1884 expedition in which Roger served his apprenticeship as an explorer had been to prepare the communities scattered along the banks of the Upper, Middle and Lower Congo, in thousands of miles of dense jungles, gorges, waterfalls and mountains thick with vegetation, for the arrival of the European merchants and administrators that the International Congo Society (AIC), presided over by Leopold II, would bring in once the Western powers granted the king the concession. Stanley and his companions had to explain to the half-naked chieftains, tattooed and feathered, sometimes with thorns in their faces and arms, sometimes with reed funnels on their penises, the benevolent intentions of the Europeans: they would come to help them improve their living conditions, rid them of deadly plagues like sleeping sickness, educate them and open their eyes to the truths of this world and the next, thanks to which their children and grandchildren would attain a life that was decent, just and free.

I wasn't aware because I didn't want to be aware, he thought. Charlie had covered him with all the blankets in the house. In spite of that and the blazing sun outside, the consul, curled up and freezing, trembled beneath the mosquito net. But worse than being a willing blind man was finding explanations for what any impartial observer

would have called a swindle. Because in all the villages reached by
the expedition of 1884, after distributing beads and trinkets and
then the aforementioned explanations made by interpreters (many
of whom could not make themselves understood by the natives),
Stanley had the chiefs and witch doctors sign contracts, written in
French, pledging to provide manual labour, lodging, guides and food
to the officials, agents and employees of the AIC in the work they
would undertake to achieve the goals that inspired the Society. They
signed with Xs, lines, blots, drawings, without a word and without
knowing what they were signing or what signing was, amused by the
necklaces, bracelets and adornments of coloured glass they received
and the little swallows of liquor with which Stanley invited them to
toast their agreement.

As the years passed – eighteen had gone by since the expedition
carried out under Stanley's leadership in 1884 – Roger
Casement reached the conclusion that the hero of his childhood
and youth was one of the most unscrupulous villains the West had
excreted onto the continent of Africa. In spite of that, like everyone
who had worked under Stanley's command, he could not fail to
acknowledge his charisma, his affability, his magic, that mixture of
temerity and cold calculation with which the adventurer accumulated
great feats. He came and went through Africa, on the one hand
sowing desolation and death – burning and looting villages, shooting
natives, flaying the backs of his porters with the chicotes made of
strips of hippopotamus hide that had left thousands of scars on
ebony bodies throughout Africa – and on the other opening routes to
commerce and evangelization in immense territories filled with wild
beasts, predatory insects and epidemics which seemed to respect him
like one of those titans of Homeric legends and biblical histories.

'Don't you sometimes feel remorse, have a bad conscience
because of what we're doing?'

The question burst from the young man's lips in an unpremeditated
way. And he could not take it back. The flames from the bonfire in the

centre of the camp crackled as small branches and imprudent insects burned there.

'Remorse? A bad conscience?' The head of the expedition wrinkled his nose and the expression on his freckled, sunburned face soured, as if he had never heard those words and was trying to guess what they meant. 'For what?'

'For the contracts we have them sign,' said Casement, overcoming his embarrassment. 'They place their lives, their villages, everything they have, in the hands of the International Congo Society. And not one of them knows what he's signing because none of them speaks French.'

'If they knew French, they still wouldn't understand those contracts.' The explorer laughed his frank, open laugh, one of his most amiable attributes. 'I don't even understand what they mean.'

He was a strong, very short man, almost a midget, still young, with an athletic appearance, flashing grey eyes, thick moustache and an irresistible personality. He always wore high boots, a pistol at his waist and a light jacket with a good number of pockets. He laughed again, and the overseers of the expedition, who with Stanley and Roger drank coffee and smoked around the fire, laughed too, adulating their leader. But Casement did not laugh.

'I do, though it's true the rigmarole they're written in seems intentional, so they won't be understood,' Roger said respectfully. 'It comes down to something very simple. They give their lands to the AIC in exchange for promises of social assistance. They pledge to support the construction projects: roads, bridges, docks, factories. To supply the labour needed for the camps and public order, and feed the officials and workers for as long as the work continues. The Society offers nothing in return. No salaries, no compensation. I always believed we were here for the good of the Africans, Mr Stanley. I'd like you, whom I've admired since I was a boy, to give me reasons to go on believing it's true. That these contracts are, in fact, for their good.'

E ighteen years later, in the disordered images the fever sent whirling around his head, Roger recalled the look, inquisitive, surprised, mocking at moments, with which Henry Morton Stanley inspected him.

'Africa wasn't made for the weak,' he said at last, as if talking to himself. 'The things that worry you are signs of weakness. In the world we're in, I mean. This isn't the United States or England, as you must realize. In Africa the weak don't survive. They're finished off by bites, fevers, poisoned arrows or the tsetse fly.'

Pentonville Prison, 1916

'Y ou hate me and can't hide it,' Roger Casement said. The sheriff, after a moment's surprise, agreed with a grimace that for an instant transformed his bloated face.

'I have no reason to hide it,' he murmured. 'But you're wrong. I don't feel hatred for you. I feel contempt. That's all traitors deserve.'

They were walking along the corridor of soot-stained bricks towards the visitors' room, where the Catholic chaplain, Father Carey, was waiting for the prisoner. Through the narrow barred windows, Casement could see large patches of dark, swollen clouds. He imagined the stalls and stands at the nearby market, in the middle of Islington's large park, soaked and shaken by the storm. He felt a sting of envy thinking about the people who were buying and selling, protected by raincoats and umbrellas.

'You had everything,' the sheriff grumbled behind him. 'Diplomatic posts. Decorations. The king knighted you. And you went to sell yourself to the Germans.'

He fell silent, and Roger thought the sheriff was sighing.

'Whenever I think about my poor son killed over there in the trenches, I tell myself you're one of his killers, Mr Casement.'

'I'm very sorry you lost a son,' Roger replied, not turning round. 'I know you won't believe me, but I haven't killed anyone yet.'

'You won't have time to do that now,' was the sheriff's judgement.

'Thank God.' They had reached the door of the visitors' room. The sheriff stayed outside, next to the jailer on guard. Only visits from chaplains were private; in all the others the sheriff or a guard, and sometimes both, remained. Roger was happy to see the silhouette of the cleric. Father Carey came forward to meet him and took his hand.

'I made enquiries and have the reply,' he announced, smiling. 'Your memory was exact. You were, in fact, baptized as a child in the parish of Rhyl, in Wales. Your name is in the register. Your mother and two of your maternal aunts were present. You don't need to be received again into the Catholic Church. You've always been in it.'

Roger Casement agreed. The very distant impression that had accompanied him his whole life was correct. His mother had baptized him, hiding it from his father, on one of their trips to Wales. He was glad because of the complicity the secret established between him and Anne Jephson. And because in this way he felt more in tune with himself, his mother and Ireland, as if his approach to Catholicism were a natural consequence of everything he had done and attempted in these last few years, including his mistakes and failures.

Not long before, a small bench had been installed in the visitors' room. They sat on it, their knees touching. Father Carey had been a chaplain in London prisons for more than twenty years and accompanied many men condemned to death to their end. His constant dealings with prison populations had not hardened his character. He was considerate and attentive and Roger Casement liked him from their first encounter. He did not recall ever having heard him say anything that might wound him; on the contrary, when it was time to ask questions or talk to him he showed extreme delicacy. He always felt good with him. Father Carey was tall, bony, almost skeletal, with very white skin and a greying, pointed beard that covered part of his chin. His eyes were always damp, as if he had just cried, even though he was laughing.

'I thank you for not asking me anything about those loathsome things they apparently are saying about me, Father Carey.'

'I haven't read them, Roger. When someone has attempted to talk to me about them, I've made him be quiet. I don't know and don't want to know what that's about.'

'I don't know either,' Roger said with a smile. 'You can't read newspapers here. One of my lawyer's clerks told me they were so scandalous they put the petition for clemency at risk. Degeneracies, terrible vileness, it seems.'

Father Carey listened to him with his usual tranquil expression.

'I believe it's better not to know what they're accusing me of. Alice Stopford Green thinks it's an operation mounted by the government to counteract the sympathy in many sectors for the petition for clemency.'

'Nothing can be excluded in the world of politics,' said the priest. 'It's not the cleanest of human activities.'

There were some discreet knocks at the door, which opened, and the sheriff's plump face appeared. 'Five more minutes, Father Carey.'

'The director of the prison gave me half an hour. Weren't you told?'

The sheriff's face showed surprise. 'If you say so, I believe you,' and he apologized. 'Excuse the interruption, then. You still have twenty minutes.' He disappeared and the door closed again.

'Is there more news from Ireland?' Roger asked, somewhat abruptly, as if he suddenly wanted to change the subject.

'It seems the shootings have stopped. Public opinion, not only there but in England too, has been very critical of the summary executions. Now the government has announced that all those arrested in the Easter Week Rising will pass through the courts.'

Roger Casement became distracted. He looked at the tiny window in the wall, also barred. He saw only a tiny square of grey sky and thought about the great paradox: he had been tried and sentenced for carrying arms for an attempt at violent secession by Ireland, when in fact he had undertaken that dangerous, perhaps absurd trip from Germany to the coast of Tralee to try to stop the uprising he was sure would fail from the moment he learned it was being prepared. Was all of history like that? A more or less idyllic fabrication, rational and coherent, about what had been in raw, harsh reality a chaotic and arbitrary jumble of plans, accidents, intrigues, fortuitous events, coincidences, multiple interests that had provoked changes, upheavals, advances and retreats, always unexpected and surprising with respect to what was anticipated or experienced by the protagonists?

'It's likely I'll go down in history as one of those responsible for the Easter Week Rising,' he said with irony. 'You and I know I came here risking my life to try to stop that rebellion.'

'Well, you and I and someone else,' Father Carey said with a laugh, pointing up with a finger.

'In Africa,' Roger said, 'I often saw blacks as well as whites fall suddenly into a crisis of despair. In the middle of the undergrowth, when we lost our way. When we entered a territory the African porters considered hostile. In the middle of the river, when a canoe overturned. Or in the villages. I was never afraid of death until now. I saw it at close range many times. In the Congo, on expeditions through inhospitable places filled with wild animals. In Amazonia, in rivers replete with whirlpools and surrounded by outlaws. Just a short while ago, when I left the submarine at Tralee, on Banna Strand, when the rowing boat capsized and it seemed we would all drown. I've often felt death very close. And I wasn't afraid. But I am now.

'If the petition is rejected, will you be with me until the end?' he asked, not looking at the priest.

'Of course,' said Father Carey. 'You shouldn't think about that. Nothing has been decided yet.'

'I know that, Father Carey. I haven't lost hope. But it does me good to know you will be there with me. Your presence will give me courage. I won't make an unfortunate scene, I promise.'

'Would you like us to pray together?'

'Let's talk a little more, if you don't mind. This will be the last question I'll ask you about the matter. If I'm executed, can my body be taken to Ireland and buried there?'

He sensed the chaplain hesitating and looked at him. Father Carey had paled slightly. He saw his discomfit as the priest shook his head.

'No, Roger. If that happens, you'll be buried in the prison cemetery.'

'In enemy territory,' Casement murmured, trying to make a joke that failed. 'If you like, we can pray now, Father.'

Whenever he prayed he thought of his mother, a slim figure dressed in white, a broad-brimmed straw hat with a blue ribbon that danced in the wind, walking under the trees in a field. Were they in Wales, in Ireland, in Antrim, in Jersey? He didn't know where, but the countryside was as beautiful as the smile shining on Anne Jephson's face. Praying like this brought back to him a childhood when, thanks to his mother's presence, everything in life was beautiful and happy.

They parted with a handshake. In the long, damp corridor, without having planned it, Roger Casement said to the sheriff: 'I'm very sorry about the death of your son. I haven't had children. I imagine there's no more terrible pain in this life.'

The sheriff made a small noise with his throat but did not respond. In his cell, Roger lay on his cot and picked up *The Imitation of Christ*. But he couldn't concentrate on reading. The letters danced before his eyes and in his head images threw out sparks in a mad round. The figure of Anne Jephson appeared more than once.

What would his life have been like if his mother, instead of dying so young, had been alive as he became an adolescent, a man? He probably would not have undertaken the African adventure. He would have remained in Ireland or in Liverpool and had a bureaucratic career and an honourable, obscure and comfortable life with a wife and children. He smiled: no, that kind of life wasn't for him. The one he had led, with all its misfortunes, was preferable. He had seen the world, his horizons had broadened enormously, he had a better understanding of life, human reality, the innermost core of colonialism, the tragedy of so many peoples caused by that aberration.

If the subtle Anne Jephson had lived, he would not have discovered the sad, beautiful history of Ireland, the one they never taught him in Ballymena High School, the history still hidden from the children and adolescents of North Antrim. They were still made to believe that Ireland was a savage country with no past worth remembering, raised to civilization by the occupier, educated and modernized by the Empire that stripped it of its tradition, language and sovereignty. He had learned all this in Africa, where he never would have spent the best years of his youth and early maturity or ever come to feel so much pride in the country where he was born and so much rage because of what Great Britain had done, if his mother had lived.

Were they justified, the sacrifices of his twenty years in Africa, the seven in South America, the year or so in the heart of the Amazonian jungles, the year and a half of loneliness, sickness and frustration in Germany? He never had cared about money, but wasn't it absurd that after having worked so hard all his life, he was now a pauper? The last balance in his bank account was ten pounds sterling. He had never learned to save. He had spent all his income on others – on his three siblings, on humanitarian organizations like the Congo Reform Association and on Irish nationalist institutions like St Enda's School and the Gaelic League, to which for some time he had handed over his entire income. In order to spend money on those causes he had lived austerely, for example, residing for long periods of time in cheap boarding houses not appropriate to his rank (as his colleagues at the Foreign Office had insinuated). No one would remember the donations, gifts or assistance now that he had failed. Only his final defeat would be remembered.

But that was not the worst thing.

Degeneracies, perversions, vices, all human lewdness. That is what the British government wanted to remain of him.

The campaign to discredit him claimed no one would cry over this human disgrace, this degenerate that decent society would be rid of thanks to the gallows. It was stupid to have left those diaries for anyone to find when he went to the United States. A piece of negligence that the Empire would make very good use of and for a long time would cloud the truth of his life, his political conduct and even his death.

He had been weak and succumbed to lust many times. Not as many as he had written in his pocket diaries and notebooks, even though writing what he hadn't experienced, what he only had wanted to experience, was undoubtedly also a way – cowardly and timid – to have the experience and therefore surrender to temptation. Was he paying for that in spite of not really having enjoyed it except in the uncertain, ungraspable way fantasies were experienced? Would he have to pay for everything he hadn't done, had only desired and written about? God would know how to differentiate and surely would punish those rhetorical errors less severely than the sins he had really committed.

In any event, writing what he hadn't experienced in order to pretend he had already carried an implicit punishment: the sensation of failure and frustration in which the lying games in his diaries always ended (as did the real experiences, for that matter). But now those irresponsible games had placed in the hands of the enemy a formidable weapon to vilify his name and memory.

Roger recalled, in those distant years of his adolescence, that his first feelings for well-formed bodies, virile muscles, the harmonious slimness of adolescents, did not seem malicious, concupiscent emotion but a manifestation of sensibility and aesthetic enthusiasm. This is what he had believed for a long time. And this same artistic vocation was what had induced him to learn how to take photographs in order to capture those beautiful bodies on pieces of cardboard. At some moment he realized, when he was already living in Africa, that his admiration was not healthy or, rather, it was healthy and unhealthy at the same time, for those harmonious, sweating, muscular bodies, without a drop of oil, in which he could perceive the material sensuality of felines, produced in him, along with ecstasy and admiration, avidity, desire, a mad longing to caress them. This was how temptations became part of his life, revolutionized it, filled it with secrets, anguish, fear, but also with startling moments of pleasure.

And remorse and bitterness, of course. At the supreme moment, would God do the arithmetic? Would He pardon him? Punish him?

Demoralization overwhelmed him. It turned him into a being as helpless as the Congolese attacked by the tsetse fly and whose sleeping sickness prevented them from moving their arms, feet, lips, or even keeping their eyes open. Did it keep them from thinking as well? Unfortunately, these gusts of pessimism sharpened his lucidity, turned his brain into a crackling bonfire. The pages of the diary handed by the Admiralty spokesman to the press, which so horrified the red-faced assistant to Maître Gavan Duffy, were they real or falsified? He thought of the stupidity that formed a central part of human nature and also, naturally, of Roger Casement. He was very thorough and well known, as a diplomat, for not taking any initiative or the slightest step without foreseeing all possible consequences. And now, here he was, caught in a stupid trap constructed throughout his life by himself, giving his enemies a weapon that would sink him in disrepute.

Startled, he realized he was bellowing with laughter. ■

DAMON ALBARN'S

EN
O

Dr Dee

AN OPERA INSPIRED BY THE
ENIGMATIC ELIZABETHAN MYSTIC
WHO SHAPED THE BRITISH EMPIRE

DIRECTED BY
RUFUS NORRIS

Tickets
from only
£29

25 Jun – 7 Jul

ENO LIVE AT THE LONDON COLISEUM
www.eno.org · 0871 911 0200

Calls cost 10p per minute plus network extras

LION AND PANTHER IN LONDON

Tania James

THE SENSATION
OF
THE WRESTLING WORLD

EXCLUSIVE ENGAGEMENT

OF INDIA'S
CATCH-AS-CATCH-CAN CHAMPIONS

GENUINE CHALLENGERS OF THE UNIVERSE
ALL CORNERS. ANY NATIONALITY. NO ONE BARRED.

GAMA | IMAM

The Great, champion undefeated wrestler of India, winner of over 200 legitimate matches.

His brother, champion of Lahore.

(These wrestlers are both British subjects.)

£5 will be presented to any competitor, no matter what nationality, whom any member of the team fails to throw in five minutes.

GAMA, THE LION OF THE PUNJAB,
will attempt to throw any three men, without restriction as to weight, in 30 minutes, any night during this engagement, and competitors are asked to present themselves, either publicly or through the management.

NO ONE BARRED!! ALL CHAMPIONS CORDIALLY INVITED!!
THE BIGGER THE BETTER!!

Gama the Great is bored. Imam translates the newspaper notice as best he can while his brother slumps in the wingback chair. On the table between them rests a rose marble chessboard, frozen in play. Raindrops wriggle down the windowpane. It is a mild June in 1910 and their seventh day in London without a single challenge.

Their tour manager, Mr Benjamin, lured them here from Lahore, promising furious bouts under calcium lights, their names in every newspaper that matters. But the very champions who used to thump their chests and flex their backs for photos are now staying indoors, as if they have ironing to do. Not a word from Benjamin 'Doc' Roller or Strangler Lewis, not from the Swede Jon Lemm or the whole fleet of Japanese fresh from Tokyo.

Every year in London, a world champion is crowned anew, one white man after the next, none of whom have wrestled a *pehlwan*. They know nothing of Handsome Hasan or Kalloo or the giant Kikkar Singh, who once uprooted an acacia tree barehanded, just because it was disrupting the view from his window. Gama has defeated them all, and more, but how is he to be Champion of the World if this half of the world is in hiding?

Mr Benjamin went to great trouble to arrange the trip. He cosied up to the Mishra family and got the Bengali millionaires to finance the cause, printed up press releases, and rented them a small, grey-shingled house removed from the thick of the city, with space enough out back to carry on their training. The house is comfortable enough, if crowded with tables, standing lamps, settees and armchairs. When it rains, they push the furniture to the walls and conduct their routines in the centre of the sitting room.

Other adjustments are not so easy. Gama keeps tumbling out of bed four hours late, his moustache squashed on one side. Imam climbs upon the toilet bowl each morning, his feet on the rim, and engages in a bout with his bowels. Afterwards, he inspects the results. If these are coiled like a snake ready to strike, his guru used to say, all is in good shape. There are no snakes in London.

These days, when Mr Benjamin stops by, he has little more to offer than an elaborate salaam and any issues of *Sporting Life* and *Health & Strength* in which they have been mentioned, however briefly. He is baby-faced and bald, normally jovial, but Imam senses something remote about him, withheld, as though the face he gives them is only one of many. 'You and your theories,' Gama says.

Left to themselves, Gama and Imam continue to hibernate in the melancholy house. They run two miles up and down the road, occasionally coughing in the fume and grumble of a motor car. They wrestle. They do hundreds of *bethaks* and *dands*, lost in the calm that comes of repetition, and at the end of the day, they rest. They bathe. They smooth their skin with dry mustard that conjures homeward thoughts of plains ablaze with yellow blooms. Sometimes, reluctantly, they play another game of chess.

On the eighth morning, Mr Benjamin pays a visit. For the first time in their acquaintance, he looks agitated and fidgets with his hat. His handshake is damp. He follows the wrestlers into the sitting room, carrying with him the stink of a recently smoked cigar.

The cook brings milky yogurt and ghee for the wrestlers, tea for Mr Benjamin. Gama and Imam brought their own cook from Lahore, old Ahmed, who is deaf in one ear but knows every nuance of the *pehlwan* diet. They were warned about English food – mushy potatoes, dense pies, gloomy puddings – the sort of fare that would render them leaden in body and mind.

When Mr Benjamin has run out of small talk, he empties a sober sigh into his cup. 'Right. Well, I suppose you're wondering about the tour.'

'Yes, quite,' Imam says, unsure of his words but too anxious to care. It seems a bad sign when Mr Benjamin sets his cup and saucer aside.

Wrestling in England, Mr Benjamin explains, has become something of a business. Wrestlers are paid to take a fall once in a while, to pounce and pound and growl on cue. After the match, the wrestlers and their managers split the money. Occasionally these hoaxes are discovered to great public outcry, the most recent being the face-off between Youssouf the Terrible Turk and Stanislaus Zbyszko. After Zbyszko's calculated win, it was revealed that Youssouf the Terrible was actually a Bulgarian named Ivan with debts to pay off.

'And you know of this now only?' Imam asks.

'No – well, not entirely.' Mr Benjamin absently cracks his knuckles. 'I thought I could bring you fellows and turn things around. Show everyone what the sport bloody well should be.'

Imam glances at Gama, who is leaning forward, gazing at Mr Benjamin's miserable face with empathy.

'There would be challengers,' Mr Benjamin shrugs, 'if only you would agree to take a fall here and there.'

After receiving these words from Imam, Gama pulls back, as if bitten. 'Fall how?' Gama says.

'On purpose,' Imam explains quietly.

Gama's mouth becomes small and solemn. Imam tells Mr Benjamin that they will have to decline the offer.

'But you came all this way.' Mr Benjamin gives a flaccid laugh. 'Why go back with empty pockets?'

For emphasis, Mr Benjamin pulls his own lint-ridden pockets inside out and nods at Gama with the sort of encouragement one might show a thick-headed child.

Gama asks Imam why Mr Benjamin is exposing the lining of his trousers.

'The *langot* we wear, it does not have pockets,' Imam tells Mr Benjamin, hoping the man might appreciate the poetry of his refusal. Mr Benjamin blinks at him and explains, in even slower English, what he means by 'empty pockets'.

So this is London, Imam thinks, nodding at Mr Benjamin. A city where athletes are actors, where the ring is a stage.

In a final effort, Mr Benjamin takes their story to the British press. *Health & Strength* publishes a piece entitled 'Gama's Hopeless Quest for an Opponent', while *Sporting Life* runs his full-length photograph, alongside large-lettered text: GAMA, THE GREAT INDIAN CATCH-CAN WRESTLER, WHOSE CHALLENGES TO MEET ALL THE CHAMPIONS HAVE BEEN UNANSWERED. The photographer encouraged Gama to strike a menacing pose, but in the photo, Gama appears flat-footed and blank, his fists feebly raised, a stance that wouldn't menace a pigeon.

Finally, for an undisclosed sum, Doc Roller takes up Gama's challenge. Mr Benjamin says that Doc is a fully trained doctor and the busiest wrestler in England.

They meet at the Alhambra, a sprawling pavilion of arches and domes, its name studded in bulbs that blaze haloes through the fog. Inside, golden foliage and gilded trees climb the walls. Men sit shoulder to shoulder around the roped-off ring, and behind them, more men in straw boaters and caps, standing on bleachers, making their assessments of Gama the Great, the dusky bulk of his chest, the sculpted sandstone of each thigh. Imam sits ringside next to Mr Benjamin, in a marigold robe and turban. He is a vivid blotch in a sea of grumpy greys and browns. He feels slightly overdressed.

Gama warms his muscles by doing *bethaks*. He glances up but keeps squatting when Roller swings his long legs over the ropes, dauntingly tall, and whips off his white satin robe to reveal abdominal muscles stacked like bricks above the waistband of his wrestling pants.

They take turns on the scale. Doc is a full head taller and exceeds Gama by thirty-four pounds. Following the announcement of their weights, the Master of Ceremonies bellows: 'No money in the world would ever buy the Great Gama for a fixed match!' To this, a hailstorm of whooping applause.

Imam absently pinches the silk of his brother's robe, draped across his lap. Every time he watches his brother in a match, a familiar disquiet spreads through his stomach, much like the first time he witnessed Gama in competition.

Imam was eight, Gama twelve, when their uncle brought them to Jodhpur for the national strongman competition. Rajah Jaswant Singh had gathered hundreds of men from all across India to see who could last the longest drilling *bethaks*. The competitors took their places on the square field of earth within the palace courtyard, and twelve turbaned royal guards stood sentinel around the grounds, their tall gold spears glinting in the sun. Spectators formed a border some yards away from the field, and when little Gama emerged from their ranks and joined the strongmen, laughter trailed behind. Gama was short for his age, but hale and sturdy even then.

When the Rajah raised his hand, Gama began, up and down, steady as a piston. His gaze never wavered, fixed on a single point of concentration in the air before him, as if his competitors and critics had all dissolved into the heat. At some point, Imam wanted to sit in the shade, but his uncle refused to move, too busy staring at Gama as if with every *bethak*, the boy was transforming into something winged and brilliant. When Imam complained about the sun, his uncle said, 'Look at your *bhaiya*. Does he complain?'

Imam looked at his brother: serene and focused, impervious to pain – everything Imam was not. There was a gravity about Gama in his youth, as if he had been schooled from the womb in the ways of the *pehlwan*, to avoid extremes of emotion like rage and lust, to reserve his energies for the pit. Their father had begun Gama's training at age five and died three years later, before Imam could prove himself worthy of the same attention.

The *bethak* contest lasted four hours, and by the end, only fifteen men remained standing. Rajah Singh yanked Gama's hand in the air, declaring him the youngest by far, and thus, the winner. Greased in sweat, Gama wore a dreamy expression, listing slightly before his knees buckled. Seeing him this way – limp, waxy, the crescent whites of his eyes between his lashes – made something jerk in Imam's chest.

He could not move. At that moment, Imam began to hate his uncle. He hated the Rajah for coming up with this stupid contest, and he hated every person who herded around his brother, claiming him as if he were theirs.

The bell clangs, and the match with Roller begins. Gama slaps his thighs, beats his chest, charges. He plunges at Doc's leg. Doc evades him the first time, but not the second. With a smooth backheel, Gama fells him and finishes him off with a half nelson and body roll. One minute and forty seconds.

The second fall happens in a blur – Doc laid out on his belly, sweat-slick and wincing at the spectators in the front row, who lean forward with their elbows on their knees. Roller gives in, and then: bedlam. The MC yanks Gama's hand into the air; men mob the mat like sparrows to a piece of bread. Mr Benjamin wrings Imam's hand, then shoulders his way through the crowd. Imam hangs back, Gama's robe in his arms, craning his neck to see over all the hats and heads between him and his brother.

Over the next few days, Gama defeats two more challengers, sends them staggering to the mat like drunken giants. The newspapers have begun to take notice. Sometimes, while warming up, Gama and Imam spot a reporter watching from the road, the brim of his hat shadowing his eyes as he scribbles something in his notebook. Imam doesn't like being ogled while doing his *dands*, but Mr Benjamin has told them not to shoo the scribblers away. Press, he says, breeds more press.

Mr Benjamin is right. These days, he brings more clippings than ever before, and Gama wants to digest every word, his appetite inexhaustible. Imam would rather play chess, the only game in which he consistently beats his brother. The journalists rarely, if ever, mention him.

'Gama the Great,' writes Percy Woodmore in *Health & Strength*, 'has so handily defeated all his European challengers that one can only wonder whether the Oriental strongman possesses some genetic advantage over his Occidental counterpart.' Imam can recognize barely half the words in this sentence, but he understands the next. 'Will the Hindoos ever lose?'

'Do you know,' Gama interjects, 'these sahibs have so few counters – only *one* to the Cross Buttock Hold.' He shakes his head in bemusement, and just when Imam thinks he cannot stand him a minute longer, Gama adds: 'Wait till they see you in the ring.'

Imam is beginning to wonder if that day will ever arrive. He feels the distinct weight of malaise, just as he used to suffer in school. When they were children, Gama got to train at the *akhara* with Madho Singh while Imam had to recite English poems about English flowers. After Gama's triumph at Jodhpur, people talked as if the boy could upend mountains, greater than all the *pehlwan* ancestors who had preceded him.

Sometimes, if Imam was sitting alone, sullenly reciting his multiplication tables, Gama took pity on him. 'Come on, *chotu*,' he'd say, taking Imam outside to show him a new hold. Gama was the only one who called him *chotu*, a word that raised his spirits when nothing else would.

By the age of twelve, Imam was fed up. He began cutting school and hovering around the *akhara*, where the only language that mattered was the heave and grunt of bodies in constant motion, whether climbing the rope hanging from the neem tree, or hoeing the wrestling pit, or swinging a giant *jori* in each arm, spiky clubs that surpassed him in height. Moving, always moving. The *akhara* seemed a splendid hive unto itself, sealed off from mundane concerns like school and exams and the sting of the teacher's switch. Here was his classroom. Here, among the living, was where he belonged.

Finally Mr Benjamin arranges a match for Imam. He is to take on the Swede Jon Lemm, who has won belts from both the Alhambra and Hengler's tournaments.

They meet at the Alhambra, to a sold-out arena. Imam has the advantage of height but feels gangly next to Lemm, who is a stout tangle of muscle, and pale, with eyes of a clear, celestial blue.

The referee summons them to the centre of the mat. Lemm gives a cordial nod and locks Imam in a hard handshake, before releasing him to his corner. Imam can feel the spectators watching him, murmuring. There is a proverb that their forefathers minded for centuries: *Make your mind as still as the bottom of a well, your body as hard as its walls.*

Imam touches the mat, then his heart.

The bell clangs. Lemm hurls himself at Imam, toppling him with a backheel. Imam slips free, darts around Lemm, quick as the crack of a whip. He does not see Lemm in terms of ankle and knee and leg. Instead he tracks Lemm's movements, listening for one false note – the falter, the doubt, the dread.

At one point Lemm stalls, a fatal mistake. Imam lunges, lifts him up and hurls him to the mat. He flips the bucking Swede and pins him. Three minutes and one second.

Not long into the second bout, Lemm is sprawled out on the mat, Imam on his back. Imam can feel Lemm struggling beneath him, trembling down to his deepest tissues until, with a savage groan, he deflates. One minute and eight seconds.

Imam gets to his feet, heaving. Something bounces lightly off his back. He whirls round to find a beheaded flower at his feet. Someone else tosses him a silver pocket watch. Imam turns from one side to the other; the men are roaring. It takes him a dizzying moment to realize they are roaring for him.

Of the fight with Lemm, a reporter from *Health & Strength* goes into rapture: 'That really was a wonderful combat – a combat in which both men wrestled like masters of the art . . . Let us have a few more big matches like unto that, and I tell you straight that the grappling game will soon become the greatest game of all.'

In the two weeks that follow, Gama and Imam defeat every wrestler who will accept the challenge. Though Gama the Great commands the most public attention, a dedicated sect of Imam devotees takes shape. They mint him with a new name: the Panther

ENJOYING YOURSELF?

Have *Granta* delivered to your door four times a year
and save up to 38% on the cover price.

'An indispensable part of the intellectual landscape'
– *Observer*

```
*********************************
*                               *
*              UK               *
*            £36.00             *
*     (£32.00 by Direct Debit)  *
*                               *
*            EUROPE             *
*            £42.00             *
*                               *
*       REST OF THE WORLD★      *
*            £46.00             *
*                               *
*********************************
```

Subscribe now by completing the form overleaf,
visiting granta.com or calling UK free phone 0500 004 033

*Not for readers in US, Canada or Latin America

GRANTA.COM

GRANTA

THE MAGAZINE OF NEW WRITING

SUBSCRIPTION FORM FOR UK, EUROPE AND REST OF THE WORLD

Yes, I would like to take out a subscription to *Granta*.

GUARANTEE: If I am ever dissatisfied with my *Granta* subscription, I will simply notify you, and you will send me a complete refund or credit my credit card, as applicable, for all un-mailed issues.

YOUR DETAILS

MR / MISS / MRS / DR ....
NAME ....
ADDRESS ....
....
POSTCODE ....
EMAIL ....

☐ Please tick this box if you do not wish to receive special offers from *Granta*
☐ Please tick this box if you do not wish to receive offers from organizations selected by *Granta*

YOUR PAYMENT DETAILS

1) ☐ Pay £32.00 (saving £20) by Direct Debit
   To pay by Direct Debit please complete the mandate and return to the address shown below.

2) Pay by cheque or credit/debit card. Please complete below:

   1 year subscription: ☐ UK: £36.00 ☐ Europe: £42.00 ☐ Rest of World: £46.00

   3 year subscription: ☐ UK: £96.00 ☐ Europe: £108.00 ☐ Rest of World: £126.00

   I wish to pay by ☐ CHEQUE ☐ CREDIT/DEBIT CARD
   Cheque enclosed for £_____ made payable to *Granta*.

   Please charge £ _____ to my: ☐ Visa ☐ Mastercard ☐ Amex ☐ Switch/Maestro

   Card No. ☐☐☐☐☐☐☐☐☐☐☐☐☐☐☐☐☐☐

   Valid from *(if applicable)* ☐☐☐☐   Expiry Date ☐☐☐☐   Issue No. ☐☐

   Security No. ☐☐☐

SIGNATURE .... DATE ....

Instructions to your Bank or Building Society to pay by Direct Debit
BANK NAME ....
BANK ADDRESS ....
POSTCODE ....
ACCOUNT IN THE NAMES(S) OF: ....
SIGNED ....
DATE ....

DIRECT Debit

Instructions to your Bank or Building Society: Please pay Granta Publications direct debits from the account detailed on this instruction subject to the safeguards assured by the direct debit guarantee. I understand that this instruction may remain with Granta and, if so, details will be passed electronically to my bank/building society. Banks and building societies may not accept direct debit instructions from some types of account.

Bank/building society account number
☐☐☐☐☐☐☐☐

Sort Code
☐☐☐☐☐☐

Originator's Identification
9 1 3 1 3 3

Please mail this order form with payment instructions to:

Granta Publications
12 Addison Avenue
London, W11 4QR
Or call 0500 004 033
or visit GRANTA.COM

of the Punjab. They contend that the Panther is really the superior of the two, citing the blur of his bare brown feet, so nimble they make an elephant of every opponent. Gama may be stronger, but Imam has the broader arsenal of holds and locks and throws, as seen in his victories over Deriaz and Cherpillod, the latter Frenchman so frustrated that he stomped off to his dressing room midway through the match and refused to come out. Within a year or two, they claim, Imam will surpass Gama.

Gama listens in silence when Imam relays such passages. He betrays no emotion, though his fingers tend to tap against his glass of yogurt milk.

Baron Helmuth von Baumgarten is the only critic to speak in political terms, a realm unfamiliar to both Gama and Imam. 'If the Indian wrestlers continue to win,' the Baron writes, with typical inflammatory flair, 'their victories will spur on those dusky subjects who continue to menace the integrity of the British Empire.'

And where most articles include a photo of Gama or Imam, this one displays a photo of a young Indian man in an English suit, with sculpted curls around a centre parting straight as a blade. This is Madan Lal Dhingra, the Baron explains, a student who, several months earlier, walked into an open street, revolver in hand, and shot a British government official seven times in the face. Before Dhingra could turn the revolver on himself, he was subdued, arrested, tried and hanged.

Gama looks over Imam's shoulder at the article. They stare in silence at the soft-skinned boy with the starched white collar choking his throat.

Gama folds the paper roughly, muttering, 'Half of it is nonsense, what they write.' He tosses the newspaper on a side table and goes upstairs. This clipping they will not take back home.

Imam remains in the sitting room, waiting until he can hear the floorboards creaking overhead. From his kurta pocket, he removes the pocket watch he has been keeping on his person ever since it landed at his feet. The silver disc, better than any medal, warms his palm. He draws a fingertip over the engraved lines, each as fine as a feline whisker.

As word spreads of the Lion and the Panther of the Punjab, all the European wrestlers fall silent but one – Stanislaus Zbyszko, winner of the Graeco-Roman world championship tournament at the Casino de Paris four years ago, ranked number one in the world before his more recent scandal with Youssouf the Terrible. This time, Zbyszko is looking to rebuild his name and promises a match with no foul play. He and Gama will face off at the John Bull Tournament in early July.

'This is it,' Mr Benjamin says to Gama. 'You pin him, you'll be world champion. You –' Here, he jabs a finger at Gama's chest. '*Rustom! E! Zamana!*' Mr Benjamin's pronunciation, earnest yet terrible, brings a smile to Gama's face.

Imam is less amused. He detects a growing whiff of greed about Mr Benjamin in the way he goads Gama towards desire and impatience, the very emotions they have been taught to hold at bay. Just as troubling is his refusal to offer a clear figure of ticket sales, though he promises to give them their earnings in one bulk sum at the end.

Out of habit and innocence, Gama puts his faith in Mr Benjamin. Through him, Gama dispatches a single message in *Sporting Life:* he will throw the Pole three times in the space of an hour.

Imam has seen pictures of Zbyszko, the fused boulders of muscle, the bald head like the mean end of a battering ram. Even hanging by his sides, his arms are a threat. Gama has seen the pictures too, but they rarely speak of Zbyszko, or his size, or his titles. They refer only to the match.

News of the bout spreads to India. Mr Mishra, their Bengali patron, writes Gama a rousing letter, imploring him to prove to the world that 'India is not only a land of soft-bodied coolies and clerks'. Mishra rhapsodizes over Bharat Mata and her hard-bodied sons, comparing Gama to the Hindu warrior Bhim. Regarding

Europeans, Mr Mishra has only one opinion: 'All they know is croquet and crumpets.'

Imam isn't sure if Mr Mishra knows that Zbyszko is a Pole. He considers writing back before recalling the article with Dhingra's picture, the words 'traitor' and 'treason' that captioned it. Once, a journalist asked Gama and Imam about their political leanings, whether they consider themselves 'moderate' or 'radical'. Imam turned to Gama, each searching the other for the correct answer, before Gama, bewildered, said, 'We are *pehlwan*.'

Those words return to Imam, later, as he sets a lit match to the letter. They do not want trouble. He holds the burning letter over the sink and then rinses the ash down the drain.

A week remains until the John Bull Tournament. Life now consists only of wrestling and meditation, *bethak* and *dand*, *yakhi* and ghee and almonds. Food is fuel, nothing more. They wake at three in the morning and retire at eight in the evening, their backs to the sunset slicing through the crack between the curtains.

For all their time together, Imam has never felt further from his brother. He can detect some deep tidal turn within Gama, a gravity at his core, pulling him inward and inward again into a wordless coil of concentration. He declines all interviews. His gaze is a wall.

Lying in bed, Imam imagines entering the ring with Zbyszko. He pictures himself executing an artful series of moves never witnessed on these shores, the Flying Cobra perhaps, an overhead lift, a twirl and a toss. The papers would remember him all over again. Twitching with energy, he can hardly sleep.

One day, he upends Gama with the Flying Cobra. Imam knows he should withdraw, but something snaps in him, and it happens in a blink: he dives and pins his brother.

Imam lies there, wide-eyed, panting. Beneath him is Gama the Great, *Rustom-e-Hind*, Boy Hero of *Bethaks* with his cheek against the mat. No one has ever pinned him, until now.

'Get up,' Gama says.

Imam springs to his feet, embarrassed. He knows better than to offer his brother a hand. Somehow he wants Gama to strike out at him, to rear up in anger or indignation.

Gama sits for a moment, catching his breath, before he hoists himself up and shifts his jaw right and left, back into place.

'Again,' Gama says, tugging at his *langot*. 'Again.'

July arrives, and on a damp evening, the John Bull Tournament. Gama and Imam enter a music hall with cut-out cartoons of clowns between the windows, and a painted lady in a twirling skirt, her knees exposed. Imam does his best to ignore those ivory knees. White lights reading HOLBORN EMPIRE silver the cobbled street below, the stones shining like fish scales.

Inside, the arena smells unpleasantly of wet wool. Mr Benjamin keeps twisting round in his seat to take in the hundreds of spectators. 'Sold out,' he enunciates to Imam, turning his hands upward. 'No more tickets. None!'

Imam says, 'Yes, splendid,' unable to remove his gaze from Zbyszko. He stands in the opposite corner of the ring, twisting his torso from side to side. He seems larger than in his pictures, his head so prominent and bald that his ears are reduced to small pink cups. In the ring, Gama does one *bethak* after another, taking no notice of his opponent.

The bell clangs. Gama lunges, felling Zbyszko with a neat foot hook. He clamps Zbyszko with a half nelson, flings him over, and pins his shoulder to the mat. Zbyszko keeps his other shoulder raised as long as he can, quivering. Imam leans forward, wills the other shoulder to kiss the mat.

But now, a shock: Zbyszko wriggles out of Gama's clutch.

Zbyszko then deploys a move so bizarre that Imam thinks it a practical joke. Without warning, Zbyszko falls to the mat on all fours. Like a farm animal.

Gama tries to push him over or pull him up by the waist, but Zbyszko bears down, muttering as if to brace himself against the

100

hurled curses of the spectators. He will not move. Gama tries the wristlock, the quarter nelson – every hold he can imagine – but Zbyszko will not be thrown, nor will he attempt a throw.

A tiresome hour passes in deadlock. People bark, pitch insults and peanut hulls, cursing Zbyszko more than Gama, though neither is spared. Imam sits with his hand propped against his mouth, speechless. Even if he could be heard over the din, he wouldn't know what to say.

At one point Gama's hands fall to his sides. He looks helplessly at Imam, who shakes his head.

A crumpled wad of newspaper bounces off Zbyszko's rounded back. Spectators thunder to the exits. The match is eventually stopped, and it is decided that both parties will wrestle again the following Saturday.

Imam opens the door to Gama's bedroom. In all the weeks they have been staying in this house, he has never seen his brother's room until now, the day before they are leaving. He enters to find a vast bed, Gama's suitcase lying open upon it. On the nightstand is a glass of water, a few yellow wild flowers wilting over the rim. Imam stares at the sullen blooms, unable to imagine his brother bending to pick them.

Gama gets up suddenly from the window seat, as if caught in a private moment. He asks if Imam has packed.

'I was helping Ahmed,' Imam says. 'His is the heaviest trunk.' The cook brought an endless supply of ghee and almonds, not knowing when they would return.

Imam runs a hand over the oak footboard and peers into the suitcase. Among the clothing, Gama has nestled a trio of paper-wrapped soaps for their mother and a tin of Crawford Biscuits in the shape of a barrel organ, with finely painted green wheels and a tiny monkey extending its hat. Mr Benjamin procured the gifts for them. He has promised to send along their earnings once their bills are settled up, a promise that Gama doesn't care enough about to question.

Wedged in between the gifts is the John Bull belt. Imam holds it up to his face. The leather is soft and pliant, the centre plate broad and bordered in gold scrollwork. On the plate is a painting of a heavyset man wearing breeches tucked into his boots and a black top hat. This, presumably, is John Bull, and peering from behind his ankles is a bulldog who shares his build. Englishmen and their dogs – Imam will never understand the attraction. There are a great many things he will never understand.

Gama was awarded the belt two days before, after showing up for the rematch, only to learn that Zbyszko had fled the country. Gama won by forfeit. Only a handful of people clapped as Gama received the belt from the referee and raised it limply over his head. He never even removed his turban and robe.

The next day, a journalist called at the house, wanting a comment on Percy Woodmore's recent opinion in *Health & Strength*, which stated that Gama 'showed a surprising ignorance of strategy' in the match against Zbyszko. The journalist also referred to rumours, hinted at in Woodmore's piece, that Zbyszko had secretly agreed to flee the country if Gama paid him a percentage of his winnings. The journalist said, 'Hello?' several times before Imam set the phone back on its hook.

Imam replaces the belt and peers round it. 'You forgot the newspapers,' he says. 'Everyone will want to see them.'

Gama shakes his head. 'There's no room.' He shuts and buckles the suitcase. Imam moves to help him, but Gama has already hefted the box in both hands, and eases it onto the floor, next to his battered leather valise.

He smoothes down the bedspread and, with his back to Imam, casually asks if the newspapers have said anything about the John Bull Tournament.

'Just the usual nonsense,' Imam says.

'But someone called yesterday. You looked upset.'

'Oh, what does it matter?' Imam squints through the window, as if the sky has claimed all his attention. He can feel Gama's eyes on him.

'We are going home.'

'You aren't telling me something.' When Imam doesn't answer, Gama raises his voice. 'I am not a child, Imam.'

Imam turns to face his brother, who stands rigid with irritation. 'Some are saying you paid that Zbyszko to run away. They say that's how you got the belt.'

Gama blinks as this news crashes over him. He takes a step back, his hand fumbling for the edge of the bed before he sits. He has never looked more like a child, Imam thinks, even when he was a child.

'But who . . .' Gama begins, then drops his gaze to the floor and does not speak for a long time.

'It's just a rumour,' Imam says quickly. 'A stupid rumour. Back home, you are a hero.' He tells of the telegram that just arrived from Mishra, reporting the top headline from the *Times of India*: GAMA THE GREATEST – INDIA WINS WORLD CHAMPIONSHIP.

Gama gives a weak smile. 'Is that what they've decided?'

'You have the belt to prove it,' Imam says. For a long moment, Gama looks over his shoulder at the suitcase but does not go near it. 'It's true –'

'No, *chotu*. I am just a pawn.'

He says this so softly he could be talking to himself, if not for that one tender word, which Imam has not heard from him in years. It is as if they are eight and twelve again, and Gama has set him apart from everyone else – *chotu*. Imam feels himself rising to the word. Inglorious as it is, this is something that for once only he can be. Only he knows to say nothing, to rest his hand at the back of his brother's neck, to let his grip say everything, or simply: *Not to me.* ■

The Self-Illuminated

i.m. Peter Porter

As your hand turns white upon the book
we'd biked across so you might see it done,
only you could, at a time like this,
put me in mind of that rum business
with St Fillan of Glen Dochart, whose brief entry
in the *Breviarium Aberdonense*
tells of the stone he spat when he was born,
and of how, denied a candle in his cell,
he found his left arm light up from within
so he could read, till sleep turned out his skin.
His relics are five: the carved head of his crook,
his once-candescent bones, his flying bell,
and two long lost – one, perhaps his psalter,
the other, a manuscript, or a portable altar.

THE DIG

Cynan Jones

The boy had not slept. He was gawky and awkward and had not grown into himself yet.

When his father came to rouse him he found the boy awake with expectation.

Warm, remember, said his father.

The boy nodded loosely in the way he had. The way was to have a minute hesitation before doing things. This came from trying to be eager and cautious at the same time around his father.

He was long and thin and he could have looked languid without this nervousness but instead he looked underdeveloped. When he got out of bed in his T-shirt and shorts it emphasized the awkward gangliness of him. He had the strange selection of muscles teenage boys' bodies either grow or don't but the skin on his face was a child's.

He got dressed and went downstairs. In the kitchen he sat at the table with the kind of extra-awakeness not sleeping can give you and started automatically to spread paste onto the sliced bread. He had a low-level excitement running through him. A day off school. He felt the same illicit closeness to his father as he did when they went lamping and in these times he was capable of forgetting that his father did other things.

His father put the tea on the table and filled the big flask and then they sat and blew on the tea and drank it. Then they went out.

They took the dogs from the run and got them in the car and drove off the estate. The boy found the smell of the sawdust and dog shit in the run hard to bear in the early morning. The smell of it was a strange note against the deodorant he enveloped himself with.

He had not been digging before and was trying to imagine it.

He imagined it frenzied and was excited by this. He did not know it would be steady, unexciting procedural work and that it would not be like ratting at all.

He had broken his own dog to rats himself and this gave him pride. When they picked on him in school he kept his pride in this. He hung on to it.

The boy's father parked up the car and they sat seeing the dog runs and the broken machinery and the boy was momentarily stupefied by the darkness and emptiness about the place. In the car lights he could see just beyond the runs the bodies of cars like some disassembled ghost train littering the field.

The big man heard them pull up outside and saw the car lights catch and reflect on the mesh of the run and came out to them. The boy had a brief inarticulate awareness that his father shied a little when he saw the big man come from the house. He hadn't seen that in his father before. The boy thought the man looked like some big gypsy.

The man leaned into the window and the dogs in the back came alive at this new presence and set off a yapping, which set off a yapping in the dog sheds beyond. The car was full of a deodoranty smell that got into your mouth.

They yelpers? asked the big gypsy.

They're good dogs, said the boy's father.

It stinks, said the man. It's a girl's bedroom.

The big gypsy looked accusingly at the boy and the boy felt himself redden. He felt the nervous flush go up in his throat.

They're good dogs, said the boy's father.

We can't have them hard-mouthed, said the man.

No. They're good dogs, the father said.

We can't work with hard-mouthed dogs, the big gypsy said. The big gypsy was looking at the terriers, taking them in. The boy could feel there was a grown-man tension.

Then his father said: They're not hard-mouthed, mun. They're good dogs.

There were three terriers in the back. One was the big Patterdale, Jip, thirteen inches at the shoulder and a solid fourteen pounds. He was about as big as you'd want for a badger dig without being too tall in the shoulder to suit the holes. It was why the man had called the boy's father, thinking of the big boar.

What's the pup? said the big gypsy. He nodded at the boy's dog and the boy felt the redness on his throat again.

He's just along, said the boy's father. The big gypsy looked at the pup.

He's not going down, said the big gypsy. He had to take the badger and there was too much risk the young dog would not be able to hold him. The boy felt this shame and the crushed feeling from school came up in him.

He's just along, the boy's father said.

They parked up in the machine yard of the big farm and got the dogs out and coupled them dog to bitch with the iron couplings. This was one of the bigger, richer farms locally and had years ago been one of the manor farms that worked under the big house. You could tell the historical management of it by the wider fields and the way the big oaks were spread out in them.

In the east a powder of light was just coming and in the barn the tractors looked immense and military. At the edges of the fields the trees were still a solid deep black.

They coupled the boy's pup to the older dog and coupled the gypsy's older bitch to the big Patterdale. They had to couple the right dogs. Dogs that could work together at rat could fight at a badger dig, as if they sensed the individuality of the process.

They got the tools and divided them up to carry; then they took the big five-litre tubs of water from the van and the bag with the tin drinking bowls and the food and gave them to the boy. They weighed on him immediately. It was crisply cold and with their thin handles the weight of the water bottles burned on his fingers.

They went through the gate and down the lane, letting the dogs run in front of them, passively aware of which dog took the lead of the other as they rooted in and out of the hedgeside at the dying scents laid down in the night.

Mud had gathered in the track and the overnight rain left it wet and the boy, alert and cold and over-awake, took in the sucked sounds underfoot and the clinking of the coupling chains and the body sounds of the dogs as they pushed through the undergrowth of the bank. He was using the gulping sounds of the water sloshing in the tubs as a kind of rhythm to walk by.

The thin light was beginning to increase and the few bean-shaped flowers on the gorse stood out with unnatural luminosity. The men's feet went down hard and solidly in the lane, but the boy constantly tripped on the loose stones the winter's rain had brought down, as if he didn't have enough weight to himself.

They went off the track and whistled the dogs in as they went over a field, the lambs prone and folded next to their mothers. Some of the smaller lambs wore blue polythene jackets against the rain and they looked odd in that first light and overprotected.

The boy could hear the ewes crunching and one or two faced the dogs and banged a foreleg on the wet ground, giving a thump that sounded like kicking a ball. He wished he could play, really play, but he was clumsy against the other boys. He loved the idea of himself playing and his inability was just another little cruelty. Even now, he looked out across the lightening field and saw himself catch a high kick, the crowd of trees a fringe of spectators coming to their feet as he took the ball. But then – the school field, the ball smashing off his fingers to the laughter of the other kids, the teacher's shouted scorn. That was the reality of him and it brought up a wad of sick and anger.

They worked their way down through the topped reeds that stubbled the slope at the base of the field and stopped by the brook and the boy set the water down. They put the dogs to lead. His pup was shaking a little with excitement.

He's got rats somewhere, he said. The sentence came out on the swell of pride and he realized it was the first time he had talked in front of the man.

The man lifted up a tub of water and unlidded it and took a rough swig.

Keep them in, he said. The bank's snared.

The mink had made their way up from the fur farms by now. They were not indigenous and so it was righteous to kill them. They took out the fish and the waterside birds, even kingfishers from their nests in the burrows, and had annihilated the watercourses as they came up.

It was as well to be able to produce something they could legitimately hunt if by chance they were stopped. It would explain the dogs. In reality, though, they should shoot the mink to make it look like they'd run it into a gun.

The boy was made thirsty by the river and wanted to drink but he did not like the idea of drinking the water after the big man had drunk from the tub.

In the relative openness of the lane and across the field the dawn light had been enough, but here things closed in and they checked the snares with the torchlight.

Bar the one, the snares were empty. The boy heard the dogs whine with the scent of something and the man signalled them to hold back and the boy put the water tubs down and stretched his fingers. Then the boy heard the dull crack of the mink's skull and for a while did not register what the sound was. The man had hit it with a foldaway spade.

They went on. The water had become convincingly heavy to the boy now. The scrub began to encroach the bank until it was thickened and difficult to pass and after a while they cut away from the stream. It was heavy going but somehow the big man had mobility in it and seemed to fit into the countryside in a way the other two did not.

The dogs sniffed in and out of the torch beams ahead of them and the men pushed through the sprawling holly as they drove into the wood. Every now and then they disturbed something, and there was a clatter in the branches or the tearing of undergrowth as something fled. The wood thickened. Everywhere there were branches down and in the strange beams of light some looked animal and prehistoric.

F rom working with the hunts the big man knew most of the land roundabouts. The hunts called in the terriermen to bolt their foxes, or sometimes to dig them out if they had gone to earth, and in the country covered with the dogs he'd had more than a chance to scout the land and get to places most people would never go. He had noted the vast majority of the local setts, and the information was a paying commodity for him, and he checked the setts regularly in the way a herdsman might his flock.

Some of the setts he knew of had been there for generations, and in other districts he had heard of those, particularly in the more impregnable places, in the harder chalk soils and rocky hillsides, that went back centuries.

Each clan of badgers had a group of setts, swapping between them periodically, sometimes with the seasons, and he needed always to know which of these was occupied. He tried not to take badgers from the same clan too regularly, to allow the family groups to recover and breed, and in this it was like he farmed the animals to ensure there were always badgers to be had.

T hey staked the dogs some way from the sett and poured them water and took a drink themselves. The boy had a queer feeling about the man's mouth being on the water and still did not want to drink it.

The trees had opened up a little and you could see the light finally coming through. There was a moment of greater coldness, like a draught through a door, and the boy felt an unnerving, as if something had acknowledged them arriving there. They had made a lot of noise moving through the wood and when they stopped they heard the birdsong and the early loud vibrancy of the place.

First dig? said the man.

The boy nodded, with that hesitancy. They could hear the dogs lapping and drinking at the water bowls.

The big man had been up to the sett the afternoon before and seen the heap of freshly scuffed soil and the drawn-out bedding outside the entrance. The sett was on a slope and looked to head deep in and there was much undergrowth and thin sycamore on the cover.

He'd gone out a little from the entrance and found the dung pit that in the colder weather was often close to the sett this time of year. The fresh spores looked soft and muddy from the badgers' predominant diet of earthworms. In the mud around were scrapings and footprints and from their impress he knew it was a big full-grown boar. A sow would put up a better fight if she had cubs to defend, but there was something more competitive to the size of a big forty-pound boar. They wanted a spectacle.

On the nearby trees were the unhealed scars where the badgers had cleaned their claws and rubbed off the dirt from their coats.

The main hole's up there, said the gypsy. He gestured up the slope. We'll put in the dog, he said. He meant Jip, the big Patterdale.

His own bitch was by his feet, with her distant, composed look against the other dogs.

I want to put her in next. He indicated. Better be a dog goes in first. He was thinking of the big tracks and the possibility of the big boar. A bigger dog would have more chance up front. They knew if you put a bitch down after a bitch, or a dog down after a dog, there were problems most times; but if you changed the sex the other usually came out with no trouble.

The boy's father nodded agreement. He was checking the locator, checking the box with the handset.

The boy was thirsty and looking at the water, not wanting to open the other tub in front of the man.

Take him round and block up the other holes. I'll do the other side.

The gypsy brought out the map he'd drawn of the holes and went over it with the boy's father. The gypsy asked the boy if he understood and the redness came to his throat under the zipped-up coat collar; but he was feeling the rich beginning of adrenalin now. He was dry and thirsty and had a big sick hole of adolescent hunger but he could feel his nerves warming at the new thing and began to feel a comradeship of usefulness to the man.

They unwound the sheets of thick plastic and went off and systematically blocked the holes with stones and sheets of plastic and laid blocks across the obvious runs with heavy timber and then went back to the dogs. Then they went up the slope with the two first dogs and gathered around the main entrance and stood the tools up in the ground.

There was old bedding around the hole, the strange skeletal bracken starting to articulate its colour in the grey light. Jip started to bounce on the lead and strain for the hole as if he could sense the badgers. The strewn bracken might have meant the badgers had gone overnight, but from the way the dog was behaving there was a fresh, present scent.

The boy looked at the dog straining on the lead and could feel the same feeling in his guts. He felt the feeling he did before the first rats raced out and the dogs went into them.

The boy's father knelt with the excited dog and checked the box and collar over again and Jip let his enthusiasm solidify into a determined, pointed thing and stood stockily facing the hole, a determined tremble going through him.

The boy's father studied the locator once more and checked the signal, then they sent the dog in.

The boy was not expecting the delay of listening for the dog. He could feel his stomach roll though. He could feel a slow soupy excitement. This was a new thing. Then deep in the earth the dog yelped. Then again; and his father was instantly by the hole, prone, calling to the dog, calling with strange excitement into the tunnel.

Stay at him, boy. Good Jip. Good Jippo.

The boy glanced at the man as his father called this out, as if it had revealed what he was thinking about the way the man looked. But the big gypsy seemed to be rapt, a pasty violence setting in his eyes as he listened and watched Messie, his bitch, solidify, focus. Finally, the dog let out a low whimper of desire.

You could hear the barks moving through the ground now and they came alternately sharp and muffled until they seemed to regulate and come with a faraway percussive sound.

The big man moved across the slope. He seemed to swirl in some eddy, then came to a halt, as if caught up on something.

The big man moved again, listening, and the boy's father tracked across with the locator until the two men stood in the same place, confirming the big man's judgement.

Here, he said. They brought up the tools and they started to dig.

It was very early spring and the bluebells were not out but made a thick carpet that looked newly washed and slick after the rain. They cut through this carpet and cleared the mess of thin sycamore from the place and the big gypsy cut a switch and bent it into a sack mouth and laid the sack down by where they would dig.

The ground was sodden with rain and sticky and they worked with the sharp foldaway spades, cutting through the thread roots. The smell of rotted leaves and dug-up soil strengthened. When they came to a thicker root, they let the boy in with the saw. Then they started to dig for real.

The big man swung the pick and the father and boy shovelled. Within minutes the boy was parched with thirst and hunger and could not shout properly when they called constantly to the dog below. He was dizzy with effort. He was afraid of not being able to keep up with the men. As the hole deepened they shored up the sides of the hole with the plastic sheeting and the work steadied to a persistent rhythm.

The badger was going nowhere and it was not about speed but persistence now.

After two hours they stopped for a drink and ate some of the paste sandwiches. The big man ate nothing. The dry soil on the boy's hands was tide-marked with water from the blisters that had torn and were flaps of skin now and there was a type of dull shock in his back.

He had been expecting more action, not this relentless work, and he didn't understand it.

The dog had been down for two hours and had continually been barking and yelping and keeping just out of the badger's reach for that time.

Every so often, the boar rushed the dog and the dog retreated and the badger turned and fled; and Jip went after him through the tunnels and junctions until they reached the stop end.

Then the badger turned and ran at the dog again. It was nearly two and a half times the weight of the terrier and armed with fearsome claws and a bite that would crack the dog if he landed it properly. But the dog was quick and in his own way very dangerous. Jip kept barking. Yelping. The badger faced him down and every now and then turned to try and dig himself into the stop end. But then Jip moved in and bit his hindquarters, and the big boar swung round again in defence.

In the confined tunnel of the sett, the constant yelps were deafening and confusing like bright lights in the brain of the badger and it was unsure what it could do. It was then a stand-off. A matter of time.

They sent the bitch in and Jip came up. He looked like he was grinning. His mouth was open and flecked with spit. The dog was exhausted and thirsty but gleamed with the event somehow and when they took off the box and collar, steam came into the morning air off his body. The boy was confused that they ignored the thick obvious blood that came out of the Patterdale and spread down its throat.

The boy kept looking nervously at the exhausted bleeding stubborn dog. The fresh blood seemed a synthetic colour against the dun-green slope.

Messie's good, said the big man. She'll hold him for the rest.

The boy sat and held his blistered hands against the cold metal of the foldaway spade. He had gloves but he did not feel he could wear them. Steam rolled off from the plastic-flask cup of tea and it came off the body of the injured dog. Steam came too off the lifted soil, but no birds came as they might to a garden, as if they knew some dark purpose was at work.

The man's bag hung on the tree and the head of the mink protruded. The boy looked at it. The mouth was drawn and the precise teeth showed. He thought of one of his earliest memories, of his father holding a ferret and sewing its lips together so it couldn't gash the rabbits it was sent down to chase. The mink had the same vicious preciseness as the ferrets.

Get your dog on it, the man said. The boy immediately felt the redness at being talked to by the big man.

He nodded.

She on rats?

The boy nodded again. He had a panicky lump in his throat.

Good rat dog should take mink. Start them early.

The boy felt the swell of pride come up and mix strangely with his nervousness at the man.

Nice dog, commented the man.

They'd gone through finally into the roof of the tunnel and it looked now like a broken waste pipe and it was mid-morning when they lifted the terrier out. There was still an unnerving composure to her, a kind of distant, complete look.

The boy did not understand the passivity of the badger and that it did not try to bolt or to struggle. He had to develop an idea of hatred for the badger without the help of adrenalin and without the excitement of pace and in the end it was the reluctance and non-engagement of the animal which drew up a disrespect in him. He built his dislike of the badger on this disgust. It was a bullying. It was a tension, not an excitement, and he began to feel a delicious private heartbeat coming. He believed by this point that the badger deserved it.

The big man was in the hole alone now, his shape filling it. The boy's head pumped hotly from the work and finally his nerves sped.

Have a spike ready, his father said.

Then the badger came out. It shuffled, brow down as if it didn't want to be noticed. It sensed them and looked up and the boy looked for a moment into its black eyes, its snout circling. The boy was expecting it to have come out snarling and fighting with rage, but it edged out.

It had been trapped in three or four foot of pipe for hours and it edged out until it was by the opening and the big gypsy took it.

He got it round the neck with the tongs and it struggled and grunted and then the man swung it up and into the sack with this great output of strength. Then it kicked and squealed and you could see the true weight and strength of it and the boy didn't understand why it hadn't fought at first, at the beginning.

The badger scuffed and tried to dig and the big man punched the sack and the badger went still. At this, the boy felt a comradeship with the man again and a sense of victory, holding the iron spike there in readiness, as if he was on hand.

We'll hang him while we fill things in, said the big gypsy, stop him trying to dig.

They filled in the hole. Threw in the old roots and stones they'd dug out and finally put back down the sods of bluebells. The place was slick with mud and trodden down and the ground of the area looked like the coat of a sick dog.

The big gypsy looked at the sack hanging from the tree, at the sack-like weight of it.

It was the second time he'd dug a badger for the gang. That first time, Messie had been just a pup. He thought of the money. It was worth the risk. He made a point now and then of taking in a badger he found genuinely hit on the road to the Veterinary Investigation Centre and he carried the receipt slips in the van to produce if he was stopped. But that worked only for dead badgers, or to explain the hairs they might find. He had to move the live badger and it wouldn't matter what else was in the van if they stopped him.

The big man reached into his bag and took out the mink and threw it to the boy. Its damp weight and the limp, sumptuous ropiness of the animal surprised him as he caught it. The mouth was drawn and he could see the precise teeth.

You can keep him, the big man said. They're vermin here. It was like a payment for things.

The boy felt a glow of pride and the sudden warm teamship with the man that was alien to him and which he had difficulty with. His father looked at him with a strange grin and the redness came to him then.

He lifted the mink's lips to see the needle teeth. They were like sewing needles.

He looked at the needle teeth and felt the fur of the rope-like body. The electricity was gone out of it.

Give him a shake tonight. The big man nodded at the pup. Good rat dog be good on mink.

The boy's father was panting and looked brightened. The boy could see the sweat on his father's head through the very short hair. The adrenalin was coming in the boy now and he looked at his pup and swelled with pride. He felt a warm cruelty, standing there on the beach of soil.

I'll start her tonight, he said to himself. ∎

MA Creative Writing:
Place, Environment, Writing
(1 year full-time / 2 years part-time)

**Psychogeography • Eco-poetry • Travel writing
Creative non-fiction • The City • Edgelands
Journeys • The Rural • The Wild**

Ground-breaking collaboration between internationally renowned creative writers and cultural geographers including: **Jo Shapcott** (winner of the Costa Book of the Year Award 2011, and Queen's Gold Medal for Poetry 2011), **Andrew Motion** (former Poet Laureate, novelist and biographer) and **Tim Cresswell** (author of *Place: A Short Introduction*).

Part of the established and successful MA in Creative Writing directed by Professor Andrew Motion, this latest development focuses on writing and the environment – from wild to urban – in the modern world.

The Creative Writing MA also offers opportunities to specialize in Fiction, Poetry or Life-Writing.

Located in Bedford Square in central London, teaching takes place in small group workshops as well as one-to-one supervision.

For further details contact: **Marina.Mohideen-Moore@rhul.ac.uk**

Or visit website at: **www.rhul.ac.uk/english/** and find details of the MA Creative Writing under 'information for prospective students', 'postgraduate taught'.

To apply online go to:
https://apply.embark.com/grad/royalholloway/96/

Royal Holloway
University of London

THE GUN

Mark Haddon

D aniel stands in the funnel, a narrow path between two high brick walls that join the playground to the estate proper. On windy days, the air is forced through here then spun upwards in a vortex above the square of so-called grass between the four blocks of flats. Anything that isn't nailed down becomes airborne. Washing, litter, dust. Grown men have been knocked off their feet. A while back there was a story going round about a flying cat.

Except there's no wind this morning, there hasn't been any wind for days, just an unremitting mugginess that makes you want to open a window until you remember that you're outside. Mid-August. A week since the family holiday in Magaluf, where he learned backstroke and was stung by a jellyfish, a week till school begins again. He is ten years old. Back at home his older sister is playing teacher and his younger brother is playing pupil again. Helen is twelve, Paul seven. She has a blackboard and a little box of chalks in eight colours and when Paul misbehaves she smacks him hard on the leg. His mother is doing a big jigsaw of Venice on the dining table while the tank heats for the weekly wash.

He can see the white legs of a girl on the swings, appearing, disappearing, appearing, disappearing. It is 1972. 'Silver Machine' and 'Rocket Man'. He cannot remember ever having been this bored before. He bats a wasp away from his face as a car door slams lazily in the distance, then steps into the shadow of the stairwell and starts climbing towards Sean's front door.

There will be three other extraordinary events in his life. He will sit at dusk on the terrace of a rented house near Cahors with his eight-year-old son and see a barn on the far side of the valley destroyed by lightning, the crack of white light appearing to come not from the sky but to burst from the ground beneath the building.

He will have a meeting with the manager of a bespoke ironworks near Stroud, whose factory occupies one of three units built into the side of a high railway cutting. Halfway through the meeting a cow will fall through the roof and it won't be anything near as funny as it sounds.

On the morning of his fiftieth birthday his mother will call and say that she needs to see him. She will seem calm and give no explanation and despite the fact that there is a large party planned for the afternoon he will get into the car and drive straight to Leicester only to find that the ambulance has already taken his mother's body away. Only later, talking to his father, will he realize that he received the phone call half an hour after the stroke which killed her.

Today will be different, not simply shocking but one of those moments when time itself seems to fork and fracture and you look back and realize that if things had happened only slightly differently, you would be leading one of those other ghost lives that sped away into the dark.

Sean is not a friend as such but they play together because they are in the same class at school. Sean's family lives on the top floor of Orchard Tower whereas Daniel's family lives in a semi-detached house on the approach road. Daniel's mother says that Sean's family are a bad influence but she also says that television will damage your eyes if you sit too close and that you will die if you swim in the canal, and in any case Daniel likes their volume, their expansiveness, their unpredictability, the china greyhounds on either side of the gas fire, Mr Cobb's red BMW which he polishes and T-Cuts lovingly on Saturday mornings. Sean's older brother, Dylan, works as a plasterer and carpenter and they have a balcony which looks over the ring road to the woods and the car plant and the radio mast at Bargave, a view which excites Daniel more than anything he saw from the plane window between Luton and Palma because there is no glass and you feel a thrilling shiver in the back of your knees as you lean over and look down.

He steps out of the lift and sees Sean's mother leaving the flat, which is another thing that makes Daniel envious, because when his own mother goes to the shops he and Paul and Helen have to accompany her. *Try and keep him out of trouble.* Mrs Cobb ruffles his hair and sweeps onwards. She is lighting a cigarette as the silver doors close over her.

Sean's jumbled silhouette appears in the patterned glass of the front door and it swings open. *I've got something to show you.*

What?

He beckons Daniel into Dylan's bedroom. *You have to keep this a total secret.*

Daniel has never been in here before. Dylan has explicitly forbidden it and Dylan can bench-press 180 pounds. He steps off the avocado lino of the hall onto the swirly red carpet. The smell of cigarettes and Brut aftershave. It feels like the bedroom of a dead person in a film, every object freighted with significance. Posters for *Monty Python* and *The French Connection.* 'Jimmy Doyle is the Toughest.' A motorbike cylinder head sits on a folded copy of the *Daily Express*, the leaking oil turning the newsprint waxy and transparent. There is a portable record player on the bedside table, the lid of the red leatherette box propped open and the cream plastic arm crooked around the silvered rod in the centre of the turntable. *Machine Head. Thick as a Brick. Ziggy Stardust.*

You have to promise.

I promise.

Because this is serious.

I said.

Sean tugs at the pine handle of the wardrobe and the flimsy door comes free of the magnetic catch. On tiptoe Sean takes down a powder-blue shoebox from the top shelf and lays it on the khaki blanket before easing off the lid. The gun lies in the white tissue paper that must have come with the shoes. Sean lifts it easily from its rustling nest and Daniel can see how light it is. Scuffed pigeon-grey metal. The words REMINGTON RAND stamped into the flank. Two cambered grips are screwed to either side of the handle, chocolate brown and cross-cut like snakeskin for a better grip.

Sean raises the gun at the end of his straightened arm and rotates slowly so that the barrel is pointing directly into Daniel's face. *Bang,* he says, softly. *Bang.*

Daniel's father works at the local pool, sometimes as a lifeguard, more often on reception. Daniel used to be proud of the fact that everyone knew who his father was, but he is now embarrassed by his visibility. His mother works part-time as a secretary for the county council. His father reads crime novels. His mother does jigsaws which are stored between two sheets of plywood when the dining table is needed. Later in life when he is describing his parents to friends and acquaintances he will never find quite the right word. They aspired always to be average, to be unremarkable, to avoid making too much noise or taking up too much space. They disliked arguments and had little interest in the wider world. And if he is bored in their company during his regular visits he will never use the word *boring* because he is genuinely envious of their ability to take real joy in small things, and hugely grateful that they are not demonstrating any of the high-maintenance eccentricities of many of his friends' retired and ageing parents.

They walk across the living room and Sean turns the key before shunting the big glass door to one side. They step into heat and traffic noise. There is a faint brown smog, as if the sky needs cleaning. Daniel can feel sweat running down the small of his back.

Sean fixes the pistol on a Volvo travelling in one direction then follows an Alfa Romeo going the other way. *We could kill someone and they'd never find out who did it.* Daniel explains that the police would use the hole in the windscreen and the hole in the driver's body to work out exactly where the shot came from. *Elementary, my dear Watson,* says Sean. *Let's go to the woods.*

Is the gun loaded?

Course it's loaded, says Sean.

The woods rise up on the other side of the ring road, a swathe of no-man's-land between town and country. People park their cars at the picnic area by Pennington on the far side of the hill and walk their dogs among the oak and ash and rowan, but the roar of the dual carriageway and the syringes and the crushed lager cans dissuade most of them from coming down its northern flank.

They wait on the grass verge, the warm shock waves of passing lorries thumping them and sucking at their clothes. *Go,* shouts Sean and they sprint to the central reservation, vaulting the scratchy S-shaped barrier, pausing on the ribbon of balding grass then running across the second carriageway to the gritty lay-by with its moraine of shattered furniture and black rubbish bags ripped open by rats and foxes. All that bacteria cooking slowly. An upturned pram. They unhook the clanky gate where the rutted track begins. Sean has the gun in a yellow Gola bag thrown over his shoulder.

They pass the scrapyard with its corrugated-iron castellations. They pass the Roberts' house. A horsebox with a flat tyre, a floodlight roped to a telegraph pole. Robert Hales and Robert Hales and Robert Hales, grandfather, father and son, all bearing the same name and all living under the same roof. The youngest Robert Hales is two years above them at school. He has a biscuity unwashed smell and bones that look slightly too big for his skin. He used to come in with small animals in a cake tin, stag beetle, mouse, grass snake, but Donnie Farr grabbed the last of these and used it to chase other children round the playground before whipping its head against one of the goalposts. Robert pushed Donnie to the ground, took hold of the fingers of his left hand and bent them backwards until two of them snapped.

The curtains in the Roberts' house are closed, however, and there is no red van parked outside. They walk on towards the corner where the path narrows and turns into the trees. Slabs of dusty sunlight are neatly stacked between the branches. If it weren't for the smell of exhaust fumes you could imagine that the roar of traffic was a great cataract pouring into a ravine to your left.

They find a clearing that contains the last few broken branches of a den they built earlier in the summer where they drank Tizer and smoked four menthol cigarettes which Sean had stolen from his mother's handbag. *Let's do it here.* Sean finds a log to use as a shooting gallery and sends Daniel off in search of targets. He climbs the boundary fence and searches among the hawthorn bushes which line the hard shoulder, coming back with two empty beer bottles, a battered plastic oilcan and a muddy teddy bear with both arms missing. He feels exhausted by the heat. He imagines standing on the lawn at home, squeezing the end of the hose with his thumb and making rainbows in the cold falling water. He arranges the objects at regular intervals along the log. He thinks about the child who once owned the teddy bear and regrets having picked it up but doesn't say anything.

Sean raises the gun and moves his feet apart to brace himself. A deep cathedral quiet. The traffic stops. He can hear the shuttle of his own blood. He is not aware of the shot itself. The loose rattle of scattering birds. He sees Sean being thrown backwards, as if a big animal has charged and struck him in the centre of his chest mid-leap. The bear, the oilcan and the bottles are still standing.

Oh my God. Sean gets to his feet. *Oh my God.* He begins dancing. He has clearly never done anything this exciting in his life. *Oh my God.*

A military plane banks overhead. Daniel is both disappointed and relieved that he is not offered the second shot. Sean breathes deeply and theatrically. He braces himself again, wipes the sweat from his forehead with the arm of his T-shirt and raises the gun. The noise is breathtakingly loud. It seems obvious to Daniel that many, many people will have heard it.

What are you doing? It is the youngest Robert Hales.

They jump, both of them, but Sean recovers his composure quickest. *What do you think we're doing?*

You've got a gun. Despite the heat Robert is wearing a battered orange cagoule.

Duh.

Let me have a go.

Yeh, right, says Sean.

I want a go, says Robert. He steps forward. He is taller than Sean by a good six inches.

Just as he did in the bedroom, Sean lifts his arm until the gun is pointing directly at Robert's face. *No way, José.*

Daniel realizes that Sean may kill Robert. He is excited by this possibility. He will be a *witness to a crime.* People will respect him and feel sorry for him.

Robert doesn't move. Five, maybe ten seconds. *The Good, the Bad and the Ugly.* Daniel can't tell if he's terrified or utterly unafraid. Finally Robert says, *I'm going to kill you,* not in the way they say it to one another in the playground, but in the way you say, *I'm going to the shop.* He walks away without looking back. Sean aims at him till he vanishes. The two of them listen to the fading crunch of twigs and dry leaves under his trainers. *Spastic.* Sean lets his arm slump. *Bloody spastic.* He walks up to the teddy bear and places the barrel in the centre of its forehead. Daniel thinks how similar they look, the bear and Robert, uninterested, staring straight ahead. But Sean can't be bothered to waste another bullet. *Shit.* Robert's appearance has made the adventure seem mundane. Sean throws the gun into the Gola bag. *Let's go.*

They walk back through the woods, taking the long route that loops up the hill and comes out on the far side of the scrapyard, avoiding the Roberts' house altogether. Gnats and dirty heat. Daniel has dog shit on his left shoe that he has not been able to scrape off completely.

His sister, Helen, was unexpectedly born breech. The cord became trapped while her head was coming out and she was deprived of oxygen. Daniel is not told about this until he is sixteen.

He knows only that there is a light in her eyes which stutters briefly sometimes then comes back on. He knows only that she has trouble with numbers, money, telling the time.

She will leave school at sixteen with no qualifications, living at home and working in a furniture warehouse then in a greengrocer's. She will change doctors and get better drugs. Ethosuximide. Valproic acid. The petit mal will stop. She will be easily confused but she will be plump and blonde and pretty and people will like her instinctively. She'll meet Garry at a nightclub. Overweight, thirty-five, detached house, running a taxi firm, a big man in a small world. They will marry and it will take Daniel a long time to realize that this is a happy ending.

The noise, when it comes, is nothing more than a brief hiss followed by a clatter of foliage. Crossbow? Catapult? Then a second shot. It is the oddest thing, but Daniel will swear that he saw it before he heard it, before Sean felt it even. A pink stripe appears on the skin just above Sean's elbow. He yelps and lifts his arm. *Bastard.*

They squat on the path, hearts hammering. Sean twists his arm to inspect the damage. There is no bleeding, just a red weal, as if he has leaned against the rim of a hot pan. Robert must be somewhere further down the hill. The hole in the windscreen, the hole in the driver's body. But Daniel can see nothing without lifting his head above the undergrowth. They should run away as fast as they can so that Robert is forced to aim at a moving target between the trees, but Sean is taking the gun out of the bag. *I'm going to get him.*

Don't be stupid.

And what's your brilliant idea?

Another hiss, another clatter. They duck simultaneously. For a couple of seconds Sean looks frightened. Then he doesn't. *This way.* He starts to commando-crawl through a gap in the blackberries.

Daniel follows him only because he doesn't want to be alone. Sean holds the gun in his hand as he crawls. Daniel thinks how easy it would be for him to pull the trigger accidentally. They drag themselves between the gnarly bramble trunks. Cracked seed cases, dry leaves and curls of broken bark. Born and bred in a briar patch. He tries to pretend that they are in a film but can't do it. They are moving in the wrong direction, away from the scrapyard And this is Robert's back garden.

They find themselves under a low dome of branches just big enough for them to lie stretched out, a place where an animal might sleep, perhaps. Improbably, they hear the sound of an ice cream van, far off. No fourth shot.

What do we do now?

We wait, says Sean.

What for?

Till it's dark.

Daniel looks at his watch. At six his mother will call Sean's flat, at seven she will ring the police. He rolls onto his back and narrows his eyelids so that the light falling from the canopy becomes a shimmer of overlapping circles in white and yellow and lime green. The smell of dog shit comes and goes. Is this a safe place or a trap? He imagines Robert looking down at the two of them lying there under the brambles. Fish in a barrel. That weird keening noise Donnie made when his fingers snapped.

After twenty minutes the tension begins to ease. Perhaps this was what Robert intended after all, to scare them then go home and sit in front of the TV laughing. Forty minutes. Daniel hasn't drunk anything since breakfast. He has a headache and he can feel little gluey lumps around the edge of his dry lips. They decide to run for it. They are now certain that Robert is no longer waiting for them but the running will increase the excitement of their escape and recapture a little of their lost dignity.

And this is when they hear the footsteps. A crackle. Then silence. Then another crackle. Someone is moving gingerly through the undergrowth nearby, trying not be heard. Each heartbeat seems to tighten a screw at the base of Daniel's skull. Sean picks up the gun and rolls onto his stomach, elbows braced in the dirt. Crackle. Daniel pictures Robert as a native hunter. Arrow in the notch, two fingers curled around the taut bowstring. The steps move to the right. Either he doesn't know where they are or he is circling them, choosing his direction of approach. *Come on,* says Sean to himself, turning slowly so that the gun points constantly towards the direction of the noise. *Come on.*

Daniel wants it to happen quickly. He doesn't know how much longer he can bear this before jumping up and shouting, *Here I am!* like Paul used to do during games of hide-and-seek. Then everything goes quiet. No steps. No crackle. Midges scribble the air. The soft roar of the cataract. Sean looks genuinely frightened now.

A stick snaps behind them and they twist onto their backs just as the silhouette springs up and shuts out the dazzle of the sun. Sean fires and the gun is so close to Daniel's head that he will hear nothing for the next few minutes, just a fizz, like rain on pylon wires.

He sees straight away that it is not Robert. Then he sees nothing because he is kicked hard in the stomach and the pain consumes him. When he uncurls and opens his eyes he finds himself looking into a face. It is not a human face. It is the face of a roe deer and it is shockingly big. He tries to back away but the brambles imprison him. The deer is running on its side, wheezing and struggling in vain to get to its feet. A smell like the camel house at the zoo. Wet black eyes, the jaws working and working, the stiff little tongue poking in and out. Breath gargles through a patch of bloody fur on its neck. It scrabbles and kicks. He can't bear to look but can't make himself turn away. The expression on its face. It looks like someone turned into a deer in a fairy tale. Crying out for help and unable to form the words.

It's weakening visibly, something dragging it down into the cold black water that lies just under the surface of everything. That desperate hunger for more time, more light. Whenever Daniel hears the phrase *fighting for your life* this is the picture that will come back to him.

Sean hoists his leg over its body and sits on its chest. He presses the end of the barrel to the side of its head and fires, *bang . . . bang . . . bang . . . bang . . .* each shot sending the deer's body into a brief spasm. The gun is empty. A few seconds of stillness then a final spasm. It stops moving. *Oh yes*, says Sean, letting out a long sigh, *Oh yes*, as if he has been dreaming about this moment for a long time.

Fingers of gluey blood start to crawl out from under the head. Daniel wants to cry but something inside him is blocked or broken.

Sean says, *We have to get it back.*

Back where?

To the flat.

Why?

To cook it.

Daniel has no idea what to say. A part of him still thinks of the deer as human. A part of him thinks that, in some inexplicable way, it is Robert transformed. Already a fly is investigating one of the deer's eyes.

Sean stands up and stamps the brambles aside, snapping their stems with the heel of his trainers so they don't spring back. *We can skin it.*

He tells Daniel to return to the lay-by to fetch the pram they saw beside the rubbish bags. Daniel goes because he needs to get away from Sean and the deer. He walks past the scrapyard. He wants to bump into Robert, hoping that he will be dragged back into the previous adventure, but the curtains are still closed and the house is silent. He removes the loop of green twine and opens the clangy gate. There is a brown Mercedes in the lay-by. The driver watches him from the other side of the windscreen but Daniel cannot make out the man's face. He turns the pram over. It is an old-fashioned cartoon pram with a concertina hood and leaf-spring suspension. The rusty handle is bent, the navy upholstery is torn and two of the wheels are tyreless. He drags it back through the gate, closing it behind him.

It's a trick of the light, of course. Time is nothing but forks and fractures. You step off the kerb a moment later. You light a cigarette for the woman in the red dress. You turn over the exam paper and see all the questions you've revised, or none of them. Every moment a bullet dodged, every moment an opportunity missed. A firestorm of ghost lives speeding away into the dark.

Perhaps the difference is this, that he will notice, that he will see things in this way when others don't, that he will remember an August afternoon when he was ten years old and feel the vertigo you feel walking away unharmed from a car crash. Or not quite unharmed, for he will come to realize that a part of himself now exists in a parallel universe to which he has no access.

When they lift the deer onto the pram it farts and shits itself. It doesn't smell like the camel house this time. Daniel is certain that it would be easier to drag the body but says nothing, and only when the track flattens out by the scrapyard and they are finally free of the roots and the sun-hardened ruts does the pram finally begin to roll a little.

The man is sitting against the bonnet of his Mercedes, as if he has arranged himself a better view for the second act. He has shoulder-length black hair, a cheap blue suit and a heavy gold bracelet. Sean shuts the gate and reattaches the loop of green twine. The man lights a cigarette. *Lads.* It's all he says. The smallest of nods. No smile, no wave. He will recur in Daniel's dreams for years, sitting at the edge of whatever else is going on. Cigarette, gold bracelet. *Lads.*

They stand at the side of the carriageway. Hot dust, hot metal. Daniel sees drivers glance at them, glance away then glance back again. *Three, two, one.* The pram is less stable at speed and less inclined to travel in a straight line and they reach the central reservation accompanied by a whoosh of air brakes and the angry honk of a lorry that comes perilously close to hitting them in the fast lane.

Clumsily, they heave the deer and the pram over the barrier. This takes a good deal of time and the strip of yellow grass is not wide. *Police*, says Sean, and Daniel turns in time to see the orange stripe of a white Rover slide past, lights and siren coming on as it goes up the hill. It will turn at the roundabout and come down the other carriageway. They have a minute at most.

Now, yells Sean. And the relief Daniel feels when they bump over the kerb of the service road and heave the pram up the bank through the line of stunted trees into the little park makes him laugh out loud. *The warrens*, says Sean, panting, and they keep their momentum up past a gaggle of rubbernecking children on the climbing frame and into the little network of walled paths round the back of the estate. They stop by the peeling red lock-ups and wait. No siren. No squeal of tyres. Daniel's head pulses. He needs to lie down in the dark.

They push the pram across the parched quadrangle to Orchard Tower. An elderly lady watches them, transfixed. Polyester floral dress and varicose veins. Sean gives her a jokey salute. *Mrs Daley.*

The double doors are easy but it takes some juggling to get the pram and the deer into the lift and they leave a lick of blood across the mirror that covers one of the side walls. Sean puts his finger into it and writes the word MURDER in capital letters on the glass at head height. The chime goes, the lift bumps to a halt and the doors open.

Later when he tells the story to people they won't understand. Why didn't he run away? His friend had a loaded gun. He will be repeatedly amazed at how poorly everyone remembers their childhoods, how they project their adult selves back into those bleached-out photographs, those sandals, those tiny chairs. As if choosing, as if deciding, as if saying *no* were skills like tying your shoelaces or riding a bike. Things happened to you. If you were lucky, you got an education and weren't abused by the man who ran the five-a-side. If you were very lucky you finally ended up in a place where you could say, *I'm going to study accountancy ... I'd like to live in the countryside ... I want to spend the rest of my life with you.*

It happens fast. The door opens before Sean can put his key into the lock. Dylan stands in dirty blue dungarees, phone pressed to one ear. He says, calmly, *Cancel that, Mike. I'll talk to you later,* and puts the phone down. He grabs a fistful of Sean's hair and swings him into the hallway so that he skids along the lino and knocks over the little phone table. He puts his foot on Sean's chest and yanks at the bag, ripping it open and breaking the strap. He takes out the gun, checks the chamber, shunts it back into place with the heel of his hand and tosses it through the open door of his room onto his bed. Sean sits up and tries to back away but Dylan grabs the collar of his T-shirt and hoists him up so that he is pressed against the wall. Daniel doesn't move, hoping that if he remains absolutely still he will remain invisible. Dylan punches Sean in the face then lets him drop to the floor. Sean rolls over and curls up and begins to weep. Daniel can see a bloody tooth by the skirting board. Dylan turns and walks towards the front door. He runs his hand slowly across the deer's flank five or six times, long, gentle strokes as if the animal is a sick child. *Bring it in.*

He wheels the pram across the living room and out onto the balcony. Dylan gives Daniel a set of keys and sends him downstairs to fetch two sheets from the back of his van. Daniel feels proud that he has been trusted to do this. He carries the sheets with their paint spatters and crackly lumps of dried plaster back upstairs. Dylan folds them and spreads them out on the concrete floor and lays the deer in the centre. He takes a Stanley knife from his pocket, flips the animal onto its back and scores a deep cut from its neck to its groin. Gristle rips under the blade. He makes a second cut at ninety degrees, a crucifix across the chest, then yanks hard at one of the corners so that the furred skin rips back a little. It looks like a wet doormat. Daniel is surprised by the lack of blood. Under the skin is a marbled membrane to which it is attached by a thick white pith. Dylan uses the knife to score the pith, pulling and scoring and pulling and scoring so that the skin comes gradually away.

Sean steps onto the balcony pressing a bloody tea towel to the side of his face. Daniel cannot read his expression. Turning, Daniel sees the radio mast and the sandy slab of the car plant. A hawk hangs over the woods. His headache is coming back, or perhaps he has simply begun to notice it again. He wanders inside and makes his way to the kitchen. There is an upturned pint mug on the drying rack. He fills it with cold water from the tap and drinks it without taking the glass from his lips.

He hears the front door open and close and Mrs Cobb shouting, *What the bloody hell is going on?*

He goes into the living room and sits on the brown leather sofa and listens to the slippery click of the carriage clock on the mantelpiece, waiting for the pain to recede. There are framed school photographs of Sean and Dylan. There is a wall-plate from Cornwall, a lighthouse wearing a bow tie of yellow light, three gulls, each made with a single black tick. The faintest smell of dog shit from the sole of his shoe. Sean walks down the corridor carrying a full bucket, the toilet flushes and he comes back the other way with the bucket empty.

He dozes. Twenty minutes, maybe half an hour. The sound of a saw brings him round. It takes a while to remember where he is, but his headache has gone. So strange to wake and find the day going on in your absence. He walks out onto the balcony. Dylan is cutting the deer up. The legs have been sawn off and halved, hoofs in one pile, thighs in another. Carl from next door has come round and is leaning against the balcony rail smoking a cigarette. *I'll have a word at the chippy. They've got a chest freezer out the back.* Sean is no longer holding the tea towel against his face. His left eye is half closed by the swelling and his upper lip is torn.

Get rid of that, will you? Dylan points to a yellow plastic bathtub. Lungs, intestines, glossy bulbs of purple Daniel can't identify.

He and Sean each take a handle. As they are leaving Dylan holds up the severed head and says to Carl, *What do you reckon? Over the fireplace?* But it's the bathtub that unsettles Daniel. The way it jiggles and slops with the movement of the lift. MURDER in capital letters. The inside of a human being would look like this.

He says, *How are you?*

Sean says, *Fine.*

Neither of them means it. Some kind of connection has been broken, but it feels good, it feels like an adult way of being with another person.

They put the bathtub down and lift the lid of one of the big metal bins. Flies bubble out. That wretched leathery stink. They hoist the tub to chest height. Two teenage girls walk past. *Holy shit.* A little countdown and they heave the bathtub onto the rim. The contents slither out and hit the bottom with a slapping boom.

Upstairs, the oven is on and Mrs Cobb has put a bloody haunch onto a baking tray. Carl is helping her peel potatoes with another cigarette in the corner of his mouth. Dylan drinks from a can of Guinness. *Come here.* Sean walks over and Dylan puts an arm around him. *If you ever do anything like that again I'll fucking kill you. Understand?* Even Daniel can hear that he is really saying, *I love you.* Dylan gives Sean the half-finished can of Guinness and opens another one for himself.

Your mum rang, says Mrs Cobb. *Wondering where you were.*

Right. He doesn't move.

Because it has nothing to do with the gun, does it. The gun is one of those dark stars that bend light. This is the moment. If he asks to stay then everything will be different. But he says nothing. Mrs Cobb says, *Go on. Hop it, or your mum will worry,* and however many times he turns her words over in his mind he will never be able to work out whether she was being kind to his mother or cruel to him. He doesn't say goodbye. He doesn't want to risk hearing the lack of interest in their voices. He walks out of the front door, closes it quietly behind him and goes down via the stairs so that he doesn't have to see the blood.

Forty years later he goes to his mother's funeral. Afterwards, not wanting to seem callous by heading off to a hotel, he sleeps in his old bedroom. It makes him profoundly uncomfortable, and when his father says that he wants things back to normal as soon as possible, he takes the hint with considerable relief and leaves his father to the comfort of his routine, the morning walk, the *Daily Mail*, pork chops on Wednesdays.

There are roadworks on the way out of town and by chance he finds himself diverted along the stretch of ring road between the flats and the woods. It all comes back so vividly that he nearly brakes for the two boys running across the carriageway pushing the pram. He slows and pulls into the lay-by, grit crunching under the tyres. He gets out of the car and stands in that same thumping draught that comes off the lorries. Freakishly the gate is still held shut by a loop of green twine. It scares him a little. He steps through and shuts it behind him.

The scrapyard is still there, as is the Roberts' house. The curtains are closed. He wonders if they have been closed all these years, Robert Hales and Robert Hales and Robert Hales, the same person, growing old and dying and being reborn in the stink and the half-light.

That cathedral silence before the first shot. Slabs of dusty sunlight.

He stoops and picks up a jagged lump of broken tarmac. He imagines throwing it through the front window, the glass crazing and falling. The loose rattle of scattering birds. Light flooding in.

A stick cracks directly behind him. He doesn't turn. It's the deer. He knows it's the deer, come again.

He can't resist. He turns slowly and finds himself looking at an old man wearing Robert's face. His father? Maybe Robert himself. What year is it?

The man says, *Who are you?* and for three or four seconds Daniel has absolutely no idea. ∎

HANDS ACROSS THE WATER

Rachel Seiffert

I

Graham was eighteen and rubbish at talking to females. He looked like a grown man, only he wasn't yet; he was just all shoulders and neck, wide forehead and no talk. Everyone in the flute band was aware of this, so when they were out in the Ulster wilds it was him they dispatched to get the lunch, because it was a girl he'd have to speak to on the burger van: a fine one.

He'd been up since dawn, drumming and drinking all morning. It was his first time away from home; Graham's first Orange Walk outside of Glasgow, but nothing like the other Walks he'd been on. Same skirling flutes, dark suits, bright sashes, but no tarmac and traffic; no high flats and crowds of torn-faced shoppers. Tyrone was all wet fields and hedgerows, as far as his eye could see; and the echo of the Lambegs thudding back at them from the low hills. There were masses of folk out, too: more every village they passed through, and the field they stopped in at the halfway mark was heaving. Grannies in deckchairs with tea in flasks, wee mobs of kids in Rangers T-shirts; candyfloss and sausage suppers, smell of damp grass and frying onions. The lodges were on the far side: all the dour faces, making their speeches, reading out their Bible verses. The band stuck with the crowd, though, and the colour: more chance of a drink there. Graham hadn't paid for a pint since he got here. There were always more folk buying, especially if he told them his grandad was from Ireland; his mum's dad. And that he was in the Orange. Graham's tongue all loose with lager, he'd been telling folk ever since the ferry, but his tongue was pulled tight again by the sight of Lindsey.

Dark red hair. Wee skirt and trainers, bare arms. All those freckles. She drew all eyes in the queue including Graham's. Lindsey was taking the money; getting the cans of juice out of the fridge and adding up what was owed in her head. Half the band had set their sights on her for after, even if none of them rated their chances, and Graham could see why, when she turned her grey eyes on him:

'What'll it be then?'

She knew he'd been staring, so Graham had to look past her to get the words out. He was ordering for most of the band, or that's what it felt like. And then a couple of the flutes kept changing their minds, calling across from the grass where they'd parked themselves with the drums; chopping and changing between burgers and bacon rolls. They were doing it to wind him up, Graham knew that fine well, so he did his best not to let it show. Except the order got too hard to follow, and then Lindsey gave up on the sums and got the calculator out of the cash box.

The queue behind Graham was grumbling by that stage, but Lindsey just told them all to watch their manners. He looked up at her then, and saw how her eyes were sharp and smiling, her back straight, like she could take on all comers. She got Graham to go through the order again, roll by roll, burger by burger. And she wasn't teasing him either; she knew he was shy, but that was all right.

Graham watched her fingers on the calculator buttons; her narrow lips, repeating what he told her; the pink tip of her tongue; and all her freckles. His eyes found them on her face and hands first, then down her neck as well, and up her arms. They were all wearing the same T-shirt on the van: oversized, with what looked like a lodge number and today's date printed across the top of the chest. They had aprons on, so the rest of the shirt was covered, but Lindsey was wearing hers back to front, and knotted at the side, so when she turned round to get Graham's change, he could see the Red Hand printed on the cloth. And how long her hair was too: a long, loose plait. It stopped at Lindsey's hips, where Graham found more freckles to stare at, on a pale inch of lovely skin, just above the waistband of her skirt.

After all that, she didn't have enough coins left in the float.

'I'll bring the change over later.'

Lindsey told Graham she'd come and find him, before the lodges set off up the road again.

She looked right at him too, making her promise:

'Won't forget you, honest.'

G raham watched her while he was eating, from the safer distance of the damp grass, sitting with the rest of the band. She was the same with everyone she served – joking, familiar – and he was gutted, thinking he'd just imagined it. He'd been so sure of it, up at the van: that she fancied him. He tried to work out how old she was: could be fourteen, could be eighteen, no telling. Graham hoped she wasn't older than him.

Lindsey did come over when they were making ready to go, and she gave Graham the coins she owed. He had his drum back on already, and his gloves, so he pulled those off to take the money. He felt her fingers touch his palm, just for a second, and then she stayed next to him while the bands and lodges assembled. Graham couldn't look at her then. But he was certain again.

H e hadn't gone to Ireland thinking this might happen. He'd gone to play and put away a skinful, and then there was Lindsey.

Graham waited for her after the Walk, in the back room of the only pub. He sat there a good couple of hours, sure that she'd come, certain he'd never have the nerve to go and look for her if she didn't; and then he saw her. Coming through the bar, and looking for him, he knew she was, because when she saw him she made a beeline through the crush. She had the same shirt on, still knotted, but no apron, so now Graham could see the skin on her belly, and it was all he could do to stop himself putting his hands there when she got up close.

One drink later they were out the back and walking, past where the barrels were stacked and on, with the sun going down behind their shoulders. It was quiet out there after the pub doors fell shut, just the two of them on the empty track, and neither of them talking. Only the sound of the wind in the wheat, and the weeds growing tall beside the farm gate. They walked the length of a tumbledown wall until it got low enough to climb, and behind that was a hidden spot with just enough grass for Lindsey to lie down.

Graham shouted out when he pushed himself inside hcr. IIe didn't mean to, but it didn't matter; she didn't laugh or anything. But then after, when it was over, when she stood up and pulled down her skirt, Lindsey looked at him, and he saw it hadn't been that way, not for her.

Graham was still on his knees, and busied himself with his trousers. Tucking in his shirt, to cover his shame: gutted again. Too much drunk, he regretted the pints he'd already sunk.

Lindsey stood a moment, watching, and then she crouched down next to him reaching for her knickers. They'd slipped off her ankles, over her trainers, and she picked them up from where they'd landed.

'Where you from then?'

She was looking at him, face level with his, and close, knickers bunched in her fist. Graham told her:

'Scotland.'

And she rolled her eyes. But friendly, he thought: like she'd been on the burger van that afternoon. Graham said:

'Fae Glasgow. Fae Drumchapel.'

He named the scheme, though she'd never have heard of it, and then Lindsey narrowed her eyes a bit:

'You in a juvenile lodge, Graham? Or a man's?'

She was smiling. She'd found out his name from someone, and now she was guessing how old he was. But she was teasing as well, and that nerve was still too raw for Graham to take courage. So he shook his head:

'I'm no.'

Bad enough he was in a band; that's what his mum said; there'd be no end of nagging if he joined a lodge. But Graham wasn't about to go into all that, because Lindsey had her cool eyes on him, like she was weighing him up. She leaned in a bit closer:

'Me either. My da's Orange enough for the two of us.'

Lindsey pulled at her T-shirt, tugging the lodge number up onto her shoulder to show him, and then shoving it back again, out of sight.

The knot at her waist had gone slack. So she undid it, and then retied it, tighter; higher up, under her ribs, and she told him:

'I've never been to Glasgow. Is it good there?'

Graham shrugged, trying not to look at her skin; that strip of it on show again above her skirt.

'Aye.'

He'd never thought if Glasgow was good or not, he couldn't say.

Lindsey looked at him a second or two:

'Better than here.'

She wasn't asking, but Graham shrugged again, by way of reply, not wanting to put this place down, because he'd had a fine time. Except that made Lindsey smile, so he had to look away, and then his eyes landed on the pale scrunch of cloth between her fingers. Lindsey laughed:

'Bet it is.'

And then:

'I've never been anywhere.'

She stood up and pocketed her knickers.

Graham thought she was making to go, and so this was it now: it was all over. But when he looked up, she was waiting for him:

'You coming?'

Lindsey put two fingers through his belt loops when they got to the road. She was walking next to him, but it felt like she was pulling, like she was more than willing, and Graham got hard again, and hopeful; so hard that it was painful. And even when she led him up the front path to a house and got her keys out, even though he felt sure this must be her mum and dad's place, and they might be home and demand to know who he was, Graham couldn't think of anything but pushing himself inside her again.

Lindsey shut the door and there was no one there. Just the last bit of late sun falling through the window onto the carpet, same colour as her hair. The red-gold girl, she stood in front of him, and he put his fingers there first, where he wanted to be, and she was wet; not just from what he'd done before, he was sure, because it was different; she was full and swollen, just like he was. She kissed him, wide-eyed, open-mouthed, and she kept her eyes open, unzipping his trousers.

II

They never used to shout, Stevie's mum and dad, not when he was wee. Now he was seven, and they did it all the time; behind closed doors, sending him out if he came in the room. But Stevie still heard them through the walls. Most often they shouted about the band. His dad had been in it before Stevie was born, and now his mum yelled about him going to practice again.

Stevie's dad went on Sunday nights. Sometimes the shouting started at lunch. If his mum got angry enough, she'd slam the doors, run down the close and off down the road.

Stevie watched her go then, from the window in his bedroom; her red head bright against the tenements. His hair was the same as his mum's; everybody said so. So if she turned, he knew she'd see him, and he wanted her to do that. Their flat was a top floor, and he could watch her all the way down the hill, until she made the corner. She never looked back, but he knew where she was headed.

He went through the rooms then, looking for his dad. One time Stevie found him on the sofa, white-faced and quiet. His dad asked:

'She gone tae your gran's, aye?'

And Stevie nodded. His gran was his dad's mum. She lived on the far side of the scheme, and she said her door was always open. Stevie's dad said:

'I know whose side she's on, but.'

Not his.

He sat with his fists on his knees. Then he held his big hands up to hide his face, and Stevie didn't know where to put himself. He wished his mum had taken him with her. He didn't know why she'd left him with his dad. His dad told him:

'She reckons I'll have tae stay home now.'

Sometimes he did. He ran Stevie his bath and put him to bed. 'Warm enough, pal? Aye. Get tae sleep then.'

But sometimes Stevie's dad made their tea early and then they'd head off across the scheme, the opposite way to his mum. Stevie knew they were headed to practice, and that his mum would shout when she found out. She shouted about Shug especially.

Shug was the bandmaster, and he'd be round the back of the snooker club when they got there. Tall, with his long arms folded, standing in the doorway like he'd been waiting hours. He had pale eyes and raw-boned fingers, and he shook hands with Stevie's dad first, before he looked at Stevie:

'You with us this week, aye? You can make yersel useful.'

Shug laughed when he said it, but it didn't sound like he was joking, so Stevie did as he was told and put the chairs out. A half-circle for the flutes in the middle of the function room, so they had somewhere to sit in the breaks, and one to hold the bass drum too, in front of the stage. Stevie learned to do it fast, and right first time, leaving enough space for the snares to stand either side.

The drums were kept in lockers at the far end of the room, and if Stevie was quick about finishing the chairs, his dad gave him the key, and let him carry his drum to the stage.

'Mind an be careful.'

It was an Andante, top-notch, and it had sat locked up for years, but it cost four hundred new, near enough. Stevie knew that had come out of his dad's pocket; and his sticks too, that were hickory-wood Dutharts. His dad stood by the lockers, sorting out the best pair; resting them in his palms, testing them for weight. He said they had to balance, and he turned Stevie's hands face up, laying one in each, so he could feel it.

'Naw, naw, son. Keep your wrists easy.'

But they were over a tenner a pop, so Stevie kept his thumbs gripped tight about them.

The function room had a bar at one end, and a stage, and the rest was just wide white walls, with benches down the sides. It was a great cold hangar of a place, but Shug said it suited him: big enough to make a good noise in. Once the drums were out, Shug went down the line of them on the stage, checking the skins, bending forwards and tapping with his fingertips. Stevie watched the way he put his ear up close, twisting the screws, tight, but not too tight: Shug wanted noise, but it had to be the right one. His hair was pale, receding, and he kept it clipped, and Stevie could see his scalp creasing beneath the soft fuzz while Shug worked; all the fine blue veins between skull and skin, if he was close enough. Stevie mostly kept his distance, but he stood next to Shug when he tuned the drums up, so he could see the reddish sheen on his eyelids when he got the tone right and he closed them, the soft line of his thick white lashes.

Shug wanted the whole band to love it like he did. And put in the hours to make it worth it.

So no one was late if they could help it. Shug kept a fine box – an ice cream carton with a slit cut in the lid – and come more than ten minutes after the door shut, you'd risk a ban.

'You cannae keep time, I've nae use for you. Fuck off hame.'

'Ach away and wank, Shug.'

Not all the bandsmen would have it, especially the older ones. But some had been in other flute bands, where the instruments were all third-hand and there'd been no uniform as such, so they were quick to put down any moaners.

Pride of Drumchapel marched in royal-blue livery, made by Victor Stewart of Lurgan; Shug said the best regalia came from Ulster. He chose gold braid and epaulettes and high caps too, with short black peaks that pointed straight down your nose. They made you walk with your chin up and your back straight so as to see the way ahead. Military bearing. Shug said the lodges the Pride played for got quality: sharp turnout and tunes, and no booze until the parade was done with. And he made sure the lodges came up with proper money for it. Discipline paid, he reckoned: for uniforms and banners, and trips to Belfast.

Stevie got to like it there, in among the men. Even if it made his mum shout. Even if they could be merciless some nights, taking the piss: out of Stevie's tiny bones, and how his dad was big and thick. They made jokes that Stevie didn't get, but he knew his dad should. About how Stevie looked like his mum, a dead spit, and there was none of his dad in him. They reached up and rapped at the side of his dad's head, if he was slow to laugh:

'Emdy there?'

'Naw. Lights is on, but.'

They patted his cheeks, that had gone all flushed. It made Stevie want to ram his head into his dad's soft belly; the way he had no comeback, just an *aye, right*, shrugging them off, like he wasn't that bothered.

His dad wasn't quick with words but Stevie knew he was good on the drum, better than anyone on the scheme. He was always glad when Shug got his dad to kick the practice off. With part of a drum salute, maybe, to get them all going; his right stick knocking, while the roll was kept up with his left.

Stevie's dad had never done a full salute for the band yet. That took near-on five minutes, and he told Stevie he had to get it perfect first. It was the parts where he had to pick up a different beat that were the hardest, and on Sundays when they didn't go to practice, Stevie's dad worked on them at home in the evenings. While Stevie's mum wasn't there to hear it.

Stevie listened to him then, from his bed; going over and over the same change on his drum pads; stopping and going to the fridge, getting himself a fresh can, before he worked on the next.

Sometimes he practised before Stevie's bedtime. Shug got hold of a video for him, of a World Solo Drumming Championship. It was folk who played with pipe bands, from Scotland and Canada and Northern Ireland, but Stevie's dad never bothered with all the bagpipes and talking at the start, he just wound through to the competition. He said Alex Duthart was the finest drummer ever, and he was dead now, but everyone still played his best salute. Stevie's dad learned it by watching it; not all the way through, but broken down into bits: listen, rewind, listen, to all the different parts. He sat and played them over and over, knocking the remote against his thighs.

Stevie liked it when he practised on his pads. When his dad knocked with both ends of the sticks, turning his hands over and back, over and back; so fast, and still keeping time.

Some nights Stevie's mum came home while he was playing.

She didn't shout then, or ask how Stevie was up on a school night. She didn't come into the room either, but Stevie saw her watching from the dark in the doorway, her eyes fixed on his dad.

The Duthart was his dad's showpiece, and if Shug didn't get him to kick off a practice night with that, someone in the band would call for it, more often than not.

His dad's heels lifted as he rocked: marching on the spot, keeping the rhythm, his chin and chest going out and back like a pigeon's. But no one laughed. The band were all hushed, mindful of the skill, just like his mum had been. They all stared at his dad's hands, rapt, while the sticks flew and tapped, and his big face went soft and blank. Like it was just him there, and his drum.

When they were all playing was best, the full band, twenty-five of them, all of a piece. Stevie loved the music, the serious faces while the men played, and the thick foam his dad let him slurp off his black pint after. They usually stayed for one, and Stevie's dad said he wasn't to tell his mum. Stevie never did; that wasn't why she stopped him going. He told her something else he shouldn't have about a practice night.

It was August, the Twelfth just over a month back, and half the band were not long home from their holidays. So spirits were high and attendance was near-on full that night, and the hall got hot with all those bodies. The first half was done and the doors were open, fags were being lit and trips being made to the bogs. Shug had gone straight through to the bar. No alcohol was allowed until practice was over, but playing was thirsty work, so he always poured pints of water and diluting orange at the break.

The windows were all open, and the men were waiting. Shug was ages about the juice, and it was usually him that nagged about getting back to practice. He came back through with no glasses, just an edgy look about him. His face was shining. Most of the men were sweating, but Shug's face was different; gone all tight, and his body too, like he might slap you if your playing wasn't up to the mark. Everyone noticed the change, because no one moaned about being parched. They all just got on with playing 'Derry's Walls', like Shug told them.

The half-circle of flutes had their backs to the door, and the drums were facing them, just like always. Stevie was on the end of the line, so he could see past the flutes, and he was the first to see the door open, and the man who came in to watch them. Jeans and blue T-shirt and balaclava. He walked into the big space between band and bar, and then he stood, wide-legged, head down, his hands folded, respectful: *God bless the hands that broke the boom and saved the Apprentice Boys.*

Come the end of the third verse most in the band had seen him. They were glancing over shoulders, and missing notes, but Shug made them finish before he told them:

'We have an honoured guest. He's far from home and cannot return, but his cause is just. So let us make him welcome.'

Shug ordered 'Hands Across the Water', and there was a fair bit of shuffling before they started. But they did well, and the guest raised a hand when they got to the end, nodding his thanks. He never spoke, and he never took off the hood, but he listened all the way through the second half, sitting on one of the long benches at the wall, his arms spread out along the seat back; rock-still, save a tapping finger. A couple of times he beckoned Shug over and whispered a request. They played 'Fields of Ulster' for him and, a bit after that, 'Absent Friends'. Stevie could see the hairs on Shug's forearms, all on end, and the slow tide of sweat running down his neck. Doug and Harry were next along, both with wide, damp patches spreading downwards from their collars, and Stevie wondered if his dad was the same, on the other end of the line, only he didn't dare lean forward to take a look.

There were slick faces all around the half-circle in front of him; the men were blinking the stinging salt out of their eyes, and no one missed a beat to push at their slipping glasses. At ten o'clock Shug ordered the flutes to stand on the chairs, and the drums to surround them. They stood like that in silence, heads high for the stranger, and then they played 'The Sash' for a full fifteen minutes and longer.

They were late finishing, but the barman had already called the lock-in. Everyone stayed. It was just the band in the snooker club, sitting around the tables; a few bare-chested, his dad among them, his sodden T-shirt stuffed into his bag. Stevie sat next to his dad, and he could feel the heat off him, his skin and his jeans, his red ears. There were a lot of red ears round the tables; eyes down and stop–start conversations. Heads trying not to turn to the bar where Shug was talking with the guest. Or anyhow listening while the guest spoke, frowning serious, and then laughing at his jokes.

A bucket went round the room. Stevie had seen a bucket go round after practice before, collecting coins for sick kids or band funds. But there were no coins going in it this time, only notes, and Stevie saw his dad tuck the fiver back into his pocket when the bucket came closer. He threw in a tenner: didn't want his blue standing out among the brown and purple.

'Who was that, Da?'
It was chilly outside, and Stevie's dad pulled on his jacket over his bare shoulders, but he didn't answer.

'Who was he?'

Stevie had to trot next to him up the long wind of the hill towards home. His dad always walked fast when he was annoyed, and Stevie knew the question annoyed him, but it seemed worth knowing, so:

'Da?'

'I dinnae know his fuckiname, son. Kay?'

That was all he got.

So Stevie asked his mum, the next day when she fetched him from school. He told her about the stranger and the bucket while they were climbing the stairs, and his mum stopped still on the second-floor landing, after she'd heard him out. She took a breath:

'Tell me. What was he wearing again, this man?'

Her eyes had gone sharp and dark, and then Stevie thought he'd got the word wrong; it was a strange word, and maybe it wasn't called a balaclava at all. He said:

'A hood. Wae eyeholes, but. A black wan.'

'Bloody hell.'

She muttered it, pulling Stevie back down the stairs, down the road to his gran's. He wasn't to ask more, Stevie knew that.

Brenda didn't know what to say to Lindsey. When she showed up raging, pulling Stevie behind her, still in his school clothes. The boy looked pale, like it was all his fault, so Brenda gave him toast and jam, plenty of it, and she sat him in front of the telly. She sat with him there a good few minutes, bracing herself before she went to the kitchen to listen to the girl.

It was the band, the band, the band; it always was. But this time it was worse, and Brenda got properly scared, thinking what Shug was up to and what Lindsey might do now. She was scared for her son's sake.

Brenda had long had her doubts. Ever since Graham joined his first band, just shy of his thirteenth birthday. She'd seen three sons cross that Rubicon, and she'd been dreading another. Graham's older brothers had all gone feral. They always were a handful; so many, and so close together. But she'd kept on top of them, more or less, until their teenage years toppled her, had her living in fear. Of phone calls in the small hours and visits from the police. Brenda used to weep about it sometimes, in the watches of the night, under the bedclothes:

the wee shitebags running her ragged, sucking her lifeblood, and all the filthy looks she got from the neighbours. Her boys did come good, in the end, but Brenda didn't give herself the credit. It had taken the army to tame two of them, and fatherhood the eldest. So she'd steeled herself for Graham's wild years, but they never came. He never went missing, or set fires in closes. Never took other people's cars and did handbrake turns in the sand traps on the golf course. Graham seemed happy enough with his once-weekly band practice and his drum pads. He even got Brenda to show him how to press his uniform, and she remembered crying in bed again that night, only this time with gratitude.

It was Lindsey's turn to cry now. She spent the afternoon in tears in Brenda's kitchen, and Brenda stood with her thinking how Graham had a family now. Lindsey alone was worth more than any flute band, surely.

The girl didn't want to go home to him, it didn't matter what Brenda said. So Brenda took Lindsey's keys and she was there when Graham got in from work.

'You're no goin back tae practice.'

'How?'

'You bloody know why no. Don't gie me that.'

She followed Graham through the flat, laying into him while he looked for Lindsey and his boy.

'You needn't bother, son. They're both at mine.'

Graham stopped where he was in Stevie's bedroom. He didn't look at her, he just sat down, heavy, the small bed sagging under his bulk, and the sight of him put a halt to Brenda's tirade.

She said:

'You're a grown man, Graham. I cannae stop ye, can I? You should listen tae Lindsey, but.'

She was from over there. And she'd just spent half the afternoon telling Brenda how she'd grown up with folk like Shug and you didn't want them near you. Lindsey thought she'd left it all behind her: her dad and all her troubles. She told Brenda her dad got carried away, far too much, especially when he was in his cups: he'd have flung his week's wages in that bucket, most likely, kept the mystery man in balaclavas for a couple of years at least.

Brenda asked:

'Who the bloody hell was he, Graham?'

'He wasnae emdy.'

She looked at her son, her youngest. Out of his depth on the duvet. His big shoulders gone slack, and his jaw. He rubbed his face and then he told her:

'It was just some stunt ae Shug's. Tae bump up funds. Shug's wantin new uniforms an we cannae afford them.'

Brenda was quiet a moment. Graham didn't get carried away, not as a rule. So she sat down on the bed, next to her boy, and then she said:

'Shug'll get hissel hurt.'

'Ach, Maw. Shug's no stupit.'

Graham looked at her. And then he blinked:

'Aye, OK. So mebbe he is. A heidbanger. Just playin, but.'

'If ye say so, son.'

Half the band probably wanted it to be real, and Shug would know that. A living, breathing member of the UDA, taking a short break from the struggle to listen to their music. He was gifting them a thrill, Brenda thought; getting them closer to the dark heart, but not close enough to harm. Only she wasn't sure enough of Shug, and the thought didn't give her much ease.

'Lindsey's right, son. You're tae keep away fae him,' she said. ■

LITERATURE & SPOKEN WORD

APRIL – JUNE 2012

Bringing books to life

HILARY MANTEL

Friday 18 May

The Man Booker Prize winner discusses her new novel *Bring up the Bodies*.

KATE SUMMERSCALE

Monday 21 May

Kate Summerscale explores the social mores of the Victorian era in her new book *Mrs Robinson's Disgrace*.

HOW TO GET YOUR NOVEL PUBLISHED
Orange and Grazia Evening for Aspiring Writers
Monday 28 May

Whether you have written your first draft or are yet to write the first sentence, join us for a special writers' evening, chaired by Orange Prize co-founder and bestselling novelist Kate Mosse.

ORANGE PRIZE SHORTLIST READINGS

Tuesday 29 May

Hear exclusive readings and discussions with each of the writers shortlisted for this year's Orange Prize.

EDMUND WHITE

Wednesday 30 May

Edmund White makes a rare visit to London to discuss his writing.

HARRY BELAFONTE

Wednesday 6 June

Harry Belafonte talks about his extraordinary life as a celebrated singer and social activist.

For more great events, see our website.

TICKETS 0844 847 9910
SOUTHBANKCENTRE.CO.UK

Supported by
ARTS COUNCIL ENGLAND

SOUTHBANK CENTRE

HOME

John Burnside

A wall of Post-it notes commemorating a riot; scrawled graffiti in a backstreet alley; a housing estate scheduled for demolition. Home is makeshift. Everything we build, everything we name, everything we hold dear and would not have taken from us is temporary and in constant need of re-imagining. In this collection, the makeshift stares us in the face at every turn. We see that nothing is permanent, merely rigid. No hierarchy is just, however you spin it; and hierarchy limits the imagination and withholds essential knowledge.

Meanwhile, the real world, the wild world that is all around us, stubbornly clings onto our denatured and polluted nervous systems. It is a world of play, of spontaneity, of constant remaking and erasure. If we have lost old certainties, it is only because we are, in Philip Larkin's words, 'less deceived'. Of course, the hierarchies do still remain, as Jocelyn Bain Hogg's images of partygoers from across the class spectrum show, but they seem more hollow now. We are closer to understanding that the natural order is inimical to cynicism and injustice, and while we may still feel trapped in the ancient, decaying edifice of privilege, our imagination can transform those ruins into the signposts of a new order. Anthony Rush's lyrical and moving image of a misty decommissioned barracks estate in Omagh, with its stubborn grasses bursting through tarmac does that, as does Yinka Shonibare's ironic recreation of Gainsborough's famed portrait of Mr and Mrs Andrews, in which, along with the subjects' heads, the classicized landscape – now long polluted and littered with pylons, billboards and wind turbines – has been removed.

It would be a mistake to think that these images of the makeshift are all laments, however. On the contrary, what we find here is mostly tender, if guarded, celebration. To recognize the new values that emerge from the makeshift is to discover the earliest traces of a new direction, the first tentative steps in a spontaneous remaking of ourselves, the hazy outline of a democratizing order that imagination finds in the unlikeliest places. Here is the optimism Claire Shea finds in the aftermath of the Peckham riots, or Mishka Henner's re-humanizing of faces caught on CCTV cameras. Taken as a whole, what these works suggest is that home, or identity, can be found in cultural ruins. This is home that does not exclude, but insists on sharing its place with anyone who chooses to be there. ∎

HOME

CLAIRE SHEA
A Piece on the Peckham Riots, 2011

SARAH PICKERING
River Way (Roadblock), 2004

IBIYE CAMP
Colours in Heygate Estate, 2011

IBIYE CAMP
Pink in Heygate Estate, 2011

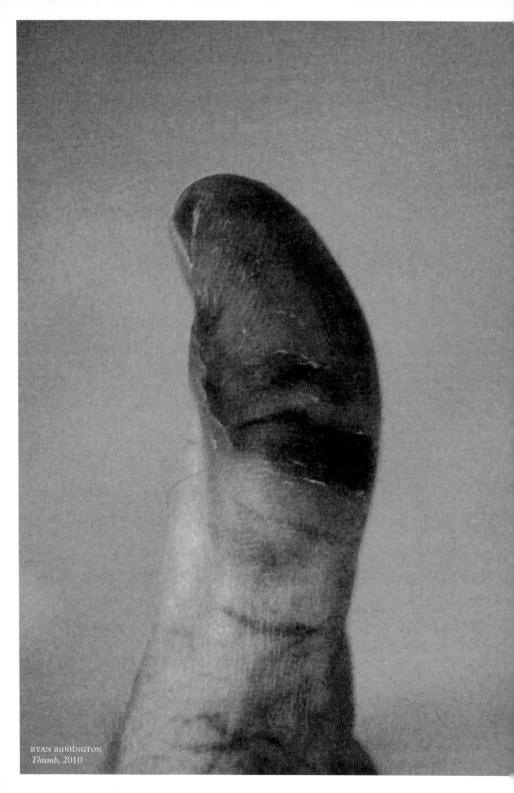

RYAN RIDDINGTON
Thumb, 2010

TINTIN COOPER
Erased, 2011

JOCELYN BAIN HOGG
British Youth, 2008–2011

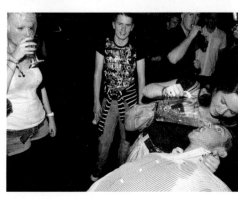

IAN TEH
Woman Walking, 2011

I grew up a son of Laurence and Elizabeth, a brother to Siobhan and Andrew.
I was the middle child, Anthony, named in memory of my father's brother who,
at eighteen months old, died in an accident within the barracks.

ANTHONY RUSH
From *Of Other Spaces*, 2011

'After, I went out and I was smoking a cigarette with them (the other officers), and I was shaking, and they were saying, "Ah, he's broke his first fucking dark, ain't he." Slapping me on the back, saying, "Good old boy, you're part of the team now, you're fucking involved." And I was just like *FUCK THAT*, I've just done something that I never thought I would do to another human being, just because I'm in a uniform and that's what they've told me to do and it's my job, and I just felt like shit, and I just thought I will never, ever do that to any one ever again.'

FLORENCE BOYD
Patrick, 2012

LÉONIE HAMPTON
From *In the Shadow of Things*, 2011

LAURA OLDFIELD FORD
Ferrier Estate (1972/1981/1995/2013), 2010

ANDREW TESTA
Muswell Hill, 2011

MISHKA HENNER
The Gleaners, 2011

GORDON CHEUNG
Living Machine, 2009

TOM HAMMICK
Compound, 2012

AFSHIN DEHKORDI
The Qajar Kings, 2012

JUSTIN COOMBES
Halcyon Song, 2011

YINKA SHONIBARE, MBE
Mr and Mrs Andrews Without Their Heads, 1998

EDMUND CLARK
Home from *Guantanamo: If the Light Goes Out*, 2010

GRANTA

THE MAGAZINE OF NEW WRITING

SUBSCRIPTION FORM FOR US, CANADA AND LATIN AMERICA

Yes, I would like to take out a subscription to *Granta*.

GUARANTEE: If I am ever dissatisfied with my *Granta* subscription, I will simply notify you, and you will send me a complete refund or credit my credit card, as applicable, for all un-mailed issues.

YOUR DETAILS

MR / MISS / MRS / DR ....

NAME ....

ADDRESS ....

....

CITY.. STATE ....

ZIP CODE .... COUNTRY ....

EMAIL ....

☐ Please check this box if you do not wish to receive special offers from *Granta*

☐ Please check this box if you do not wish to receive offers from organizations selected by *Granta*

YOUR PAYMENT DETAILS

1 year subscription: ☐ US: $48.00 ☐ Canada: $56.00 ☐ Latin America: $68.00

3 year subscription: ☐ US: $120.00 ☐ Canada: $144.00 ☐ Latin America: $180.00

Enclosed is my check for $_____ made payable to *Granta*.

Please charge my: ☐ Visa ☐ Mastercard ☐ Amex

Card No. ☐☐☐☐☐☐☐☐☐☐☐☐☐☐☐☐

Exp. ☐☐☐☐

Security Code ☐☐☐☐

SIGNATURE .... DATE ....

Please mail this order form with your payment instructions to:

Granta Publications
PO Box 359
Congers NY 10920-0359

Or call toll free 1-866-438-6150
Or visit GRANTA.COM for details

Source code: BUS119PM

CAPTIONS

CLAIRE SHEA is the curator of the Cass Sculpture Foundation. A resident of Peckham, south London, she recalls the aftermath of the riots of August 2011: 'It was incredible to see the impact several hundred Post-it notes could have. A very simple and direct method of showing support for a community that, by appearance, had been divided.'

SARAH PICKERING's Public Order series is photographed on training sites across the UK. Her monograph *Explosions, Fires and Public Order* was published by Aperture and MoCP in 2010. She was born in Durham and now lives in London.

IBIYE CAMP lives in south London. Her work explores the styles and atmospheres of the capital city through a variety of media, including oil and acrylic paint, digital and conventional photography, wool and clay.

RYAN RIDDINGTON is a London-based artist, previously resident in Leeds. He was born in the Federal Republic of Germany. *Thumb* is a photograph of his left thumb, a work he describes as a marker of lived experience that was close to hand.

TINTIN COOPER divides her time between Bangkok and London. Images of powerful leaders, athletes and icons play a central part in her collage, video and sculpture works. Using footage of well-known football players and managers, she seeks to capture the moment the heroic pose cracks.

JOCELYN BAIN HOGG began his career as a unit photographer on movie sets after studying documentary photography at Newport Art College. He has contributed images to the BBC, the *Sunday Times*, *Vogue* and other publications. In addition to the British Youth series, he is at work on a book project, *Tired of London, Tired of Life* with artists Paul Davis and designer Henrietta Molinaro. Images courtesy of VII.

IAN TEH's work is influenced by his interest in social, environmental and political issues. His photographs portray the layered and sometimes conflicting narratives that can exist in a single moment. His work has appeared in *Granta* 111: Going Back and in other publications including the *New Yorker*, *Time* and *Newsweek*. He lives in London.

ANTHONY RUSH's photographs locate personal stories within historical and political contexts. In this series he focuses on the former military barracks of Lisanelly and St Lucia, Omagh. Built in the 1880s, the 170-acre site was decommissioned in 2007 as one of the conditions of the Northern Ireland peace process.

FLORENCE BOYD is an illustrator, artist and set painter for theatre. *Patrick* is from a series in collaboration with Marc Dahl, who worked as a security officer at Yarl's Wood Immigration Removal Centre in Bedford in 2002 during a period in which a riot broke out. Boyd and Dahl are working to produce an animated documentary based on this series.

LÉONIE HAMPTON is an award-winning photographer who, in this series, documents her mother's struggle with Obsessive–Compulsive Disorder. For several years after the collapse of her first marriage, Hampton's mother, Bron, was unable to empty the packing boxes, plastic bags and accumulated artefacts of her former life. In 2007 a deal was made: Léonie would help Bron on the condition that she be allowed to document the process. *In the Shadow of Things* was published by Contrasto in 2011.

LAURA OLDFIELD FORD has, since 2005, produced a 'zine, *Savage Messiah*, which conjures an England of socio-political upheaval, squat culture, Brutalist architecture and sentimental pop tunes. Many of her drawings have focused on areas of London that were destroyed to make way for the 2012 Olympics site.

ANDREW TESTA began his photographic career in 1992 and has worked for a range of international publications. The images featured here were shot over the course of a year from the window of his bedroom in a north London suburb. Images courtesy of Panos Pictures.

MISHKA HENNER lives and works in Manchester. 'Following the riots in England in August 2011, police forces released hundreds of portraits of alleged looters into the public domain. This was an unprecedented move by authorities employing the full force of online media and broadcasting channels to target a single group.' Images courtesy of Panos Pictures.

GORDON CHEUNG is from Hong Kong and now lives in London. His multimedia works utilizing spray-paint, oil, acrylic, pastels, stock listings and ink capture the hallucinatory slippage between the virtual and actual realities of a globalized world.

GRACE ADAM's painting of a training tower for firefighters as viewed from an embankment at the entrance to an underpass examines our efforts to negotiate and influence our domestic and wider environments within an urban space. Adam lives and works in London.

TOM HAMMICK's *Compound* is part of his current exhibition, Dreams of Here, at the Brighton Pavilion Museum & Art Gallery. The piece features a panoramic image of his East Sussex garden idealized as a utopian Garden of Eden. Photograph by Leigh Simpson, courtesy of Eagle Gallery, London.

AFSHIN DEHKORDI was born in Iran and lives in London where he works for the BBC Persian Service. This series documents the annual gathering of a group of Iranians in a St James's banqueting hall in memory of their ancestors, the Qajar dynasty, rulers of the Persian Empire in the nineteenth century.

JUSTIN COOMBES's Halcyon Song is a series of photo-text vignettes. Fusing the fantastical and the everyday, the photographs inhabit the point of view of a female kingfisher as she searches for nesting sites along the length of London's Regent's Canal. Images courtesy of Paradise Row Gallery.

YINKA SHONIBARE, MBE, is a British-Nigerian artist living in London. He has exhibited internationally and was nominated for the Turner Prize in 2004. Most recently Shonibare's work, *Nelson's Ship in a Bottle*, was the 2010 Fourth Plinth Commission displayed in Trafalgar Square.

EDMUND CLARK's *Home* is part of a series exploring the consequences of control and incarceration in the wake of 9/11, illustrating three central ideas of home: the naval base at Guantanamo; the complex of camps where the detainees have been held; and the homes, new and old, where the former detainees now find themselves trying to rebuild their lives.

Unless otherwise noted, all images are copyright of the artist.

SOME OTHER KATHERINE

Sam Byers

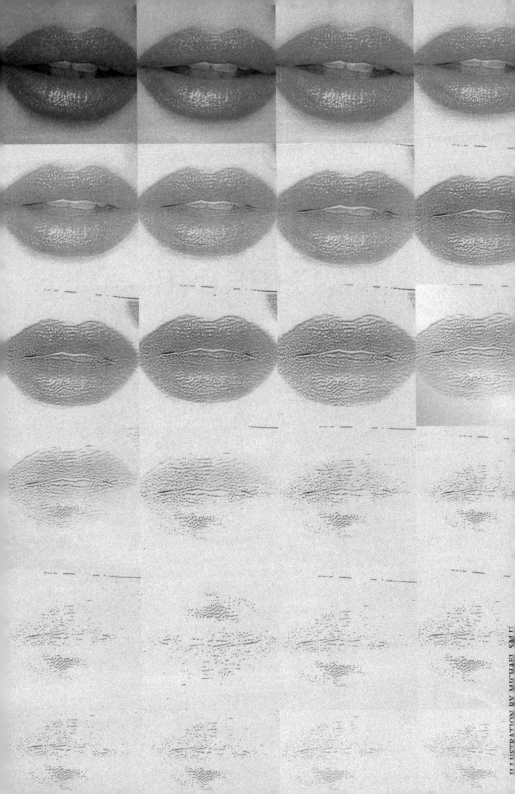

K atherine didn't like to think of herself as sad. It had a defeatist ring about it. It lacked the pizzazz of, say, rage or mania. But she had to admit that these days she was waking up sad a lot more often than she was waking up happy. Weekends were worst; workdays varied. The weather was largely inconsequential.

Time in front of the mirror didn't help. She got ready in a rush, then adjusted incrementally later. She hadn't been eating well. Things were happening to her skin that she didn't like. Her gums bled onto the toothbrush. It struck her that she was becoming ugly at a grossly inopportune time. Breakfast was frequently skipped in favour of something unhealthy halfway through her working morning. She couldn't leave the house without a minimum of three cups of coffee inside her. Recently, she had started smoking again. It helped cut the gloom.

For the past two years, Katherine, having moved from London to Norwich by mistake, had been the facilities manager at a local telecommunications company. Her job centred on the finer points of workplace management. She was paid, she liked to say, to be an obsessive–compulsive. She monitored chairs for ongoing ergonomic acceptability and suitable height in relation to desks and workstations, which she checked in turn to ensure compliance with both company guidelines and national standards for safe and healthy working environments. She performed weekly fire-alarm checks and logged the results. Each morning she inspected the building for general standards of hygiene, presentation and safety. She fired at least one cleaner per month.

She was widely resented and almost constantly berated. People phoned or messaged at least every hour. Their chairs, their desks, the air conditioning, the coffee maker, the water cooler, the fluorescent strip lighting – nothing was ever to their liking. The numerous changes Katherine was obliged to implement in order to keep step with current health and safety legislation made her the public advocate of widely bemoaned alterations. Smokers had to walk further from the building. Rooms had to be rearranged. Breaks had to be renegotiated. Her job allowed no flexibility, meaning that she frequently came off as humourless and rigid. She took comfort, however, in the ease with which she could write off enmity as a response to her job role, as opposed to her personality.

Aside from the basic majority of colleagues who couldn't stand her, there also existed a splinter group comprising the men who wanted to fuck her. Some of them wanted to fuck her because they liked her, and some of them wanted to fuck her because they hated her. This suited Katherine reasonably well. Sometimes she fucked men because she felt good about herself, and sometimes she fucked them because she hated herself. The trick was to find the right man for the right moment, because fucking a man who hated you when you were actually having a rare moment of liking yourself was deeply counterproductive, and fucking a man who was sort of in love with you at the peak of your self-hatred was nauseating.

To date, Katherine had fucked three men in her office, one of whom, Keith, she was still fucking on a semi-regular basis. The other two, Brian and Mike, had faded ingloriously into the middle distance, lost amid the M&S suits and male-pattern baldness. Brian had been first. She'd broken her no-office rule for Brian and, with hindsight, it hadn't been anywhere near worth it. She'd broken her married-man rule too, and the rule about men with kids. She resented this because it afforded Brian a sense of history he in no way deserved. The reality was, at a time in her life when Katherine had made a conscious and not entirely irrational decision to jettison so many of the rules by which she had up to that point lived her life, Brian had been in the immediate vicinity, and, moreover, had been a living exemplar

of several of those rules. Hence the sex, which had happened quite
suddenly one Tuesday afternoon after he'd given her a lift home
from work, continued through to the following month, and then
ended when Katherine began wondering if some of her rules had in
actual fact been quite sensible. Brian was fifty-something (another
broken rule, now that she thought about it), fat, and in the midst of
an epic crisis. He drove a yellow Jaguar and had a son called Chicane.
They never finished with each other. Katherine simply ceased to
acknowledge his existence and the message was quietly, perhaps even
gratefully, received.

Mike was, on the outside at least, different. He was Katherine's
age (thirty, although there was room for adjustment depending
on her mood), single, and surprisingly good in bed. Even more
surprisingly, Katherine found him to be capable of several almost-
full-length conversations when the mood took him. Their affair
(it wasn't really an affair, but Katherine liked to define it as such
because it added value to the experience and because she'd not long
previously fucked Brian and was hoping that she might be in a *phase*
of having affairs, which would of course completely legitimize her
sleeping with Mike) lasted almost two months. It ended when Mike
found out that Katherine had slept with Brian. Much to Katherine's
irritation, Mike turned out to be in possession of what he proudly
called *a moral compass*. Katherine was not impressed. As far as she
was concerned, morals were what dense people clung to in lieu of a
personality. She told Mike as much after he tried to annex the high
ground over the whole adultery issue. He ignored her. He couldn't
respect her, he said. Katherine would always remember him walking
away from the drinks cooler, shaking his head and muttering softly.

All this had been a while ago, and there had been other, non-office-
based men floating around during the same time period. Nothing had
gone well. She'd been waking up sad a lot more often. The thing with
her skin had started. She'd gained weight, then lost it, then lost a
little more. Sleep was becoming increasingly difficult. Once, during a
stretch of annual leave she'd taken purely to use up her quota, she'd

swallowed a fistful of pills and curled up in bed waiting to die, only to wake up five hours later in a puddle of vomit, many of the pills still whole in the mess. She had words with herself. She got dressed the next day and did her make-up and went into the city and collided with Keith, who suggested coffee, then food, then violent, bruising sex in his garage, her stomach pressed against the hot, ticking metal of his car bonnet.

'I remember once . . .' said Keith, lying back against the car afterwards, Katherine beside him, both of them smoking and waiting for the pain to subside. 'What was I . . . Fuck it, it's gone.'

There were days when it seemed sordid and doomed; days which, oddly, Katherine found more romantic than the days of hope. There was something doomed about Keith generally and she liked it. He was forty-one (because, she thought, once you'd broken a rule, it was no longer really a rule, and so couldn't really be said to have been broken a second time), thin on top and thick round the middle. At work he wore crumpled linen and skinny ties. In the evenings he favoured faded black denims and battered Converse. He had pale, slightly waxy skin and grey eyes with a white ring around the iris. Katherine had read somewhere that this had medical implications but she couldn't remember what they were and so chose not to mention it. She liked the idea that Keith was defective, that he might be dying. She liked the fact that he was open about what he called his *heroin years*. She even liked the way he hurt her in bed: the sprained shoulder, the deep gouge on her left thigh. Keith was different in what Katherine saw as complementary ways. He was blunt where she was sharp. He would never love her, would probably never love anyone or anything, and Katherine admired this about him. He seemed beyond the concerns that threatened daily (yes, daily by now) to swallow her whole. By definition, of course, this also placed him beyond her, but she liked that too.

She didn't live in London. There were mornings when she had to stare hard into the mirror and repeat this to herself like some sort of mantra. On a good morning she could just about say the word *Norwich*, but it was hard. After three years of dating, she and Daniel, her ex, had moved here together, ostensibly for his job, although there were unspoken implications regarding the pitter-patter of ghastly feet. But then they broke up, and London looked like it would be lonely, and now she was stuck.

Always a practical woman, Katherine's mother felt the best way to voice her concerns about Katherine's well-being was to be direct. This seemed to involve repeatedly calling to ask Katherine if she was OK, which had the effect of making Katherine feel a long way from OK.

'Are you eating enough?' her mother would say bluntly. 'Are you eating healthy foods?'

'Yes,' Katherine would say, midway through a doughnut. 'This morning I had porridge for breakfast, and for lunch I had a baked potato with tuna fish. For dinner I'm going to have grilled chicken breast.'

'Are you being facetious? Because it's unattractive, you know. And not entirely mature.'

'I'm being honest. Is that mature?'

'That depends,' said her mother, 'on what you're being honest about.'

Katherine met with Keith only on selected evenings. They fucked and drank in heroic silence, which suited Katherine. She lived in fear of him saying something interesting, which might make her fall in love with him; or something horrific, which would shatter the illusion she'd so carefully constructed. He brought her a vibrator as a present: gift-wrapped, with a heart-shaped tag that read, 'Think of me.' She donated it, tag and all, to her local charity shop. She never saw it for sale, and wondered often what had become of it. She liked to think one of the elderly volunteers had taken it home one lonely evening and subjected herself to an experience so revelatory as to border on the mystical.

'Keith,' she said one evening, deliberately loudly, in a restaurant she'd selected precisely because she knew it would be crowded when she asked the question. 'How many other people are you fucking right now?'

'Three,' he said calmly. 'You?'

'Four,' she lied.

'Is it Daniel?' her mother asked during one of her interminable phone calls. 'Because I understand, you know, I really do.'

'It's not Daniel, mother.'

'He sent me a birthday card last week. He always sends me Christmas and birthday cards. Isn't that nice?'

'It's not nice,' said Katherine. 'It's anally retentive. He sends you cards because you're on his list. It's basically an automated response. It never occurs to him to change anything.'

'Does he send you cards?'

'No.'

During the evenings she wasn't with Keith, which were numerous given that Keith had three other fucks to squeeze into his week, Katherine read and watched the news. She rarely watched anything else on television. Like much of Katherine's life, what she read and what she watched were governed by her sense of types of people: types she wanted to be; types she couldn't stand. She didn't want to be the sort of person (woman) who watched soaps and weepie movies. She wanted to be the type of person (woman) who watched the news and read the Booker list. She imagined herself at parties, despite the fact she never went to parties, being asked her opinion on world affairs and modern literature. Yet whenever talk turned to global tragedy, she found herself feeling adrift and nastily exposed. It wasn't that she didn't know what was happening, it was that she didn't see why it should cause her any distress. Once this fact became clear, it seemed to spread its tentacles into the rest of her life in such a way as to make her question, not for the first time, exactly how human she could lay claim to being. She thought of it as a certain lack of connection. Others saw it as coldness. *Unmoved* was a word that came up a lot, both in Katherine's head and in the opinions others had of her, of which she was more than aware. *Emotionally hard-to-impress*, was the way she preferred to think about it. Just as declarations of love were not enough to stir the same in her, so footage of, say, starving Haitians was not enough to cause the kind of glassy-eyed distress that seemed so automatic in others. Swollen, malnourished bellies; kids with flies in their eyes; mothers cooking biscuits made of earth. It was faintly revolting. Sometimes, when in a particularly quarrelsome mood, Katherine asked people exactly what the relevance was of such images. For some reason, people tended to find this question offensive. They cited vague humanitarian criteria. The word *children* came up a lot, as if simply saying it explained everything.

Kath, Keith wrote in an email from an undisclosed location where he was holidaying with an unnamed and un-gendered companion to whom he was almost certainly not related. *I miss you bad. I don't think I can live without you. Love me?*

Keith, Katherine wrote back. *I will never live with anyone who can't live without me. Grow up. PS: who the fuck are you on holiday with?*

'Maybe you should join a group of some kind,' her mother said. 'That's how you meet people. You've got to get out there.'

'By people do you mean men?'

'Well, who wants to meet women?'

'Fuck me like you're a child,' said Keith, back from holiday and fucking her in a way that reminded her of an animal in a veterinary collar – as if she were something to be shaken off, a constraint out of which he needed to reverse. 'Fuck me like you're scared of me.'

It proved to be too much of an imaginative leap. She fucked him like she pitied him and then told him afterwards that he was pathetic.

'You're right,' said Keith. 'You're so right. Next time fuck me like I'm pathetic.'

Lunch hours were another gloom entirely. Unable to tolerate the drab banter of the staffroom, and unable to meet Keith for fear they might be seen, Katherine roamed the city in search of stimulation, finding it, unsurprisingly, in the purchase of objects and experiences she neither needed nor could afford. Sometimes it was clothes, other times it was books. On good days it was a massage or a trip to the hairdresser's. On bad days it was just a seat in a cafe and a grandstand view of everyone else as they shopped. Even the clothes themselves were grim. On the sale rails and in the bargain bins, in shop windows and on the ageless skin of the mannequins, death was a market presence. Lines of clothing called Zero, Blank, Deathscape, Heroin. T-shirts that said Love My Bones. Life, it seemed, had become passé. Value had collapsed. Every store in town was either selling cheap or closing down. People shopped like it was the end of days, pressing stony-faced through the deals and the prophecies of closure. Fashion existed, she felt, as a way of ignoring the future, and on strong bright days, when the word seemed both capitalized and italicized in her mind, she could slip easily into the vocabulary and mindset of couture. Clothes became *pieces*; outfits were *pieces she'd put together*; old clothes in her wardrobe were *archived pieces*. When she was miserable fashion became intolerable – gaudy and false and aching with pointlessness – and so she regarded a shopping spree not as a remedy, like some, but merely as a hopeful symptom.

'Where did you go on holiday?' she asked Keith mid-fuck, having suddenly (but with careful premeditation) kicked him off her at his most vulnerable moment, sending him sprawling to the floor with only his hard-on to break his fall.

'Jesus . . . fuck, I think you . . . what?'

'Your holiday,' she said, lying back on the bed and eyeing him coldly. 'Where did you go?'

'Tenerife,' he said, inspecting his cock for permanent damage. 'Do we have to talk about it now?'

'No we don't have to talk about it now,' she said calmly. 'If you like I can just get dressed and go and we don't have to speak about it ever again.'

'I don't understand why this is suddenly such a pressing issue that you have to –'

'Who did you go with?'

'Oh, I see. You're jealous.'

'I'm not jealous. I just want to know. Who did you go with? Was it someone from work?'

'I'm going to have to go to work with my dick in a sling, you fucking –'

'Was she blonde or brunette?'

'Blonde,' he said miserably. 'Her name's Janice. Are you going to make me stop seeing her?'

Katherine was repulsed.

'What do you mean *make you*?' she snapped. 'How could I *make you*?'

'I don't know, I just –'

'How come she gets to go on holiday, that's what I want to know. How come she gets to go on holiday while I have to make do with intermittent screwing in your shabby little flat?'

'We can go on holiday,' said Keith. 'If that's what you want.'

'I'm not sure now. I'm not sure I could bear it.'

This was in fact true. The more Katherine thought about it the more going on holiday with Keith sounded like an awful idea. All those inane conversations in sunnily bland surroundings. His sweat-shined love handles; his shrivelled ball-bag in Speedos.

'Why not?' said Keith. 'What's wrong with me?'

'You want a list?' she said.

'Yeah,' said Keith. 'Give me a list.'

'Hit me,' she said.

'I can't.'

'You've done it before.'

'You weren't telling me to before.'

'Question answered,' she said, pulling on her clothes.

He called her two days later and begged, offering a last-minute booking. No one at work would think anything of it, he said. They'd stagger their days a little. Katherine agreed, victorious and relieved.

'Where are we going?' she asked.

'Malta,' he said. 'God, I'm fucking haemorrhaging money.'

In Malta, everything was clearer and more muddled at the same time. They fell into an easy routine of lazing, drinking and eating during the day, then fucking and sleeping, which after the drinking became somewhat indistinguishable. Everything seemed to pass not so much in a blur as in odd drifting snippets, as if segments of the film had been removed and only highlights remained. Here she was waking up, Keith snoring beside her, and sitting alone on the balcony staring out across the bay at the huddled, stone-cut splendour of Valletta, feeling calm and deliciously lonely. Here she was by the pool, either drifting with her thoughts or squinting through one eye at the array of flesh around her. Brown flesh, reddened flesh; German and English and Italian flesh, all pressed together and sizzling under the sun. It was erotic and vile at the same time – vilely erotic – the only kind of eroticism Katherine seemed to experience these days. Here she was at dinner with Keith, exchanging heavy clods of conversation so deadening she was tempted, at times, to cause physical injury, either to him or to herself, just to have something distinctive to discuss. He said things like, *It's hot,* and then followed that statement seconds later with a clarification (*It's really hot*) and then, after a bit of thought, some further exposition (*It's so hot I feel like I'm melting in my seat*) until finally his thought processes reached their natural conclusion and he ended with a sort of ruminative coda (*So hot . . .*).

He'd turned an odd colour – a deep leathery tan with a thin cherry varnish. This was partly to do with the dedication Keith applied to his

sunbathing. He lay in the heat with the gritty focus of a man making
a long-distance drive. He took scheduled breaks. He was careful to
maintain full attention. On the beach, by the pool, he was a faintly
ridiculous sight. There was, Katherine speculated, no possible way of
concealing his Englishness, or any English person's Englishness for
that matter. You could spot them immediately – pasty white; muffin-
bellied; Rorschached with quasi-Celtic tattoos.

Not that Katherine was immune. She had, though she was loath
to admit it, a worryingly English physique. What was it about going
abroad, she wondered, that threw all your shortcomings into howling
relief? Why did every other race seem so at home while the English
seemed determined to be uncomfortable? In the afternoons, by the
pool, it was a parade of bikinis, of flat stomachs and deep cleavages.
Keith had a way of angling his sunglasses away but then sliding his
eyes in their direction, thinking Katherine couldn't see the whites
through his Wayfarers. He lay in the sun for hours, simmering and
staring at other women's tits, and then, back at the hotel, sticky with
sweat and Ambre Solaire, he fucked her while she was still in her
bikini, the images of those other women so clearly running across his
eyes that she could almost see them, like figures in a zoetrope. Not
that she saw his eyes much when they fucked. Keith had two favoured
sexual positions: from behind or getting a blow job. If he could have
found a way to fuck the back of her head he'd have been in hog's
heaven. It saddened her that the fantasy was so depressingly clear:
the sun, the hotel room, the way he pawed at her bikini just enough to
get past it without ever actually removing it. Keith was imagining the
whole thing as a holiday romance – a sordid affair with a mysterious
stranger; the indulgence of all his sex-in-the-sun imaginings.

'Why don't we fuck in the morning?' she asked. 'Why don't we
fuck at night? Why do we always have to fuck straight after we've
been at the pool?'

'The sun revs my engine,' was how Keith put it, but Katherine
knew better, knew he needed at least four hours of unadulterated
poolside porn before he could crank up the necessary desire for

a screw. He also needed a few beers – more and more, it seemed. Katherine had a theory for this trend, developed while watching Keith's lizardly eyes dart from one bikini to the next. Keith's libido, she decided, was based on strangeness. This was true of most men, of course, but for Keith it was particularly true. He had an inbuilt urge to have sex with people he didn't know – anonymous, foreign, mysterious people with whom he would need to exchange only a few clumsy pleasantries. At first, he'd been rapacious to the point of aggression. Now he was distracted, frequently drunk and usually all-too-clearly thinking of someone else. For a while, Katherine had been concerned that Keith was thinking of a specific someone else – that there might be one bronzed beauty by the pool who'd caught his eye for longer than the others. It took her time to realize he was simply imagining that Katherine wasn't Katherine. That's what mattered, that's what got his engine going. Keith's withdrawal from anything that could have been termed a shared reality between them was precisely because that reality, or any reality for that matter, was profoundly unerotic to him. He didn't want to fuck Katherine; he wanted to fuck a stranger who looked like Katherine.

A man – old and English – disturbed her in the toilet as she was pulling up her bikini bottoms. He blushed claret and bolted. When Katherine told Keith she saw a light go on in his eyes. He told her to go back to the toilet and leave the door open. He followed her in and fucked her against the sink without removing her bikini, each of them looking themselves in the eye in the steaming mirror, Katherine all too aware of what had stirred Keith's libido: the fantasy of her as a nameless stranger, disturbed in the toilet, fucked without introduction. It was chance that excited Keith. Chance and anonymity and the infantile idea of stolen peeks at women's bodies. She could be anyone, she thought, watching Keith's reddening face in the mirror. Anyone at all and he wouldn't care.

Fuck you, she mouthed into the mirror. He didn't see. He'd closed his eyes as he came, imagining, no doubt, some other time and place entirely, some other fuck, some other Katherine.

Back at home, after a wordless flight and a relieved parting at the airport, Katherine discovered she was pregnant. Her period was a week overdue. She'd put it down to the strains of the holiday but to put her mind at rest, she pissed on a plastic stick. The stick promised total confidence. Nothing in her life had ever given her less. At the sight of the little blue bar in the stick's predictive window, she threw up. Then she went out and bought five more sticks of differing brands, all of which promised relief, reassurance, an end to doubt. She was not reassured. She was not relieved. She was riddled with doubt. She bought a half-bottle of vodka from the offie on the corner and drank it neat. She considered buying Mr Muscle or household bleach. She thought of herself as a drain that needed to be cleansed. Everything on the telly seemed to be about babies. She called Keith and said, without explanation, that she needed some space. He gave it, of course, and save for a cursory text thanking her for a great time, he made no effort at contact. She was glad and disappointed. She still had three days of her leave and spent them pacing her flat and smoking. She called her mother and told her she was fine. She thought about the pills again and decided it was simply too pathetic, too predictable, and would allow her mother to wring far too much sympathy out of family events.

At work, there was a briefly pleasing sense of furtiveness and secrecy that, not altogether coincidentally, mirrored the feelings she'd had when she'd been secretly fucking Keith (yes, past tense for that now). There was something about having a secret, she thought, that brought with it a sense of elevated moral standing or general day-to-day importance. Not telling people removed the burden of explanation, of the need to emote; it allowed her to look at the problems of others as nothing more than the problems of others. How pleasing it was to watch the women in her office – Jules and Carol and all the others – go about their daily distractions in blissful ignorance of Katherine's secret martyrdom. Secrecy was a point of pride. She wanted it, then of course didn't want it, felt hampered by it, and wanted its opposite: attention. People surprised her in their ability not to notice. Not telling them her problems meant she had to listen to theirs. The pains of the supermarket; their Very Repetitive Strain Injuries; the fact that their husbands were too 'closed' emotionally ('I try to ask him why he's angry all the time, but he's so *closed,* you know?'); and the way their neighbours were encroaching on their back garden by shifting their fence six inches over. Problems were competitive in the confines of the office. Sympathy was a contact sport. Even as she felt aloof, the injustice keened away inside her, swelling and fading and Dopplering off into her soul. She started to self-sabotage her own secrecy, not wanting to tell but desperate to impart. She favoured implication over explanation. When Jules caught her coming out of the stalls dabbing bile from her lips and tears from her eyes and asked her what was wrong, Katherine said Nothing while making all the possible facial shapes of someone who should really have had said Something. But Jules failed to notice Katherine's shuttling eyes and roving stare and quivering lip as she declared herself to be Fine, really *Fine,* just as Carol failed to notice when Katherine stared at the floor and sucked in her top lip after coming over faint in the staffroom and saying Nothing was wrong, that she was *Fine.*

Galvanized by her isolation, Katherine attempted to make inroads into her iciness. She made sure to say good morning. She asked after Jules's friend who had recently died. She stood in the staffroom and listened to Debbie go on about her son, who ate foil wrappers and had been excommunicated from the Rainbow Day Centre for whopping his willy against other children's thighs. When someone in the office either stole or inadvertently appropriated Janice Johnson's bag for life, which she had very sensibly brought in so as to allow her to transport her macrobiotic stew without it leaking all over her handbag, Katherine sent a global email that resulted, after just thirty minutes, in the bag miraculously reappearing in the staffroom.

When Dawn Rickstadt, who Smelled So Good, wafted past Katherine's desk smelling particularly good, Katherine made sure not only to note the name of her perfume (Consensual, by Chanel) but also to check how Dawn might feel if Katherine purchased the same perfume and so also ended up Smelling So Good, to which Dawn had generously replied that she had no problem at all with Katherine buying a bottle of Consensual because it was gorgeous and indeed, since she herself was nearly out, perhaps they could go shopping for it together at lunch.

'This has lovely dirty notes,' said Dawn in Debenhams, misting Katherine's wrist with Reproach by Comme des Garçons. 'It's sea breeze meets knee-trembler in a Ford Capri.'

'Is that supposed to be nice?'

'It's supposed to be sexy.'

'I don't want to be sexy,' said Katherine. 'I want to be clean.'

'Gotcha,' said Dawn. 'Something more zesty?'

'How about Mace?' said Katherine.

'Oh, I know,' said Dawn. 'You'd think with all this research they'd have come up with a reliable twat repellent by now.'

Afterwards they did lunch. After lunch they did coffee. Dawn talked about her relationships, all of which had ended badly, but about which she was still, she said, hypothetically optimistic.

'That must be nice,' said Katherine.

'It has its moments,' said Dawn. 'But anyway. Tell me about you.'

'Ick,' said Katherine.

It was, however, short-lived, just as Katherine's occasional episodes of bad-faith niceness were always rather short-lived, and always left her feeling disappointed and faintly dirty after the event. She could understand it, obviously, the whole being-nice-to-people thing. She could see its advantages over her usual tactic of abrasion which, admittedly, required a high level of effort and dedication. Yes, people

were much nicer to you if you were nice to them, but then how were
you supposed to tell if it was really you they liked, or simply the nice
things you did for them? Of *course* people liked to be around people
who were nice to them – who wouldn't – but that didn't mean they
liked you or knew you or had any sort of handle on you as a person;
and it certainly didn't mean you could rely on them to be there when
things were less rosy.

Jules was too Compassionate. Dawn Smelled too much. Debbie's
Patience was annoying. They were all annoying. They nibbled their
food in naughty little bites because they were watching their weight.
They sent global emails listing fifteen things that make you glad to be
alive. They thought capital punishment had its uses but only for really
bad crimes and only if you could be really sure the person did it. The
ones with husbands moaned about their husbands. The ones without
husbands wanted husbands. They all wanted more stuff but their
houses and flats were very cluttered and they felt they should really
get rid of some things because the minimalist look was in but then
on the other hand it wasn't *homely*, was it, the minimalist look. Many
of them wanted to do something worthwhile because they admired
people who did things that were worthwhile. Often one of them was
coming down with something, and the others would worry that they
would be about to come down with something, although often they
would not and then they would all agree that they were probably just
run down. Yogurts had a lot more calories than any of them ever really
imagined. Somehow, they had all been given computers that were
particularly recalcitrant. They liked one another only to the extent
that they themselves wanted to be liked. When one stood up to go to
the toilet or make a cup of tea the others talked about her, about how
she smelled too much or how her patience was wearing them all thin.

She went back to the charity shop where she'd donated Keith's
vibrator. She told them she'd left something in the bag by accident
and wanted it back. The woman looked blank yet suspiciously relaxed.

'I haven't seen anything,' she said. 'What was it you left?'

'A vibrator,' said Katherine.

'Oh. Um . . .'

'You can't miss it,' said Katherine. 'It's shaped like an enormous penis and on the side it says "The Widowmaker" in Day-Glo letters.'

'I don't think I –'

'I know you've got it,' said Katherine.

'I assure you I haven't.'

'Give it back.'

'I would if I could.'

'Whatever,' said Katherine.

Keen to once again reaffirm her faith in the basic degradation of humankind, Katherine took herself off to her local strip club.

Despite using the word 'executive' at every opportunity on its membership cards, its posters, even its drinks coasters, L'Après-Vie represented the cheaper end of male entertainment. The girls were foreign and got all the way naked. Private dances took place in clammy rooms that had, as Dawn would have said, dirty notes. Katherine wondered as to the etymology of all this: the precise moment in man's history when the definition of eroticism had been agreed to include a skinny, sad-eyed tween in cheap heels launching herself off a piece of repurposed scaffolding. She paid twenty quid for a private dance with a girl named Clover, who had pigtails and purple nails and a tattoo of a unicorn just above her groin.

'It's my power animal,' she said.

'I'm pregnant,' said Katherine. ∎

Cofiwch Dryweryn

'Remember Tryweryn' – graffiti near Aberystwyth

Soft water from Tryweryn reservoir
was at our fingertips
in Liverpool; no limescale clogged the taps
but imperceptible rogue molecules
ran from the drowned valley, the slate roofs and stone walls
of Capel Celyn, whose fifty souls
were cleared, while those in the Quaker graveyard
were gravelled over. Soft water from Wales
was all we knew, the shadow
of the 'giver' faded from the cup,
the singing flow like a foreign tongue
silenced by a twist. Billions of liquid tons
lie on their homes – soft, oblivious sips
which cushioned us from others' hardships.

ENCLOSURE

Jim Crace

R eap and gossip. That's the rule. On harvest days, anyone who's
got a pair of legs and arms can expect to earn supper with
unceasing labour. Our numbers have been too reduced of late to allow
a single useful soul to stay away. The children go ahead of us, looking
for the grey of any thistle heads that have outstripped our barley, then
duck below the level ears of grain to weed out nettles, teasels, docks.
'Dealing with the grievances,' we say. Then the broadest shoulders
swing their sickles and their scythes at the brimming cliffs of stalk;
hares, partridges and sparrows flee before the blades; our wives and
daughters bundle up and bind the sheaves, though not too carefully
– they work on the principle of ten for the commons and one for
the gleaning; our creaking fathers make the lines of stooks; the sun
begins to dry what we have harvested. Our work is consecrated by the
sun. Compared to winter days, or digging days, it's satisfying work,
made all the more so by the company we keep, for on such days all
the faces we know and love (as well as those I know but do not like
entirely) are gathered in one space and bounded by common ditches
and collective hopes. If, perhaps, we hear a barking deer nagging to
be trapped and stewed or a woodcock begging to make his hearse
in a pie, we lift our heads as one and look towards the woods. We
straighten up as one and stare at the sun, reprovingly, if it's been
darkened by a cloud; our scythes and hand tools clack and chat in
unison. And anything we say is heard by everyone.

O ur humour ripens as the barley falls. It's safe to spread the gossip
noisily, it's safe to bait and goad. Who's sharing wives? Which
bearded bachelor is far too friendly with his goat? Which widower

(they look at me) has dipped his thumb in someone else's pot? Which blushing youngsters are the village *spares*, that's to say those children who've been conceived in one man's bed and then delivered in another's? Who's making love to apple tubs? Who's wedded to a sack of grain? Nothing is beyond our bounds, when we are cutting corn.

So it was hardly a surprise yesterday that once 'Mr Quill', in Master Kent's close company, was attending with his survey sticks and measuring tapes to the shape and volume of our fallow field and so beyond hearing, we wondered out loud whether our visiting townsman had ever overcome his undisguised deficiencies to secure himself a willing wife. Was he a husband yet? And, if he was, what blushing pleasures might Mistress Quill take from such staggering and stiffness and from having such a likeness of her hairy private part upon her stumbling lover's chin? 'I'd like to take a scythe to him,' said neighbour John. Another said, 'I'd rather take my wooden staff to her.' And then of course the bawdiness increased with such play on the prospect of caressing Mr Quill's three-cornered beard and Mistress Quill's twin attribute that every time that evening and in our company he ruminated with his hand around his chin as was his habit, the women could barely plug their grins while their men looked on, biting their lips. 'And have you noticed his white hands?' one of our village daughters asked. 'I wonder if he's ever dirtied them . . . other than to . . .' No, she would not finish. What she had in mind did not seem possible.

It was only when the gentleman returned on the brow of the afternoon and stood at our backs on the bristle of the field to weigh and measure us that we began again to wonder what awaited these treasured neighbourhoods and to feel uneasy. What was he wanting from our soil, what were his charts securing? We saw his finger wagging on the count. We heard him numbering, until he reached the paltry fifty-eight that represented us. We know enough to understand that in the greater world, flour, meat and cheese are measured first, then sold by weight or size. Was Mr Quill the confirmation of the rumour that had gone about our doors that Master Kent was in such

narrows now he was a widower that he would need to measure, weigh
and sell our land? No earthy openness and jollity could raise our
spirits once that fear took hold. Now our observer's ready smile was
menacing.

We were slow to broadcast our alarm. But we tackled our last
barley stands more silently, less lewdly – and more scrupulously, as
we were being watched. Nothing for the gleaning. Now each barking
deer or woodcock call was a warning. Each darkling cloud reminded
us how nothing in our fields was guaranteed. We only muttered to
ourselves, too anxious to raise our voices loud enough to reach our
neighbours down the reaping line. Some of the younger men set faces
which declared they'd defend our acres with their lives or with the
lives of anyone that crossed them. The usual silent swagger. Rather
than speak up, they turned their anger on the pigeons and the rooks,
and a handful of our master's near-white doves, that had descended
on the stub and were already robbing fallen grain that should, by
ancient gleaning rights, be ours. These 'snowy devils', their out-of-
season whiteness making them seem even more coldly pea-eyed and
acquisitive than their grey-and-black companions, were feasting on
our bread and ale, they said, and sent the children to use their slings
or shower them with handfuls of grit or yell the thieves away, anything
to evidence our tenancy. The air was full of wings and cries. So our
final harvesting gained ground.

Master Kent is standing now, and drawing expectant smiles
from us. These feasting times are when, fuelled by ale, he
likes to recall for his earthbound guests the life he led before his
happy coming here. His are embroidered tales of a strange and
dangerous world: imps and oceans; palaces and wars. They always
leave my neighbours glad they'll not be part of it. But tonight his
mood is clearly not a teasing one. Instead, he has invited Mr Quill
to join him at the makeshift dining board and both of them have
clapped us quiet. Is this a moment we should fear? 'Here is my good
acquaintance, Philip Earle,' he says, taking hold of Mr Quill's elbow

and pushing him forward for us to greet and inspect. 'You will have met him yesterday, and you will see him hereabouts for one more week. He has come to us in my employ to make a map of all our common ground and land. We will prepare some vellum for his task from that veal skin which is hanging now above my head. He will take note of everything and then draw up petitions for the courts. What follows is – with your willing, kind consents – an organization to all of our advantages. Too many seasons have been hard for us . . .' At this point Mr Earle (as we will never think of him) unrolls one of the working charts he has prepared and asks us to come up to see our world 'as it is viewed by kites and swifts, and stars'. We press forward, shuffling against each other to fit within the lantern light. 'These are more complete than yesterday,' says Mr Quill, but once again we only see his geometrics and his squares. His mapping has reduced us to a web of lines. There is no life in them. Now he shows a second chart with other spaces. 'This is your hereafter,' he says.

'Yes, our tomorrows will be shaped like this,' adds Master Kent. That Yes is more uncertain than it ought to be. He pauses, smiles. 'I will be exact . . .' he promises. But not, it seems, for the moment.

Say it, say it now, say the word, I urge him silently. I don't have to be a swift or kite to know about the world and how it's changing – changing shape, as Master Kent suggests – and to hear the far-off bleating of incoming animals that are not cows nor pigs nor goats, that are not brethren. I know at once; I've feared this Yes ever since the mistress died. The *organization to all of our advantages* that the master has in mind – against his usual character and sympathies, against his promises – involves the closing and engrossment of our fields with walls and hedges, ditches, gates. He means to throw a halter round our lives. He means the clearing of our common land. He means the cutting down of trees. He means this village far from everywhere which has always been a place for horn, corn and trotter and little else is destined to become a provisioner of wool. The word that he and no one dares to whisper, let alone cry out, is Sheep. Instead Master Kent presents a little nervously a dream he's had. He hopes that if he can describe these changes as having been fetched to him by a dream, then we will understand him more and fear him less, for dreams are common currency even among commoners. Surely, we are dreamers too.

In this dream, all his 'friends and neighbours' – meaning us – no longer need to labour long and hard throughout the year and with no certainty that what we sow will ever come to grain. We have good years; we have bad, he reminds us. We share contentments, but we also share the suffering. The sun is not reliable. And nor is rain. A squalling wind can flatten all our crops. Mildew reduces it to mush. Our cattle might be ravaged by the murrain fever. Our harvest can be taken off by crows. ('And doves,' a small voice says. My own.) But wool is more predictable. A fleece of wool does not require the sun. Indeed, a fleece of wool will grow and thicken in the dark. A fleece is not affected by the wind or by the changing seasons, he says, warming to the task – for it's a task, a labour of persuasion. And, as far as he's aware, crows do not have a taste for wool, despite – he smiles, to alert us to his coming jest – their appetite for flocking.

No, Master Kent has had a dream which makes us rich and leisurely. Every day becomes a day of rest for us. We walk about our fenced-in fields with crooks. We sit on tussocks and we merely watch. We are not ploughing; we are shepherding. We are not reaping; we are shearing. We are not freezing to the bone on damp and heavy winter days picking stones out of the soil, wringing the necks of furrow weeds, or tugging out twine roots and couch until our backs are stiffer than a yoke. No, we are sitting at our fires at home and weaving fortunes for ourselves from yarn. Our only industry is shooting shuttles to and fro as if it were a game, child's play. Our only toil is easy toil – a gentle firming at the heddles, attending to the warp and weft with just our fingertips, untying snags and loosening. Instead of oxen there'll be looms. Instead of praying that the stems of crops stay straight and tall against the odds, against the efforts of the elements, and for their ears of corn to thicken and to ripen, we will be closing the sheds on broadcloth, fustian, worsted and twill. 'A stirring prospect, isn't it?' he says. Somewhere too far away to name, in places we can never see, a man is putting on a coat that we have shepherded and then made up with our own hands, a woman pulls a scarf across her head and smells our hearths and country odours in its weave. We start off with the oily wool on the back of our own livestock, our Golden Hoofs, and end up with garments on the backs of noble folk. It is a dream that, surely, none of us find vile. And still he has not said it: Sheep. Am I the only one to recognize what the dream is trying to disguise?

Master Kent has timed his revelation well. The veal is his. The ale is his too. We are no longer hungry. We're certainly not sober. We're in his debt this evening and know him well enough to want to trust his word, at least for now. His plans might be five years away. Or ten. Tonight's what matters, and tonight he's satisfied us with his feast. He only has to raise a hand to wave away anxieties and allow the drinking to continue. We have become like animals in our individual ways, precisely as the brewer's ballad says: goat drunk and lecherous; dog drunk and barking mad; bull drunk and looking for a brawl; pig drunk and obdurate. But mostly we are as drunk as post-horses – their thirsts are never satisfied – and so, for this evening at least, beyond anxiety. ■

GRANTA

SUGAR
IN THE BLOOD

Andrea Stuart

M y earliest identifiable ancestor, George Ashby, was one of the many thousands of Englishmen who 'took ship' for the New World in the first half of the seventeenth century. His destination, Barbados, was in those days the most popular colony in the region, a magnet for swashbucklers and other restless hopefuls who considered mainland America prosaic in comparison.

And so George Ashby left England in the late 1630s a humble blacksmith, and arrived in Barbados 'a fighting farmer', with a hoe in his hand and a sword at his belt. He landed in a country that was different in every way from the one he had left behind. Instead of the English palette, which was permanently tinged with grey, the Caribbean was a chaos of colour, bombarding the senses with dazzling light, heavy scents, unfamiliar sounds. And so a man habituated to winter's shortening days, the turning of the leaves and cold nights crouched around heat-giving fires had to become accustomed to the eternal heat and days that were divided equally all year round. The lifestyle too was radically different. The population of Barbados, in new conurbations such as Bridgetown, was teeming with young men on the make (only 1 per cent of the early settlers were women): a motley assortment of English planters and privateers, Dutch traders and French merchants, as well as a sprinkling of – largely enslaved – black and Amerindian faces. Freed from the social constraints of the old country, these men cursed and fought and drank assiduously, coming together in rustic 'tippling houses' to reminisce about the old country and share information about the new, but most importantly to find consolation in the companionship of their fellow migrants and assuage the loneliness and uncertainty that assailed them in this strange and unfamiliar place. Only to separate at the end of the night and return to their isolated plantations, where they would resume their ongoing battle with the hostile wilderness of their plots of land. The work was brutal, the crops – tobacco, cotton, indigo – yielding at best a meagre benefit.

But then came the economic miracle that rescued George Ashby and his contemporaries from a life of abject poverty, exhaustion and deprivation: sugar. This 'noble condiment', which had been virtually unknown in the West before the Crusades, became by the fifteenth century as valuable as pearls and as sought after as musk. Over the next century it became accessible to the merely wealthy, and hunger for it grew exponentially. From the sixteenth century it was evident that the soil and temperature of the New World were perfect for the crop. When production began in Barbados, it was a machine that could not be turned off. Availability stoked desire and desire stoked production; soon sugar was known as the 'white gold' and the planters grew desperate for a workforce large enough and strong enough to harvest it.

And so another migration took place, this time a forced one. The trade in slaves had begun as a trickle when the first colonists settled in America but it soon became a flood, once the financial potential of sugar became apparent. Many times I have imagined the journey undertaken by my first slave ancestor: a warrior captured in a raid, a girl stolen for her beauty, an overdue debtor. I picture them leaving behind a scorched village, spirited away in a dusty caravan by black traders and white slavers. By the time they arrived at the coast, whether it was Togo, Dahomey or western Nigeria, they were already dull-eyed, ulcerated and weak. They were then incarcerated in slave forts, markets or prisons called barracoons, where they were branded with irons and then left to fester for months. Many did not survive. Those who did were loaded on board the 'wooden worlds' which would transport them across the infamous 'middle passage', that terrible voyage from the African subcontinent to the port cities of the New World. A passage on a slave ship was truly a voyage of the damned – its talisman 'instruments of woe' included: manacles and neck-rings, locks and chains, cat-o'-nine-tails and the speculum oris (designed to prise a slave's mouth open so he could be force-fed). I picture my forefather here, manacled and starved in this purgatory, with death all around him. And yet he survives, though his head is filled with memories of the bodies abandoned along the journey to the coast, the shame of his body being displayed on the auction block, and the shit-smeared holds below decks.

When the slaver arrived in Barbados, a month or so later, it was straight to market. There the slaves stood trembling, their skin rubbed with oil to remove the greyish pallor it had acquired on the journey and their sores camouflaged with ash. Then they were pushed and pulled, foreign fingers thrust into their mouths and other orifices. A price agreed, they were dragged away from their countrymen and families and propelled on another forced march to a plantation. There, slaves were stripped of their names and their language, and taught to endure a life of torture and servitude. I can only imagine the ocean of their grief, the pain of their multiple losses: homeland, identity, family and friends.

Almost one third of slaves died within that first year, whether it was on the long trek across the African subcontinent or on the middle passage or during the 'seasoning', those terrible first months in the New World. Expiring as a result of disease or murder, suicide or misadventure, abuse or grief.

Somehow, my unnameable ancestor managed to survive.

The planters of the Americas justified their kidnap, enslavement, torture and murder of millions of Africans by espousing pseudo-scientific theories that labelled their charges as brutish heathens and their exploitation as an act of manifest destiny. Over time they created a society predicated on race, where skin colour determined the social place and the life chances possible for each individual. In the process, George Ashby and his contemporaries, who had for most of their lives barely conceived that they had an ethnicity, invented a new description for themselves: 'white', and used it to separate themselves from the people they exploited, who became 'black'.

The plantation, that unique fusion of farm and factory, was the stage on which this epic played out. Here, in this tinderbox, where sugar and slavery commingled, blacks and whites lived cheek by jowl, one group attempting to impose their will on the other through a regime of violence and cruelty, the other attempting to survive while resisting their enslavement at every turn. It was a situation so explosive that the French revolutionary Mirabeau once described planters of the region as 'sleeping on the edge of Vesuvius'.

Even after Emancipation in 1833 sugar was still the biggest game in town, so it made good business sense that my great-grandfather, a brown-skinned descendant of George Ashby, bought a plantation in Barbados called Plumgrove, which has been the heart of my family ever since. Here my grandfather struggled to make a living in the waning days of sugar and my mother and her siblings were born. The mixed-race descendants of planters and their slave mistresses (female slaves they had exploited and occasionally even loved), my grandparents and their progeny acquired both social and financial advantages from their white forebears and, in some cases, their warped ideas and curious predilections. As a result, they became part of a privileged caste poised between the white planter elite at the top of the society and the majority of blacks at the bottom: the bedrock of today's post-sugar middle class.

Almost three and a half centuries later, my family and I reversed George Ashby's journey, travelling back to England in the summer of 1976. Unlike my first ancestor, we did not have a long sea journey to accustom us to our change in homeland. In his day one's sense of the world altered slowly and the traveller had time to become used to new physical conditions; but for us, air travel meant our lives were changed in just a few hours.

So there we stood, two teenagers, their little sister and parents, in the cavernous confusion of Heathrow International Airport, shivering in our too-light cotton clothes. More than anything, we were struck by the gloom: it was as if the sky had been lowered and a grubby canopy had been draped over us. We reached into our carry-on cases for sweaters and shawls. Ironically, a legendary heatwave would begin a few weeks later, lulling us temporarily into a false sense of familiarity.

That autumn we settled into our first English residence, a dour if substantial detached construction in a leafy Surrey suburb. (I think my parents chose it for its proximity to the Barbados ambassador's residence: a link to the security of the place of their birth.) It was a typical rental, denuded of all those personal items that make a house a home. Instead of the nightly orchestra of cicadas and tree frogs that lulled us to sleep in the Caribbean, we listened to the distant rumble of the South West Trains Hampton Court to Waterloo service. So much else about our new home was mystifying. Why did all the rooms have a light switch, except the bathroom, which was illuminated by pulling a grubby string cord with a plastic nobble at the end? Why, despite central heating, did the house never feel really warm?

Sometimes it seemed that nothing was the same. I had no idea that I had an accent, until people began to mimic my Caribbean drawl. Even the way I walked, the slow glide that is necessary to negotiate the heat of the tropics, seemed parochial in contrast to the fast, bobbing walk of the Northern urbanite. And all those white faces! In the Caribbean, Caucasians are a minority, often tourists who look out of place: skin stung by the sun, faces glossy with sweat. Here, I – cold and hunched, my dark skin covered in goosebumps – was the outlandish one: the interloper.

We had a new life to learn, and like many migrants, in our bewilderment, we turned to the television to decipher the customs of this strange new land. But once again we were confounded. The English sense of humour escaped us. The spectacle of Tommy Cooper – a large shambolic man in a fez, performing lame magic tricks while mumbling indecipherably – left us wide-eyed with incomprehension. Nor could we understand why the sight of a straight man pretending to be a gay man, prancing around screeching 'I'm Free!', in double-entendre-fest *Are You Being Served?*, was so hysterical. The absence of black faces on British television in this decade was so marked that when an African Caribbean or an Asian person appeared on our set, we were apt to run out of the room shouting, 'There is a black person on TV!'

Unbeknown to us, 1970s Britain was a cauldron of bitter rhetoric about race and immigration, which had in turn triggered an upsurge in racism. The country was in recession and unemployment was rising, and a vociferous minority were demanding that 'coloured' migrants be sent home. Their most respectable spokesperson was the Conservative MP Enoch Powell. His infamous 'rivers of blood' speech criticizing Commonwealth immigration, delivered at the Conservative Association meeting in 1968, had warned that Britain would disintegrate into open conflict if the repatriation of these people did not take place. I got used to seeing his gargoyle-like face whenever the issue was discussed in the newspapers or on television. Indeed, race was the leitmotif of the era: the press was awash with race-related riots and demonstrations. The National Front was thriving, and its logo and slogans were everywhere. Every time we commuted into the capital, we had to pass the graffitied slogan STOP COLOURED IMMIGRATION, painted in white capitals as high as the train itself, on an embankment alongside the tracks just before we pulled into Wimbledon station. It remained there for several years, an enduring reminder of how unwelcome we were in this new land.

And then it became personal. It was one of those incidents that every black person has endured: not life-threatening, no permanent damage, just searing for the soul. Early one evening I went into London to visit a friend over from the Caribbean. And just as I was about to ascend the escalator at Leicester Square Underground station, I was surrounded by a group of Millwall football fans, their faces engorged and red with drink, chanting, 'I smell a nigger!' The people in front of me moved forward as the men encircled me, and they continued chanting until we got to the top. The whole thing couldn't have lasted more than a couple of minutes, but it felt like the proverbial lifetime as I stood there, all five foot three inches and seven and a half stone of me, in my best red dress, shivering with fear. And then they walked on, glaring at me triumphantly, laughing and slapping one another on the back. These men knew nothing about me; they didn't know or care about my long links to Britain, they didn't even understand their own history; all they saw was the colour of my skin, and that was enough to justify the abuse. I was a nigger and that was that. Britain had shown me what hate looked like.

Living in a racist society has a profound psychological impact. It produces in its victims a sort of hyper-vigilance, as the individual attempts to read those around them and so anticipate the hostility that might assail them. This is a work of self-protection that is as exhausting as it is necessary because so often these verbal assaults seem to come out of the blue; just at the moment when one is caught up in one's own thoughts or walking in a park. And so in order to protect oneself from these random moments of pain and the shame, one becomes acutely watchful; anything to avoid the shock and vulnerability that these incidents induce. One wonders: is that person staring at me out of hostility or desire? Is this unfamiliar pub going to be a hostile environment or a benign one? Will this new friend, in some unguarded moment, say something that reveals a malignant inner core, which precludes you from ever trusting him again?

It was a bewildering time for my family. We were socially isolated, as most of my parents' contemporaries had resettled in the US or Canada. We were, in addition, isolated by our class position. We were the sort of black family that did not then exist in the British imagination: affluent, professional, cultured. Our mother would take us to the opera or the ballet or to piano recitals at the Southbank. Every day I set off for my exclusive private girls' school, where I was the only pupil of African-Caribbean descent. My brother and sister went off to their respective schools, where they were in a similar position. We clung together in our loneliness, bewilderment and shock. We had few familial or social links with the *Windrush* generation, and our life experience was very different. One of my acutely class-conscious Caribbean aunts, when studying in the UK, remarked, 'We wouldn't talk to them there, so why should we mix with them here?' What should have been a source of solidarity and comfort – the nearby presence of compatriots – so often felt, at that time, a source of yet more isolation.

As I grew up I realized that my perpetual sense of displacement, the fate of most migrants, was something that would never leave me but that I could make a life nonetheless. I understood that migration was a kind of death, in which one's old self must be buried in order for a new self to be born and that this experience has made me who I am today. Inevitably, however, my feelings about the 'mother country' are ambivalent. So much here is now familiar and so much remains completely strange. My colour still enters the room before I do, and in some situations I have to work inordinately hard to make others put it aside. I know that despite the privileges of my upbringing, some people see me as just another inferior, troublesome black face. And I cannot help resenting the notion that while I am, according to some, not good enough to be British, my ancestors were nonetheless good enough to help build the country, defend it and die for it.

I have settled in a country where the epic forces that created my family – settlement, sugar production and slavery – are still shaping English life, unacknowledged and unremarked, shifting and moving beneath the surface of daily life. Sugar surrounds me here. Each year, thousands of locals and tourists visit the grand Tate galleries without remembering that its collections were funded by the voracious sugar company Tate & Lyle. They wander though the grandeur of All Souls College, Oxford, without being aware that it was paid for by the profits generated by the slaves who toiled and died at the Codrington estate in Barbados. Sugar built the magnificent Harewood House in Leeds and many of the lovely mansions in Bristol's majestic Queen Square, while much of the wealth that the West Indian proprietors collected in compensation for their 'losses' at emancipation fed back to the City of London, shoring it up and helping make it the dynamic, global business centre it has become.

Just as it is easy to forget that the 'white gold' of sugar paid for the bricks that built many of the grand buildings, homes and museums that make up England's cultural heritage, and enabled its cities to flourish, so too we ignore the impact of the trade in 'black ivory', despite the many-hued faces that throng these streets. We allow ourselves, and each other, to remain ignorant of or resistant to understanding the forces that brought our ancestors together from opposite ends of the world. We understate how these forces continue to shape our communities and our life chances to this day. Over 150 years after slavery was abolished, Africans and the descendants of Africans remain markedly disadvantaged compared to the descendants of those who promoted the trade against them.

Slavery is a ghost that keeps haunting modern Britain, because we have never fully exorcised it from our past. Like any nation, Britain is what the academic Benedict Anderson describes as an 'imagined community'; its self-image is determined by what it decides to recall and what it decides to disregard. Abolition is warmly remembered and commemorated as the heroic action of a civilized society and the hundreds of years of barbaric slavery that preceded it conveniently forgotten.

In all fairness, I probably came to Britain too late to ever feel British. I was halfway through my teens when I arrived here and the ingredients of my identity were already in place. Most of us are irrevocably shaped by the place in which we are raised. Especially a place where frangipani perfumes the luminous night, where mangoes bear fruit so sweet you giggle with pleasure, and where birds in shimmery colours surprise the eye. The Caribbean is impressed on my eyes, my ears, my skin: all my senses. It is my first love, and its presence is stained on my heart; its terrain that lost lover's body, its cliffs and carapaces their curves and contours, its smells, their odours and fragrances; a paramour unforgettable and unbested.

More than two centuries ago someone put it better. Then, the ex-slave called Ignatius Sancho, attempting to navigate the vicissitudes of a racist eighteenth-century London, explained his place here thus: 'I am only a lodger – and hardly that.'

I go back 'home' most years; and when I 'deplane' at Grantley Adams International Airport the heat welcomes me; I am assailed by the smell of the tropics; that warm fulminating scent of exuberant life. Though the other arrivals are predominantly white, weary refugees from the northern hemisphere dreaming of palm-fringed beaches and white sands, the faces in the terminal are predominantly black, chattering in a patois that sounds uncannily like English spoken with a West Country accent. The taxi journey to our holiday home passes the supermarkets, office buildings and gas stations that one would expect, as well as field after field of sugar cane. In an hour or so there will be one of the island's famous fuchsia sunsets, and a brief twilight in which the bats will fly and the cicadas will begin to sing in the dark.

The island's colonial past is evident everywhere. To wander through the streets of the capital Bridgetown is in many ways to walk through a reproduction of an English town, except the heat is shimmering off the buildings and market ladies sit on crates selling fish sandwiches and snow ice. Here is the crescent-shaped harbour that welcomed the Englishman George Ashby when he arrived more than three and a half centuries ago. Here are the parliament buildings, constructed during his lifetime, which, along with the town's other official establishments – courts, police headquarters and banks – are so reminiscent of those in the mother country. It even has a statue of Nelson, which was erected before the more famous one, now in Trafalgar Square.

In Barbados, as with the rest of the Caribbean, the legacy of the sugar boom and the slave trade is not easily ignored or forgotten. Although sugar is no longer the vibrant industry it once was, it is still cultivated and the vista of endless fields of cane remains emblematic of the region, as is the sweet syrupy smell of the fields as they are fired and razed. Sugar has transformed the landscape and changed the region's ecosystem. It has shaped our economies, traditions and our national identities. Indeed, by pulling together the unique racial mix of the islands – black, white, Amerindian, East Indian, Syrian, Chinese – it is written across our very faces. The continuing politics of colour – the association of lighter complexions with status and influence, and darker skins with poverty and powerlessness – persists, particularly among older people who remember the plantations with both horror and nostalgia. Many families like my own are mixed race on both sides, blending the histories of both oppressor and oppressed.

George Ashby spawned a succession of descendants who were raised in a place that he could never have even conceived of before he arrived there. The world that became their home was a land of sunlight and warmth where they grew accustomed to different foods, traditions and beliefs. They mutated from a traditional English family to a multi-hued one with white, brown and black faces. As for George Ashby's descendants who migrated in their turn, their fates have been as varied and complex. Many of them suffered extreme hardship, while others achieved great success and happiness. The pattern of their movement – to other islands in the Caribbean, to the US and UK, to Canada and as far away as Australia – has mirrored that of their fellow islanders. Those who remained in Barbados have done well, but perhaps suffered more from the complex psychological pressures that evolved from slavery, since it is still a country deeply influenced by the interactions of colour and class. My mother's two sisters found out for themselves how slowly social change comes about. One fell for a dark-skinned Barbadian; but even in the seventies, the familial pressure was such that she felt she could not marry him. Meanwhile the other fell in love with a married white man. He loved her in return but would not leave his wife for a brown-skinned woman.

When I return to Plumgrove, the family plantation, I am at the scene of my earliest, most vivid memories: being enfolded in my grandmother's warm and perfumed arms, eating roast pork and plantain around the large wooden dining table, and at night looking out of the windows at the rustling cane, which swayed like an army of stick-like shadows against the starlit night. Some of the wider changes that have occurred across the island are mirrored in the land around me. There is no trace of Waterland Hall, the sugar plantation from which Plumgrove was carved. Because real estate is now more valuable than cane land, its endless fields of sugar cane have largely been replaced by residential districts. The plantation, too, is a different place. Within the span of a few decades, most of its acreage has been converted from the cultivation of sugar to a modern housing development built for middle-income Barbadians; the little wooden houses that once perched so precariously on their coral blocks have now been replaced by sturdy stone dwellings. The land hums with the incessant noise of engines starting, tractors rolling, nails hitting plywood as houses are constructed. This burble almost overwhelms the perennial soundtrack of the plantation: the strangely soothing and sad noise of the cane.

Sitting here now – with cane behind me, and the development in front of me, the main road and its busy stream of cars just out of sight – Plumgrove's great house still provides the perfect vantage point to feel both the rural isolation of the plantation and the busyness of modern Barbadian life. The plantation house is fated to be converted to condominiums, but perhaps, however sad, its demolition is fitting: a way of finally laying the ghost of the plantation system to rest.

For me, this land is haunted. It is a place that harbours restless souls for whom not even death has proved a release. These spectres disturb the air, waiting for me to face and name them: as all our ghosts do. Every time I visit, Plumgrove catches my heart so intensely that I'm left dizzy by the force of emotion. I am immediately carried back to my childhood self, jumping from hot paving stones onto cool green grass, chasing my brother and sister around the garden or hiding behind gigantic tamarind trees, trying to catch fireflies in the starlit Caribbean night.

As a child, it was my exotic and wonderful playground; as an adult, I can almost taste the aura of unhappiness that surrounds it. I can sense the spirits of my ancestors here – George Ashby, and all his descendants, some familiar, some with names I will never know – who strived and suffered on this island. The plantation house our family still owns stands as a monument to things lost: not just my youth, my sense of belonging, my Caribbean self, but also my predecessors, their hopes, dreams, and despair. When I visit Plumgrove I am assailed by existential questions. Where do I belong? Who am I? And I realize that the sight and sounds and smells of this place have permeated my thoughts and shaped my personality in ways that will last a lifetime – just as my ancestors' plantation experience did theirs. ■

AFRICAN WRITING *online*

ISSN 1754-6672   No.11

many literatures, one voice

African Writing appears in both print and online with fiction, poetry, think pieces and reviews by new voices from Africa and the diaspora.

The *African Writing* website (www.african-writing.com) gives you a chance to buy individual issues, sample content, or subscribe to print and online editions. You can also read free, exclusive online-only writing in our Blogs section.

ISSUE 11 OUT NOW

INTERVIEWS with Tendai Huchu, P. Adesanmi and Ellen Banda-Aaku (Photo top left)

FICTION
Sesotho Speakers by Ret'sepile Makamane, *Bad Hair Day* by Tendai Huchu, *The Teacher* by Ibrahim al-Koni (Photo left), *Dodo is Yoruba for Fried Plantain*, by F. Fetto, *Befriending A Lie* by Christian Uwe, *Invisible Woman* by Mamie Kabu, *Making Connections* by Bashir Adan, and *The Wonderful No. 1 Recliner* by E. Chiew

POETRY BY
Malika Assai, Ayodele Morocco-Clarke, Stephen John Rae, Isoje Iyi-Eweka Chou, Isaac Anyaogu, Essia Skhiri, Magdalawit Makonnen

MEMOIR
My Son is a Story by Juliane Okot-Bitek (Photo left)

in print... online... www.african-writing.com

GRANTA

THEATRE
OF FORTUNE

Nikolai Khalezin and Natalia Kaliada

INTRODUCTION BY TOM STOPPARD
TRANSLATED FROM THE RUSSIAN BY YURI KALIADA AND CHRIS THORPE

Introduction

The Belarus Free Theatre announced itself seven years ago by email. Along with a few other playwrights, I received a letter asking for 'a message of support'. It didn't seem much to ask. So after further exchanges of messages I went to Minsk to meet the group. Nikolai (Kolia) Khalezin and Natalia Kaliada, husband and wife, both writers, were at the airport to greet me. Hefty Kolia with his fair hair pulled back into a ponytail and dark gamine Natya, smiling and waving.

Aware that the 'Democratic Republic' of Belarus was a police state, I was as surprised as I was alarmed to see that Kolia was wearing a 'protest' T-shirt emblazoned with the faces of four men who had crossed the dictator, Alexander Lukashenko, and had subsequently 'disappeared'. They had been murdered, Kolia explained, and he spoke the truth.

Much has changed since that day we met in the summer of 2005. Back then, the spirit of rebellion was in plain sight. Nobody wears a protest T-shirt in Belarus now. The change happened literally overnight. In the presidential election of December 2010, Lukashenko, who had felt himself secure as the figurehead of national independence, found he had lost the confidence of the voters. He annulled the election and cracked down on every trace of opposition. The former Soviet Republic is now a throwback to the lost world of Communist dictatorships.

Meanwhile, things have changed for that outlawed theatre group. As the Belarus Free Theatre, the troupe has built up an international reputation in exile. They have many troubles but they endure. It has been a privilege to witness their journey.

Tom Stoppard, London, February 2012.

Just after midnight on New Year's Eve 2010, we clandestinely crossed the border into Russia. It had always been an open border – or at least we considered it open – but since the events of 19 December 2010 in Minsk, security police have controlled the road. More than 700 people, arrested during the protests against rigged presidential elections, were in prison. Four dozen of those prisoners were held in facilities run by the KGB, charged with 'planning the overthrow of the state'. We had spent ten days in hiding to avoid arrest, or, in Natalia's case, rearrest.

We met our friends in the border town of Orsha. They had brought a van: I was to lie on the floor, covered with blankets. Our daughter was to lie on top of the blankets to conceal me. Closer to the border, we shared sips from a flask of brandy, deliberately creating the alcoholic fug of a Russian family returning home after celebrating New Year in neighbouring Belarus. It was a useless disguise, and we knew it. The next day our friend admitted that he wouldn't have stopped if the security police had tried to wave us down: *I'd have headed into Russia so fast they wouldn't have been able to catch us*. In the event, they did nothing. As we crossed, five police officers sat in a roadside cafe, peacefully downing vodka. Their two jeeps sat idly outside.

Three years earlier, in the summer of 2007, all the members of our theatre company, the Belarus Free Theatre, had been arrested, along with the whole audience that night – about sixty people in all. By then, we had already become outcasts in our own country. Members of the group had suffered arrests, beatings, expulsion from university, job terminations, and revocations of their Soviet-style right of residency. The security apparatus tried to discredit us abroad, editing our Wikipedia entries to identify us as a totalitarian sect.

All the doors had slammed shut in Belarus, from established theatres to local bars. We had ended up performing in a tiny house belonging to a friend in the outskirts of Minsk. The first time we saw it, we had to decline the offer – the rooms were too small for us to rehearse, never mind perform. Our friend then took a hammer and smashed down a dividing wall. With that gesture he created the stage for the only underground theatre company in Belarus.

There were so many deaths. For a while we felt like we were in a bad film, overstuffed with murders. In September of 2010, after a period of relative peace, we found ourselves at yet another funeral. Our old friend Oleg Bebenin, journalist and founder of charter97.org, who in recent years had exchanged jokes with us almost every morning via Skype, had been found hanged at his dacha.

Oleg's five-year-old son, Stepa, told his mother on a visit to his father's grave, *Now I know where to look for you when you die.*

On the eve of the December 2010 presidential election, the sports store was packed with people looking for thermal underwear. The weather forecast for Sunday was minus eleven degrees. People planning to demonstrate need warm clothes.

Elections are always in the cold season in Belarus: it reduces the numbers of protesters. The main question this time was how many people would take to the streets in Minsk – five thousand, ten, twenty, fifty, or a hundred thousand? In fact, hundreds of thousands of demonstrators gathered, and about fifty thousand converged in the evening on October Square.

Natalia went up on the stage, to read out a message from Václav Havel. The rally was in full swing when we heard the sound of breaking glass – a few people, later proven to be agents provocateurs, were smashing the glass doors of Government House. All of us who were there tried to stop them, but it was impossible.

Half an hour later armed Special Forces men filled the square. They ripped through the crowd, shouting, wielding batons and shields. Natalia was arrested early on – we had been separated by a column of riot police. Five people were already lying face down on the floor of the police van when she was forced inside. Ten minutes later there were sixty-eight people in the van. Several of them fainted from the lack of air. Natalia sent me a text with the names of everyone in her van, and I passed it on to journalists and human rights advocates. From each police van someone was sending names out, so in the end human rights activists had a complete list of the 700 arrested.

At the prison, the detainees were forced to stand in columns facing the wall, hands behind their heads. The men were separated from the women. Any attempt to sit down or make the slightest movement was punished with blows from a truncheon, and threats: *We're going to make you think the Nazis were just playing*, they said. And: *I'm going to take your clothes off and show you what I can do to a woman with a chair leg.*

Toilets, water and sleep were prohibited. In the middle of the night about twenty men were brought to the women's floor. One man (his wife was with the women) was asking to go to the toilet. One of the guards responded: *You want to overthrow the man who is in power. You want to humiliate all of us people who stay in power. So shit your pants in front of all the whores who are with you, and understand what humiliation is.*

At home the following morning, our dog barked. I was giving an interview to an Israeli radio station when our daughter Dana ran into the room to say we were being raided. She had seen six security officers through the peephole. We sat in silence in an interior room. The KGB came back three times that morning. In the short time between one of their visits and the next, we managed to slip away.

The same day, the legal conveyor belt began for Natalia. The judges had hundreds of cases to get through, so each defendant got ten minutes or less. The majority of the sentences were fifteen days, in cells with no bedding or hot water, and twelve people crammed into a space meant for five or six.

Natalia was saved from prison time on a technicality – the judge had been given documents meant for another person with her name, who'd also been held. The judge deliberated for a while, deciding whether it was worth correcting the mistake, and eventually made a 'compromise' ruling of a fine, and she was released. In the turmoil, the authorities let her go, and so the two of us escaped incarceration while some of our friends were charged with offences carrying up to fifteen years in jail.

Following our escape, we embarked on a tour around the world with more than a dozen members of our company. Wherever we found ourselves, we woke up and went to bed intent on our screens, reading the bleak news from Belarus. Continuing arrests and searches. The offices of independent newspapers wrecked. We read the names of friends, colleagues, acquaintances and relatives. On Skype we helplessly watched our eldest daughter, still in Belarus, weeping. My father, who had recently survived a heart attack, was stoically bearing the raids on his house. Natalia's parents had to tolerate endless hours of a single question posed over and over by intelligence officers: *Where are your children?* Six of our closest friends were detained in a KGB facility. We could find out almost nothing about that facility. Lawyers were not allowed in, and a thin and ominous trickle of information about torture seeped out.

On 19 January, we were in New York. The PEN American Center had held an event in our honour. Sitting in a bar after that evening, our friend Jakab Orsós, from PEN, said, *I wanted so much for your actors to enjoy tonight, because so many great people were gathered here to support them. But they never found the strength to be happy.*

They never found the strength to be happy.

They never found the strength to be happy . . . and certainly not on that day. As we held our evening performance in New York, in

Minsk, Nikita Volodko, one of our students and the partner of Free Theatre performer Yana Rusakevich, had been arrested. Later, Yana was herself summoned and interrogated by a KGB officer. After the 'conversation', which lasted several hours, she messaged us on Skype. We asked how things had gone. She wrote simply, *They want you. Do not come back under any circumstances.*

Home was gone. The home in which our people were always waiting for us; where my joker of a father-in-law used to meet me at the door as we came back from touring, carrying a tray with a glass of cold plum brandy and a fish sandwich; and where our dog, Jay, woke us in the morning, poking our cheeks with her nose.

It is quite difficult to see yourself as homeless. When I'd previously considered it, I'd imagined stories of degradation, the irresistible pull of circumstances, a gradual sinking to the bottom – the lower depths as described by Gorky. We began to explore our new circumstances, and the principles that governed them. One of the main principles was that we should buy nothing, because while flying from country to country a person can't take more than their allotted twenty-three kilograms. It turned out not to be that difficult, living within a twenty-three-kilogram allowance.

Another principle: remember in which country, and with whom, you've left the suitcase with your winter clothes or vital props.

By the middle of August 2011 friends in Belarus had installed a computer in our Minsk flat, and taught Natalia's mother to use Skype. One day, during a break in rehearsals, she called. She didn't turn the webcam on while she spoke about everyday things, and her voice was strangely detached. Natalia finally asked her, *Mum, what's happened?* She exploded into sobs. My father had died.

He had died of a heart attack on 16 August – the same day my mother had died four years earlier. Constant KGB raids, searches and interrogations, our enforced escape, separation from me, his granddaughters, Natalia, whom he adored – all of that had rolled together into a single blow on the anniversary of the death of the woman he had loved and lived with for fifty years.

I couldn't fly home to attend his funeral. I couldn't say goodbye to him.

In the months after my father's death I was tortured by one simple question: *How can I get through all this?* There's no heroism in it – endurance, coming to terms with the death of loved ones, losses. It boils down to a simple banality: you either decide to live, or you don't. And if you decide to live, that's what you have to do. It's your only remaining choice. Rhetorical questions become irrelevant, as does any pride in the suffering you experience.

In December 2011, Václav Havel, one of the patrons of the Free Theatre, and a good friend, passed away. The last document he signed in his life was the Artistic Manifesto in which cultural figures demanded the release of Belarusian political prisoners. Two days before his death he sent a message through his assistant: *I'm sorry that this is the only thing I can do in my condition.*

When we arrived at Heathrow, we switched on our phones. We learned that our friend Andrei Sannikov, detained in a harsh regime for months, had been sentenced to five years in prison. His wife, Irina, had received a two-year suspended sentence. Andrei's sister Irina Bogdanova, and her husband, Tony, were at Heathrow to pick us up. The drive to their house in Aldershot was quiet – we simply didn't have the energy to talk. We had heard leaks of Andrei's torture, and he had not been allowed legal visits for months. It had been difficult to keep track of all his transfers. He is still in prison, along with many others. And we are trying to find the strength to be happy. ∎

Baffler #19, the first from new editor John Summers, features salvos from **Thomas Frank**, **Chris Lehmann**, **Barbara Ehrenreich**, **Rick Perlstein**, and **David Graeber**; fiction by **Kim Stanley Robinson** and **Ludmilla Petrushevskaya**; plus poetry, photography, and satirical art.

It's the magazine abrasive, and it's back.

SUBSCRIBE NOW BY VISITING
thebaffler.com Individual: Print + Electronic Access **$25**
Individual: Electronic Access Only **$20**
Published three times a year by the MIT Press.

1964

Under the gritted lid of winter, each
ice-puddle's broken plate
cracked to a star. The morning
assembling itself into black and white, the slow dawn
its developing tray. Cold steams off the grass;
the frosted yarrow and sea holly
smoke in the new sun.

*

In the barber-shop mirror, I study this museum of men
through glass: their shaving brushes, talc and whetted razors,
the bottles of bay rum, hair tonic, astringents; long
leather strops; those faded photographs of hairstyles,
that blue Barbicide jar on the counter
dense with pickled combs and scissors like a failed aquarium;
the special drawer full of Durex, copies of *Parade*.

*

The plane from England scores a skater's track
across the icy sky; on the promenade, frost thistles
the railings above the turning sea. You hear the drawl
of the wave, the gulls, raucous at their litter bins,
the day's first Labrador, his tail flogging the surf.
The quarantined city lies behind, bilge-deep in cobbles,
listing: flying the Yellow Jack, typhoid in its quick-work.

*

On the floor of the butcher's,
blood has rolled through the sawdust
and become round and soft.
We found the blood-buds
in corners as the shop was closing, and gathered
the biggest ones in handkerchiefs to take them
to the woods, break them open for their jelly.

*

In the light from the blaze, there's a fox
nailed to a fencepost: the tricked god
hanging from his wounds. We have nothing to feed
to the snap and nip of the fire's many beaks
but some mealy apples and a bottle of Hay's Lemonade,
which explodes. I dig in my pockets and find
a Salvation Army picture of Jesus; tender it to the flame.

*

We'd skip school lunches for some milk,
a rowie and a mutton pie. A twist of penny sweets:
cherry lips, gobstoppers, liquorice sticks.
On special days, some hard bonfire toffee
and a lucky bag, watching the third-years fight
in the kirkyard, in among the graves: one boy
holds the other's hair so he can kick him in the face.

*

Creels are swung from boat to shore, filling
fishboxes in silver rows. A slush of ice and gulls
all day till nightfall. Then all you hear is the ice
tightening back together
and the cats crying that dreadful way they have,
like the sound of babies
singing lullabies to other babies.

*

I knew how children came, so I look for the stork
in the cliffs over the mussel pools,
in the quarry ledges, the chimney stacks,
all along the walking pylons –
search for her everywhere
in the gantries of the storm woods, in the black pines,
that she might take me back.

London: A History in Verse Edited by *Mark Ford*

Poet Mark Ford has assembled the most capacious and wide-ranging anthology of poems about London to date, from Chaucer to Wordsworth to the present day, providing a chronological tour of urban life and of English literature. The result is a cultural history of the city in verse, one that represents all classes of London's population over some seven centuries, mingling the high and the low, the elegant and the salacious, the courtly and the street smart. **Belknap Press of Harvard University Press** £25.00 | HB

The Event of Literature *Terry Eagleton*

In this characteristically concise, witty and lucid book, Terry Eagleton turns his attention to the questions we should ask about literature, but rarely do. Freewheeling through centuries of critical ideas, he sheds light on the place of literature in our culture, and in doing so reaffirms the value and validity of literary thought today. **Yale University Press** £18.99 | HB

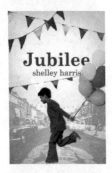

Jubilee *Shelley Harris*

1977, the Queen's Silver Jubilee: at a street party a photographer captures a moment forever. Right in the centre of the frame, a small Asian boy stares intently into the camera. The photograph becomes iconic, but the harmonious image conceals a very different reality. Fast-forward to the present and that boy, Satish, is now a successful paediatric heart surgeon. A message about a proposed reunion of the photograph throws his life into turmoil as he thinks back to Jubilee Day, and the events that changed his life forever. **Weidenfeld & Nicolson** £12.99 | HB

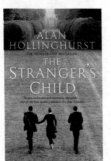

The Stranger's Child *Alan Hollinghurst*

Picador is thrilled to present the magnificent novel from Man Booker Prize winner Alan Hollinghurst. Powerful, absorbing and richly comic, *The Stranger's Child* is a masterly exploration of English culture, taste and attitudes over a century of change: it is an enthralling novel from one of the finest writers in the English language. A great British novel. **Picador** | PB

CLOUGH

Jon McGregor

The missing girl's name was Emma-Jane. She was five. She hadn't been seen since three o'clock the previous afternoon. She'd been out on the moor with her parents. They'd lost sight of her when the weather had turned, and chased around in the dark for over an hour before running down to the village to get help. They weren't local. They were staying in one of the Harvey family's barn conversions. They'd enjoyed being there so much last summer that they'd immediately booked again for Christmas. They were absolutely beside themselves.

This had all come from Irene, who did the cleaning on changeover days at the Harveys' and had come round last night claiming to remember the girl from the summer. She was bright as a button, apparently. A dear little thing. The story going round was that when she'd sat down and refused to go any further, they'd walked on ahead and assumed she would follow. They'd waited round the corner for no more than a minute or two, and when they'd gone back to scoop her up, their patience running thin and the weather threatening, she'd vanished.

It was strange, Richard thought, to give a girl two names like that. As if one wasn't quite enough.

There were handouts already, with a photograph of Emma-Jane and a description of what she'd been wearing: denim jeans with embroidered butterflies on the pockets, pink wellington boots, a red duffel coat. The photograph matched the description exactly. It must have been taken just before she'd disappeared.

The police helicopter had been out for most of the night, its searchlight skimming across the heather and peat and surging brown streams. Jackson's sheep, in the lower meadows, had taken the fear and scattered through a broken gate, some of them as far as the reservoir, and his boys were out with the dogs and the quad bikes now to bring them all back in. But the helicopter hadn't found anything, and the police officers on the ground with their torches hadn't found anything, and so a public search had been called. It hadn't taken much to raise the volunteers. Word had gone round quickly. People had stayed out late into the evening, talking on front steps, or in the pub, or clustered around the incident van, which the police had set up outside the village hall.

It was unwise to have gone up on the moor at all in the middle of winter, let alone at that time of day and with a young child. But her parents weren't to know how quickly the weather could turn, nor how dark it could get up there. They weren't locals, after all. Some of the people who came for holidays in the area had never known real darkness before. They had no idea. They didn't know how easy it was to get lost, up on the hills. They didn't seem to know, some of them, that there were places where their phones wouldn't work.

She's probably hiding under a bush somewhere, people had been saying. Or she'll be down in a clough. She'll have turned her ankle and be waiting to be found. She'll be scared of getting in trouble, that's all. It's mild for the time of year. Someone else will have found her and taken her to the hospital. She probably thinks this is all a game. There's time yet.

Sometimes, Richard thought, people just felt the need to open their mouths and talk. They didn't seem to mind what came out.

It was barely light when they set out. The mist hung low across the moor and the ground was frozen hard. It had rained long into the night, and the air was still cold and damp. It was no kind of a day to be walking up on the hills. It was no kind of an hour to be up and about at all. Richard pulled his scarf up over his mouth, and clenched his fists inside his gloves, and watched where he was putting his feet.

It had taken him by surprise, seeing Cathy in the car park like that.

He'd been so careful about avoiding her while he was home that he'd almost forgotten she'd be around. They'd caught each other's eye at the same time, and opened their mouths without knowing what to say. And because they were still standing there when the word came to move off, they'd been paired up and sent on to the hill together. He'd followed her over the stile and up the first rise, their boots slipping and crunching on the stiffened ground and their tracks fading behind them as the heather sprang back into shape.

He watched her walking ahead of him now, her steps as light and sure as he remembered them. She looked older, of course, but she seemed to be carrying it easily, as just one more thing that needed to be carried. He wondered if she'd even recognized him, down there in the car park. If she'd seen anything of what she'd once seen, when the two of them used to walk up here together.

The climb to the first ridge was steeper than he remembered. He was sweating already, in spite of the cold air, and he stopped to undo his jacket. Cathy turned back, waiting for him, and they both looked down towards the village. She was breathing less heavily than he was. The mist was already beginning to clear. They could hear a helicopter further down the valley, towards the reservoirs.

They walked on, keeping their eyes to the ground and prodding at clumps of heather with their sticks. They didn't find anything. They started to talk, quietly. He told her about Irene saying she knew the girl. Cathy nodded, and said she supposed Irene would have seen her at the Harvey place. She'll have been slow making the beds and still been there when the family arrived, she said. He poked at a scrap of old sheep-feed bag. That sounds about right, he said.

The family was from London, Irene had said. A lovely couple. Seemed quite old to start having children but that's what people tended to do these days. Especially the professional types, which these seemed like. That's mostly who you get staying at the Harveys' anyway, with the prices they charge. Probably got plenty of money because they both worked: she seemed like one of those career-women types. This had all been said before Irene was even through the front door, saying she couldn't stay long, she should get back to the Harveys' and see if anything needed doing. The police might want to speak to her, she'd said. They'd probably be doing door-to-doors but they'd want to start with anyone who'd had contact with the family. With the little girl. The dear little girl.

Cathy caught her breath suddenly, stooping towards the ground. The state they must be in, she said. The parents. It doesn't bear thinking about. They must be going absolutely spare.

She asked how his mother was keeping. If Irene was keeping an eye out for her, if that was why she'd been there. Richard said he supposed that was partly it, and partly just that they were friends anyway. He wondered what she meant by keeping an eye out.

It had been a shock, actually, when his mother had opened the door and he'd seen all her bedroom furniture crammed into the front room like that. Jackson's boys came and moved it for me, she'd said, as if that was an explanation. When she'd been living on her own for so long, and so comfortably. He'd never needed to worry about her before. She wasn't ill. She wasn't using a stick, although she looked like she could probably do with one soon. She didn't even look frail, really. But she was slowing down, and it was clear that this would be the start of something. He would have to talk to his sisters, he knew. They must have known about this, and not told him. About the time it was taking her to get up out of her chair, to walk through to the kitchen and get the kettle on. He wondered how she was managing to get to the shops, to the post office. There were people who helped her, presumably. Neighbours. Irene.

Cathy asked what he was doing back home. He told her he was just here for Christmas, that he was due to fly out again the next day and be in a meeting by lunchtime, local time. He told her he'd been worried about his mother, and that his sisters hadn't been able to make it. He asked how she was, and whether her sons were home from university. She said they were, and that she was fine, all things considered. He realized that she must know he knew about Patrick, and so he said that he'd heard, that he was sorry, that he was sorry he hadn't been able to come back for the funeral. She shook her head and said she hadn't expected him to; it would have been a long way to come.

They reached the top of the first ridge. They stopped, breathing hard and looking down into the shallow valley ahead of them. The mist had lifted, and they could see the others strung out in a long line across the moor, each pair of volunteers no more than twenty or thirty yards apart. Police officers in bright yellow jackets were dotted along the line. A helicopter clattered overhead, and they saw, fanning out ahead of them, half a dozen police dogs crouching low along the ground, pulling their handlers behind them.

The missing girl's name was Emma-Jane.

By the time they were halfway across the valley, the line had started to straggle. He was beginning to realize how big an area they might have to cover, and how long it might take. He wondered, and then wished he hadn't, whether food and drink would be provided.

A whistle blew, and they watched a couple of police officers run over to a man with his hand raised in the air. The three of them crouched down together, looking at something, and then the two police officers returned to their places and waved everyone on. Richard looked at the man who'd raised his hand.

Is that Bruce's dad? he asked.

Martin? I think so – yes.

Is he still running the shop?

No. Oh, no. That closed down five or six years back. At least. Might be longer. He's working at the new Tesco's in town, on the meat counter.

What about Bruce?

Disappeared a few years after we left school. There was some kind of blow-up about something. He went to Manchester, apparently. Martin and Ruth split up after he left. She's still around; she's running the shop over in Harfield. They're doing organics.

He remembered Bruce's parents working in the butcher's shop, their white aprons splashed with blood, the huge knives thunking down onto the bowled wood of the chopping block, the cuts of meat being wrapped in waxed paper and swung up onto the scales. He'd imagined, as a boy, that the slaughtering of the animals was done right there on the premises, and that when Bruce's father ducked out into the darkened back room it was to slice through another bleating windpipe, while Bruce's mother smiled, and wiped her hands on the front of her apron, and asked Richard what she could get for him today.

They watched Martin shuffling across the moor, head down, poking at the heather with his stick. A much younger man was walking beside him.

That's Stuart he's with, Cathy said. Stuart Harvey. He was a few years below us at school. He bought the timber yard after Patrick died. I hung on to it for a bit; I thought the boys might be interested in taking it on once they were done at university, but they're really not. And it needed someone to keep it going straight off. Stuart offered us a good price. I've never liked the Harveys, to be honest. But it was a good price.

They clambered down into a clough, sheltered from the cold wind for a moment before struggling up the steep crumbling bank on the other side. He held out his hand to help her up.

He asked her what she thought they were actually looking for. She caught her breath again.

Oh, God. Richard. Anything. Like the policeman said. Clothes, shoes, gloves. Anything that might have been dropped. You know.

You don't think they think we might find –

Bloody hell. Richard. How should I know? I don't know.

They heard a cry and saw, away to their right, a white-haired woman falling over, her legs skidding out from under her and her arms flinging out to the side as she hit the ground. She lay quite still for a moment, winded, or worse, and then allowed herself to be pulled to her feet. Everyone walked on. Oily brown water seeped up around their boots. He asked about her sons, about university and what their plans were. About what it was like not having them at home any more. She said it was strange. She said it had been nice having them both back for Christmas. He asked how they were coping, after Patrick. He noticed himself not being quite able to say the word death. She said that two and a half years was a long time, at their age.

They reached the foot of the second ridge. The ground was steeper now, and softer, the peat giving way beneath their feet. They both stumbled a couple of times. He stopped to catch his breath again, and looked back at the village. When they were younger – when they were doing A levels, and walking up into these hills together – all they'd ever talked about was getting out of the village, going to university and finding work elsewhere and getting away. He'd never disliked the place, or held a grudge against the people who lived there. It had just seemed natural to want to leave.

Patrick had never mentioned leaving. It had probably never occurred to him. He'd never talked about the future at all. There was no need. He just kept working in his father's timber yard after school, while his shoulders got broader, his hands rougher, his wallet fatter. Everyone knew, without Patrick having to mention it more than once, that he would inherit the family timber yard once his father retired. It was the sort of certainty, Richard realized later, that some girls found attractive.

He looked at her now, and wondered if she was thinking about any of this. It seemed impossible that she wouldn't be.

There had been other women. He wanted to tell her this. There had been relationships. Perhaps she knew this anyway, or assumed it. Perhaps it didn't need to be said.

He looked past her, along the line of volunteers curving away around the hill, their heads lowered. The sky was clearing, and there was an occasional flash of light from the traffic on the motorway, just visible along the horizon. The reservoirs were a flat, metallic grey. He saw, in the distance, a thick band of rain moving towards them.

She asked about his mother again, and he said he didn't think she was coping at all. She asked if he thought he should even be taking his flight tomorrow; if he shouldn't stay with his mother until one of his sisters could make it back. The job can always wait, she said pointedly. It wasn't as simple as that, he told her. There were people relying on him.

He trod on something dark and heavy and wet. He prodded at it with the stick, lifting it clear of the heather. It was an old pair of jeans, half buried and blackened by the peat. He let them fall, and they walked on, and then the rain came, as suddenly as always, rearing up from behind the ridge and breaking over them like a wave. They pushed on for a few minutes, barely able to see where they were going. They heard whistles blowing on either side, and shouts for attention, and they saw people waving and gesturing back down the hill. It was finished. A man with a peaked cap came hurrying towards them, walking away from the commotion, his waterproof trousers swishing against the heather. He had his head down, concentrating on keeping his footing across the boggy ground. Richard put a hand out to stop him, and asked what had happened.

His mother was on the kitchen floor when they got back to the house. She was lying on her back, and she smiled up at them as they came into the room. She looked quite comfortable. She asked if they'd found the girl. Cathy helped him lift her up onto a chair, with some difficulty, and he crouched beside her, asking if she was OK, if she'd fallen, how long she'd been down there. She said she was fine, and that she would have got up in a minute or two if she hadn't heard them coming in anyway. She asked if they'd found the girl, and Richard said no, not yet, the search had been called off because of the weather. He asked her if it hurt anywhere, and she told him again that she was fine. She sat there, smiling, brushing down her skirt and fidgeting with the back of her hair. She looked at Cathy, who had moved back into the doorway, and seemed to register her presence for the first time.

Cathy, she said. How lovely to see you. It's been a fair while, hasn't it? Cathy smiled apologetically and agreed that it had. Her hands hovered over the buttons of her coat, as though she wasn't quite sure whether to stay. You'll have a cup of tea, his mother said. You must be chilled to the bone. Richard moved to put the kettle on, and heard, behind him, the rustle of Cathy taking off her coat. His reaction caught him by surprise. It was such a thrilling sound, even now. He kept his back turned and concentrated on making the tea.

In the evening, after supper, he sat with his mother and watched television pictures of the search party strung out across the side of the moor. His mother asked which one was him, but he couldn't really tell. The stooping figures all looked the same. They showed a photograph of the girl, from the handouts, and then a glimpse of the parents being helped into a car and driven through the gateway of the Harveys' place. A police officer was standing guard beside the gate, his hands clasped behind his back.

She would be dead by now. She must be. People must have realized that. It had been too long. If she'd been out there for a day and a night, with the weather they'd had. Or if she'd fallen down a hole. Or if she'd been taken.

They would go on searching, of course. There wasn't any choice. We can't give up now, people would say. The parents would say. And besides. These things did still sometimes turn out fine. Some boy falls down a well, and lands on something soft, and happens to have a carton of juice and a packet of biscuits stuffed in his pocket, and when they haul him back into the world a week later he's got nothing worse than a broken arm and a snotty nose to show for it.

But really, to be logical about it. The chances were slim.

It was dark when he left the next morning, kissing his mother while she lay in bed and saying that he'd make sure someone called in. The roads were already busy with police vans and journalists' cars. It was raining heavily. He wondered if they were going to reconvene the search.

This was all the village would be known for now, he realized. No matter what happened, this would be what people thought of when they heard the name. It seemed unfair.

People stood in huddles beneath umbrellas, looking up at him as he passed. He glanced through the open door of the village hall, and saw a woman setting out cups and saucers on a white cloth laid across a trestle table. He drove past the old butcher's shop, with the heavy wooden chopping table squatting in the middle of the empty floor and the faded *Eat British Meat* posters on the walls. He drove past the church, and the playground, and the new houses at the edge of the village, and he saw what he assumed were Jackson's sheep, back in the lower meadows. One of Jackson's boys was already working on the broken gate, the sawdust turning to a creamy sludge in the pouring rain. He came to the mini-roundabout by the quarry entrance, and circled the car back round towards the village. He drove past the village hall again, and the post office, and the pub, and he stopped outside Cathy's house.

She'd asked him to call round on his way to the airport. For a coffee or something, she'd said, as she'd stood on his mother's doorstep buttoning up her coat. He didn't know quite what she meant. He wondered if she wanted to make him feel guilty about his mother, or if she might find some other reason to persuade him to stay. He waited in the car.

He could see her in the kitchen, standing over the table while her sons ate breakfast. The room was brightly lit against the rest of the house, the colours spilling into the dark morning. He watched her lean across them to take a piece of toast. He watched the relentless way the boys were eating, talking and laughing while they crammed food into their mouths. He looked at their broad shoulders, their expansive gestures. They made the room look full. Complete.

The engine was still running. The car radio was on. The newsreader started talking about the missing girl. He saw Cathy shushing the boys, and realized they were listening to the same station. He saw the turn of their heads, the concentration in their bodies. He watched Cathy, with her back to him, lift her hair in both hands and twist it into a knot. He remembered her doing the same thing years ago. He knew, before she turned to the window, that there would be a hairband pinched between her lips, ready.

They listened to the radio. The police were appealing for further information. The parents were being comforted by friends. There were no new leads. The search would resume at first light. ■

Award-Winning Fiction from **Grove Press**

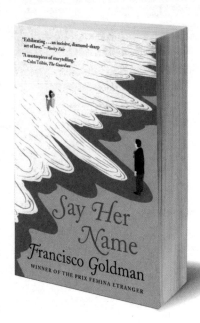

Say Her Name Francisco Goldman

Winner of the Prix Femina Etranger

"A masterpiece of storytelling."—Colm Tóibin

"The book of the year. . . A soaring paean to a brilliant young woman and to the infinite invincible power of love."
—Junot Díaz, *New York*

A BEST BOOK OF THE YEAR:

American Library Association, *The New York Times, San Francisco Chronicle, Entertainment Weekly, Boston Globe, New York, Pittsburgh Post-Gazette, Publishers Weekly, The Guardian, The Independent, Evening Standard*

Turn of Mind Alice LaPlante

Winner of the Wellcome Prize

"An unputdownable page-turner . . . Combines murder mystery with family drama, bringing new meaning to the term 'psychological thriller.'"
—Susan Cheever, *Vanity Fair*

A BEST BOOK OF THE YEAR:

Newsday, Chicago Tribune, The Washington Post, The Guardian, Kirkus Reviews

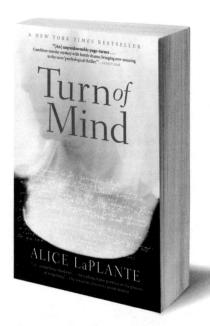

NOW AVAILABLE IN PAPERBACK

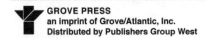

GROVE PRESS
an imprint of Grove/Atlantic, Inc.
Distributed by Publishers Group West

www.groveatlantic.com

GRANTA

DREAMS OF A
LEISURE SOCIETY

Adam Foulds

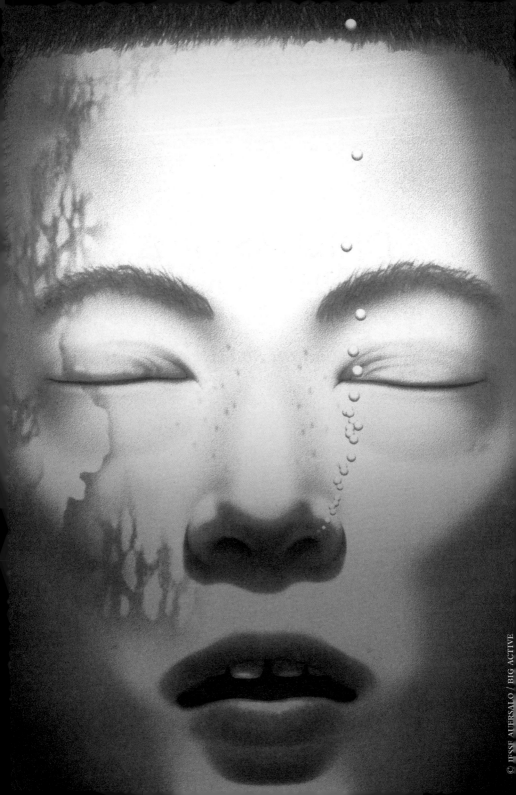

Simpson held his mask to his face and dropped with a crash into the grip of cold water. The weight of his equipment was lifted suddenly. It swayed now on its straps. He caught hold of the ladder and started the slow descent into darkness and pressure. The growling and pinging he could hear was the sound of the sea around the massive iron of the rig.

The correct way to breathe was slowly, in and out, like the strokes of an oarsman. The loud bubbles of each exhalation rose together, a silvery spinal column snaking its way back up to the surface. Simpson pressed a button on the side of his watch to check his depth. He read the dim red figures in a square industrial font like something from the *Alien* films: almost there. The weight of water tightened around his skull. His ears whined. He adjusted them, holding his nose and blowing, and the painful lumps of pressure shifted. More downward steps, the ladder reaching into depths that were out of sight. He checked his watch again. This was the place. He searched around, cloudy particles racing through the narrow beam of his torch, and found it, the crack he had to work on.

Simpson picked up the welding torch and ignited it, he wasn't sure how. Then there it was again: the endlessly thrilling small miracle of fire under water. Livid as a dog's erection, two inches of white-hot flame extended from the nozzle. Around it the chill water warped with rolling currents. Simpson angled the flame onto the crack in the great iron strut. The metal blistered, wept, slowly healed together. He became entirely absorbed in his task, hanging there, working, feeling the power of the ocean all around him. He looked up only once when the slow shapes of a school of whales swam by.

'What time is it?'

Simpson lifted one hand from the vibrating handle of the torch and looked at his watch. Through the glare and tumbling murk he couldn't make out the numbers.

'I dunno . . . It's . . . I think it's thirty-three something.'

Jay snickered and mumbled more words that Simpson couldn't hear. His voice appeared as a dark circle that pulsated like a jellyfish for a few moments then vanished. Simpson got back to work.

Afterwards, Simpson's lips were dry, scorched and papery. His head ached. He went to the bathroom to wash his face, rubbing at his skin with the clean water. He laid a fat worm of paste on his toothbrush and scrubbed inside his head too, spitting out the copious foam. As he did so, Simpson noticed the plant that lived in the bathroom in a plastic pot on a saucer. He hadn't looked at it for ages, if ever. It had a frizzy, sudden shape, with fronds of many tiny leaves. Dark green, it sat in its pot in total silence absorbing the grey London light. The fact that it was alive, an organism, struck Simpson. Philosophically it was an interesting question as to whether it had a will or not. It certainly looked like it did, pursuing its slow, pointless life beside the toilet. Simpson thought it looked mildly hostile.

He made himself a cup of tea. Milk, on the turn but only just, imparted a slight animal sourness to the brew. Lisa came into the living room and dropped backwards onto the sofa. She was wearing just a big T-shirt and nothing else. Simpson didn't like it when she did that. The insolent whiteness of her bare thighs. There was something humiliating about it.

'Where's Jay gone?'

'Is this all that's on?' She gestured at the TV, a programme about home renovation.

'No. Flick about if you want. Where's Jay?'

'Went out to get some food. Blood sugar, he said. Been a long day.'

'I'm fucked.'

'And he wants you to go to the hospital with him tonight.'

'Fuck's sake.'

'He got a message from Special K. Oh, that's better.'

On the television, two men in blue fleeces somewhere in Scotland were releasing an otter back into the wild. There was a close-up of its whiskered face while it cowered in the back of the cage, then it crept out, undulated quickly over some rocks and disappeared into the water. Lisa scratched her leg.

Low cloud. A persistent wind made them hunch their shoulders and squint. Dull between doses, the world looked worn thin to Simpson, threadbare, inadequately real. They waited in the appointed place in the car park of St George's, out of sight of any cameras. Jay smoked a roll-up. Simpson watched his lips reach forward to the wet end of the cigarette, seeping dense smoke. The movement accentuated the slight muzzle in Jay's face, the protruding circle of his mouth. He had dark eyes, dark brows, coarse eyebrows. This made him look thoughtful even when he wasn't. Jay looked back at Simpson.

'What?'

'Nothing.' Simpson stared down at the grey composite substance of the tarmac at his feet, the square grains packed together.

'Do you owe me money?' Jay asked.

'No.'

'I feel like you owe me money for something.'

'But I don't.'

Simpson dragged his toe in an arc along the ground. 'And I'm out here working,' he said.

'Yeah, this is working. Cunt.'

Jay liked to bully Simpson. Mostly, Simpson didn't mind. It was better than paying rent and he just couldn't find it in himself to care. He just took it. In a way he quite liked it. It was nice knowing someone was in charge. And it never got really nasty. It didn't matter. Jay said he was a masochist and a lazy fucker.

They fell silent while an old woman rattled past in a wheelchair. Her head wobbled. Her throat was made of long pleats of loose skin.

Dark plastic shoes rested on the foot supports. Carrier bags of stuff hung from the handles at the back. The woman pushing her said, 'Nearly there, Mum.'

'And she gets it all for free,' Jay commented when they had gone. 'What's the point? Look at her. Just let her die and get on with it.'

Finally Dr Kumarasami came jogging over to them. He took his hand from his pocket, thrust it into one of Jay's coat pockets, depositing something, then withdrew it again empty. Quick as that, like two birds fucking on a fence. Jay reached in and felt, shaking the bottle.

'Doesn't feel like much.'

'There's forty in there.'

'Forty? Forty's not a business.'

Dr Kumarasami shrugged. 'It is what it is.'

'And what is it? Where will it take us?'

'Beg pardon?'

'Up or down or round and round?'

'Oh, that.' Young, good-looking Dr Kumarasami was nervous. His hands travelled into his pockets, out again, down the slippery silk of his tie. 'I can't be too long,' he said. 'They'll make you pain-free. Very strong.'

'Side effects?'

'Could pop a weak heart. Other than that it's a nice warm bath. Hypnagogic imagery, possibly. And your sense of time goes a bit funny apparently.'

'Sweet.'

Inside a handshake, Jay passed to Dr Kumarasami a tightly folded rectangle of twenty-pound notes.

'Great. Look, I can't do much more of this. They're changing systems . . .'

'No worries. Thanks for your trouble, Special K.' Jay grinned. 'We'll take whatever. And you're not our only friend.'

'Good.' Smoothing one eyebrow with a thumbnail, Dr Kumarasami looked as though he were about to say something else. He didn't. He turned and headed back to the hospital.

'Nice,' Simpson said. 'Take these back for a test drive.'
'If you're lucky. I will anyway.'

'**W**hat do you reckon?'
'It's very warm.' Simpson stood up to his thighs in the sea, a coppery sunset pouring down over him, while cars drove past behind the scenery. In the room there'd been the longest twilight, darkness settling along his forearms like soot. 'It's nice.'

'Yeah.' Jay exhaled the full length of a breath. 'Magic biscuits.'

Simpson felt carefully the bridge of his nose and the warm skin of his forehead.

The room banged white as the inside of an ambulance.

'Fuck's sake. Don't do that.'

'Jesus, sorry.' Lisa switched the light off again. 'It's pitch black in here, you know.'

The boys didn't answer her. Jay said, 'I got beans. In the cupboard.'

'Nice,' Simpson said. 'With toast. Loads of margarine. I'll do that in a minute.'

Lisa turned on the television.

Chris was the first to arrive. In his cycling gear, he looked insectile, alien. The cleats he wore hobbled him slightly and he walked with a teeter, threw orange sunglasses onto the table and sat down on the edge of the sofa.

'So, boys, what are we looking at?'

Meds weren't like other drugs, the ordinary dirty junkie drugs. Meds were technology. They attracted a certain clientele. Jay liked to use the word 'boutique' of his operation. Simpson thought he sounded like a twat when he did that. All it meant was that they were small-time, dealing for friends. But Jay had ambitions.

Meds came from the glossy impersonal facades of big pharm multinationals or ingenious illegal labs and their users were often bright people. They liked to explore. They read books. They were talkative along lines of haywire brilliance that often routed into conspiracy theories. Their folklore was of new compounds the companies would never release, perfect payloads of harmless euphoria that would deliver people from their illusions and stop them working for the machine. There was talk of drugs that opened the third eye, that enabled remote viewing and clairvoyance. They were citizens of a multidimensional universe and they liked to get high.

'Opioid. Quite a serious mother. Nice and fuzzy and time goes gloopy.' Jay held up the gleaming capsule between thumb and forefinger. 'Give it a try?'

Half an hour later Chris was lying back in his seat, a placid smile on his face. 'Hmm,' he said thoughtfully. Then after a while he said, 'Sim, you doing that scuba course?'

Simpson was looking for a particular CD somewhere in the slithering heap by the machine. 'No. Haven't started yet. Need cash, innit. Also, might not be the right thing. I don't just want to do like holiday scuba.'

'Nice job, diving. Being in a . . .' he paused. '. . . in a different, totally different element.'

'It's more than normal scuba. Industrial diving. So you've got to be like a technician.'

'Dangerous.'

'But that's why it pays.'

'Engineer. Deep-sea engineer. Don't you need a degree?'

'I don't think so.' Simpson bit his finger. He felt uncomfortable when people treated his fantasy like it was a serious proposition and he might actually have to do something about it. 'I'm still like looking into it. It's technical. Like being a repairman underwater.'

'He's never gonna do it,' Jay said. The doorbell rang. 'That'll be Mikey and Jerome.' He got up to let them in.

Mikey walked in and immediately sat down. Jerome stayed standing, entering the room slowly in his nervous way. He fiddled strands of wind-blown hair back into place with long fingers.

'OK.' Mikey clapped and rubbed his hands. 'Let the dog see the rabbit.'

'Weapons-grade opioid.'

'Man,' Jerome said. 'It's always violent imagery. Why not like colour intensities or lumens? Candles, isn't it? We should measure them in candles.'

'You what?'

'I'm going to make a cup of tea.'

Jay gestured at Chris. 'Look how happy our friend is.'

Chris giggled. 'I'm happy.'

Jay screwed open the bottle and shook out a couple of doses.

Mikey swallowed his immediately and sat back with his hands behind his head. 'So what else is going on?'

Jerome came back in. 'Your milk is on the way to being a whole new organism. There's like clustering of proteins going on. I think it breathed at me.'

'Get over the disappointment with one of these.'

'Oh, yeah. Thanks.' Jerome took the pill and swallowed it. 'Mind if I put a CD on? It's something I've been working on. It's not harsh or anything.'

'It's a free house.'

Simpson recognized the sound of Lisa's footsteps on the stairs outside. She bustled in with carrier bags, looked round the door at the sprawled figures with their relaxed, thoughtful, mindless faces, nodded at Jay and went to wait it all out in their room.

Simpson said, 'She's not happy.'

'Like you know or not.'

Simpson had to wait it out too. Before he could make up his bed, the boys had to go – which eventually they did – and Jay had to leave the room. Jay was slumped in the armchair, staring up at the ceiling. There were tensions inherent in Simpson's situation, living on the edge of an unhappy couple, but things were basically all right. After dropping out of uni, Simpson had fallen through various different households, crashing on beds and sofas and floors. People kept running out of patience with him. One friend of a friend, a new father with a dog scuttling round the kitchen, told him after kicking him out, 'I'm trying to help you but in the end you have to save yourself.'

Save himself from what? From not wanting what they had – jobs and relationships, paperwork, two-week holidays, a car? Simpson's secret, his problem, was that he was perfectly happy doing what he did.

While Jay crashed around in the bathroom, Simpson set up his bed. At night the street lights outside lit everything a mellow orange. Objects in the room were haloed with a fuzzy tennis-ball outline. Simpson noticed that Jay had left the bottle of pills on the windowsill. Timing it with the noise of the toilet flush Simpson shook out two and swallowed them. Never trust a pleasure-seeker. Knowing the chemicals were in him and about to get active, he said a duplicitous 'night' to Jay on his way into the bathroom.

'Don't wank on my sofa,' Jay said.

Two worked. Two was good. Everything outside melted off, the sound of Jay and Lisa arguing, the room, all faded in the heat. It didn't let him think about his future employment. He couldn't think cold and industrious, only a tropical sea, wavering bands of sunlight over coral and luminous darting fish. He could hear the tiny sand grains dragging. Big rays shaped like stealth bombers flew past with slow undulations of their wings. Parrotfish cropped at the coral with sharp beaks, cracking through the hard formations. The strength of them was comical somehow. It made Simpson laugh out a gust of bubbles. The parrotfish were striped yellow and violet. The individual scales were iridescent as the little square holograms on credit cards. Bug-eyed prawns sat tensely on rocks. A flatworm swam past, flexing its whole body that was really a single scarlet frill. It flung itself back and forth and somehow ratcheted through the water. The bright blue silk of the surface rippled a few metres overhead. Everything was lit up down there like a suburban fish tank with a castle and constant bubbles. *Fuck me*, Simpson laughed. *I'm at the dentist's.*

'Oi, cunt.' A thump on his chest. Simpson woke up panicking. He found a cushion on top of him. Jay had thrown it. 'Did you take two of these last night?'

'What?'

'I've counted them.'

'Look –'

'Oh, fuck off. Don't even talk. We're supposed to make money. I mean we need money and what are you doing?'

'What about that thing you said about Dan?'

'What about not being a thieving cunt?'

'I'm sorry, I –'

'Fuck's sake. He's apologizing. Just don't.'

Jay left the room. He left the flat, slamming the front door hard enough to get that special noise of finality: the letter box flipping up and smacking back. Simpson felt his forehead. More noise: Jay had woken Lisa and she was getting up, groaning, stumbling, pissing in the bathroom, flushing, then clumsily busy in the kitchen. She came into the room with a bowl of cereal.

'Morning. Arsehole's gone out,' she said.

'Don't you ever wear trousers?'

'You don't have to look,' she said. 'Unless you can't help it. In here all on your own.' She picked up the remote and put the telly on. 'Jay thinks you look.'

'Is that what you were arguing about?'

'No. That was something else. There are infinite things. The main one is he's an arsehole.'

'And you're like never a bitch.'

'Says the fucking perv.'

'I'm not. Why do you always –'

'Pretending you don't look. Dirty fucker. Put your hands where I can see them.'

'Jesus Christ, I'm just lying here. What's wrong with you?'

Simpson felt Dan's scar when they shook hands. It recorded the desperate but effective gesture Dan had made when two blokes with blades tackled him in a car park – a knife darting in towards Dan's face had met his defending hand and striped across. Those were the early days and that sort of thing wasn't unexpected when establishing your own club nights. Dan had gone on to bigger things since then and now was almost sentimental about the scar. He'd tell you about it, about the blood soaking his new trainers, seeing his own thin white bones in the ragged tear. From the back, his hand now looked perfectly normal. Upturned, it looked like two mismatched pieces of jigsaw had been mashed together.

Simpson suspected Dan enjoyed the small shock communicated when he gripped your hand, the flinch of uncertainty in people's faces, already wrong-footed, out of their depth. Dan was a pretty fierce character, his energy always rising and expanding on uppers, terrifyingly friendly, or small and hard, watchful and bitter. His head was shaved. He wore a designer motorcycle jacket and a T-shirt that was tight around his square torso. His watch was a large rectangle of coloured metal. He sucked coffee through the lid of a takeaway cup and said, 'From what I can hear you've got nothing. Why are you here again?'

Jay picked up a flyer from the desk and glanced at it. A fracturing sphere issuing rays of light; 'Karmageddon' in a Hindi-style font. 'Yeah, but I'm here,' he said, 'more like to talk about when we do. We've got some prospects.'

'You have, have you?' Dan looked at them both. The direct gaze of his tired, wired blue eyes hit Simpson with some force. He wriggled in his seat. 'I'd say it's more like you're here on a fishing trip. And anyway why would I want to be involved in your nonsense? I don't need it as an income stream.'

'We do,' Simpson murmured. Dan ignored him. Jay tutted.

'However, I would say it is good to have around for the clientele, which is why it's actually convenient you two twats have turned up. I've got some arrangements to make for a couple of new venues. I don't know you,' he said to Simpson. 'But Jayzee boy I know from back in the day. So what it is. I give you a serious connect, and I mean serious. You don't fuck about with them. They're very steady and you'll have like a full portfolio, still club stuff only, a lot of it too new actually to be illegal. I introduce you to security and the team. They ignore you and you're in the clubs like a couple of those olden-days cigarette girls.'

'And we're independent?' Jay asked, acting as though he might turn the offer down.

'What difference?' Dan sat back, his jacket creaking. He pulled his phone from his jeans pocket and tossed it on the desk. 'But if that makes you happy. And anyway, yes, you're definitely not working for me. Problems you sort out on your own. You'll make money and I collect taxes.'

'Man,' Jay said. 'Look how you're all grown up. You're organized.'

Pleasure meant simplification. It was all coming clear. Simpson liked working in the club. Jay didn't trust him to deal with the suppliers so he was simply given his stock, nodded in by the bouncers and left to hang out at a corner of the bar. People came over to him, nervous and needy or confident, slapping him on the back, and he took their money and helped them out. They moved away and became dancers, moving in the hammering lights, human figures flashing in changing postures. The club was a machine to simplify the world, make it loud and mad and enjoyable. On the dance floor, people became two-dimensional, just shapes in the sudden colours. Not Simpson. He remained fully operational. He knew the unsmiling bouncers, the Africans selling lollipops and squirts of perfume in the toilets. He knew what the back office looked like. For the first time in his life, Simpson felt himself part of a business, at one with the forces of commerce, and it felt good. He was powerful. He was working. He sipped energy drinks and tried to think like Dan, looking at the clubbers and counting them, seeing churning numbers and money.

Simpson could see that there were still kids hanging out by the flats before he got out of the minicab. He wondered about them, what with his pockets puffy with crumpled cash. But there was no other way through. Confidence. Pace. He paid the driver and walked straight through the loitering figures and one stepped straight out in front of him. At his heels, this kid had a squat, nasty dog. Its short breath through its spade-shaped jaws was so rasping it sounded like somebody filing through metal. The kid said, 'You scared? I think he's proper scared.' Simpson didn't say anything. The kid's face was shadowed. He couldn't make it out. The features were grey and moving, unresolved. He stepped around the little fucker and kept walking. The kid called after him, 'Follow you home, innit. Find out where you live. Put a bullet in your head!'

In the flat, Simpson washed his trembling hands and face while Jay and Lisa argued. Jay's hours were wrong, apparently. He messed with girls in the clubs. He never thought about . . . He reminded her that they were getting rich. Look at the new plasma screen, his clothes, that restaurant the other night. She should be grateful.

Simpson brushed his teeth then went and made up his bed in the front room.

The following night was a night off. Jay was out wanting to talk to Dan about something and Simpson was relaxing, lying in his bed with quiet music on, drifting in a shallow dose. It was good always having money and means, nice to be able to order lavish takeaways.

Lisa walked into the room wearing her T-shirt. 'Don't say anything,' she said, and climbed on top of him.

'Jesus, what are you doing?'

'What the fuck do you think I'm doing?'

'If this is like revenge –'

'I said shut up. Why are you always so pathetic?'

'Are you drunk?'

'Just fucking lie there like you always do.'

'This is wrong. We shouldn't –'

She pulled her T-shirt off over her head. She started to unfasten Simpson's clothes. Experimentally, he reached up and took hold of one of her breasts, squashing it in his hand. She let him. This was actually happening. She was busy pulling at his penis. When it was hard, she pulled her pants aside and sat down on him.

'Holy fuck, holy fuck,' he said.

She worked back and forth on top of him, fiddling with her clitoris. Her skin was orange from the street light, her nipples large and black. When he tried to touch her, she frowned and twisted away. She was busy and she ignored him, going after her orgasm. It felt as though her orgasm was something he had in his possession that she was slowly wrestling from him, wrenching out of his grasp. She groaned when she got hold of it finally, shaking and spluttering above him. Afterwards she pulled strands of loose hair away from her mouth. Staring down at him she said, 'Well, go on then,' and Simpson raced to catch up with her, thrusting upwards into her slipperiness while she grimaced and waited. Finally his climax fluttered up into the strong arch of her body.

'Told you you wanted it,' she said, climbing off. She picked up her T-shirt and walked out of the room.

Simpson felt his genitals, warm and wet. 'Holy fuck. Holy fuck.'

At Jerome's, Simpson ignored his phone.

Jay had laid some very heavy emotional shit on Simpson, getting louder and louder. Finally he exploded in physical attack. A buckle at the cuff of Jay's new designer leather jacket had cut Simpson's cheek. A fast, straight, incredibly painful punch on the nose had made Simpson's eyes flood with tears. That single, comical direct hit was humiliating. Blinded, bent double, Simpson filled with a childish rage for justice – Lisa had fucked *him*! He'd sort of tried to stop her! It was in this state that Simpson made his huge mistake. Jay had slammed out of the flat, telling Simpson to be gone when he got back. Simpson did as he was told. On his way, he took everything: all the money, all the drugs. Jay had recently been for resupply and there was a lot of both. Simpson left clothes behind so there was room in his rucksack for the bags of pills and bricks of cash.

A big mistake. Simpson had taken it all for security, for the reassuring affluence that meant he would get by for a while without having to worry. But it made the opposite true. Now Simpson was the guy in the movie with a briefcase handcuffed to his wrist and everybody after him. In the films that guy was always moving swiftly and quietly through an airport and Simpson realized that he had that

ADAM FOULDS

option. He could leave the drugs, take the money and go, fly away, somewhere abroad. But then what? He decided to postpone that decision. In the meantime he prevailed on the hospitality of nervous, helpless Jerome.

Jerome was a nice guy, very generous. He didn't want Simpson in his place but he wouldn't kick him out. For a couple of days, they sat around sampling the merchandise and listening to Jerome's music. As he sat cross-legged on the floor, a thought lifted Jerome's head. He told Simpson that he should get away to Scotland if he wanted to go through with the whole becoming a diver thing because that's where the oil rigs were. Simpson thought about that. He turned his heavy head slowly and looked out of the window at the cars and the ordinary street. The street didn't look right, or it looked too right, too empty, like an abandoned set for a TV show. Jerome pulled Simpson out of this thought when he said, 'Seriously, though. I'd get out of here. I'm getting messages from Jay. He doesn't know where you are but it sounds bad. He says it's out of his hands.'

'What's that mean?'

'Like it's not just him. I mean, it isn't him any more. It's gone up the line.'

'I should go somewhere. I should move.'

'Yeah, I would sort of appreciate that in a way.'

'Would you?'

'Yeah. Or you should just go back to him and sort it out.'

'Hmm.' Simpson turned his head again. 'That makes sense. Sort it out. I could do that. I mean, I'm definitely going to think about that.'

Two days later, Jerome said, 'Come and look at this car.' Simpson pushed himself up from the sofa and went over to the window.

'Doesn't look right, does it?'

'Not really, no.'

The car was long and low, darkly gleaming, too expensive. Simpson stared at it, became absorbed in the sky reflected across its bonnet.

282

Jerome said, 'Maybe we should get out of sight. Probably they can see us.'

'I don't know . . .'

The passenger door opened. Jerome flinched downwards, grabbing Simpson's wrist.

'Shit.'

They both crouched out of sight. They looked at each other when they heard the solid *thunk thunk* of both car doors slammed shut.

Simpson laughed. 'You have paid the TV licence?'

'Seriously, though. I mean, fuck.'

Twenty long seconds later they listened to the doorbell ringing, thumps on the door, the door jumping in its frame, the letter box flipped open and shut then held open and someone calling through, 'Peter Simpson! Peter Simpson, we know you're in there. Come on, Pete. Don't annoy us. Open the door. Open the door and let's get this sorted.'

Jerome's mouth was open. He stared at the carpet. Simpson put a hand on his shoulder.

The voice said, 'Pete, don't be like this.' There was a pause, then, 'Fine, we'll be back later.' A kick at the bottom of the door and then silence.

Simpson and Jerome waited there until they heard the heavy car doors shut and the car drive away.

'Fucking hell,' said Jerome.

'I know. I know. I know. I know.'

'What are you going to do?'

'Haven't got a fucking clue.'

'Just give them the stuff.'

'Definitely I'll do that. Or I could leave. Just slip away.'

'And then they'll come back here and I'll be here and you won't be here.'

'They won't do anything to you.'

'Like you fucking know that.'

'They won't. I'm gonna, fuck, I don't know. I'm gonna go out and get some air and buy some proper fags so I can think and then I'll work out what to do.'

'You'd better come back.'

'I'm coming back. Don't worry.'

As he pulled on his coat, Simpson wondered whether maybe it would be better not to come back, to just go to a Tube station, pop up on the other side of town somewhere random and disappear. But as soon as he opened the front door, an arm shot forwards and grabbed his neck. Simpson was thrown backwards. Noise, force, the powerful wave of – he thought – two men coming through the door. He strained his head upright and looked along the arm and saw the man's eyes. There was hatred in them but also amusement, relish. The door frame bounced against his right shoulder blade and the back of his head and then he flew across the room, landing with one arm underneath him on the carpet. He looked round to see Jerome pleading, 'It's him! He's Simpson!' before receiving one dismissive whipping backhand punch and crumpling. Simpson had a brilliant thought. He lunged towards the coffee table and snatched the bag of pills. He pulled some out and quickly swallowed them down like a starving man with a fistful of rice. A foot landed on the small of his back and he felt his nose and forehead bounce against the floor.

When they were gone, Simpson sat on the sofa. He was tired as though after a long session of violent physical exercise, but the drugs were working, he was pain-free. He sat. Sitting was good. His body was as heavy as a bucket of water. He felt warm. He remembered the beating with flashes of faces and sound. It had been very long, repetitive, laborious, both spiteful and disinterested, almost medical. Simpson looked across at Jerome who was sitting on the carpet. His mouth had swollen to a soft beak. His eyes looked rinsed and scalded by tears. Simpson realized that he was looking at him because he'd just said something which was, 'You're going to have to go.' Simpson said, 'I know. I will. I just need to rest for a little bit.'

A while later, Jerome was sitting on a chair watching the telly and drinking tea, wincing as he sipped.

Simpson said, 'Do I look like you?'

'You look a fuck of a lot worse.'

Simpson giggled. He rubbed a throbbing spot at his right temple. Black fragments of dried blood came away on his fingertips. He flicked them onto the floor. 'I'm starting to feel myself again.'

'Rather you than me.'

'You hungry? I'm really hungry.'

'Actually, I am hungry. I sort of forgot about that.'

'I could go out and get us some chips.'

'Yeah, you could.'

'I think I've got some change in my coat.'

'You're wearing your coat.'

'Oh, yeah.'

Simpson got up to prepare himself. He washed blood from his face with cold water. He watched the red spiral wind calmly out of sight down the plughole. His body ached. There were many individual areas of pain. He had to walk carefully to keep them all separate and quiet. He fastened his coat with the careful concentration and weak, inaccurate fingers of a small child. He felt proud of himself when he'd done so.

Outside a wind was blowing in the same direction that Simpson walked. He felt it rushing against his back. It was still light outside. In fact, it was early. Kids were walking home from school. A bus pulled up. Its doors jerked open and an old woman stepped out onto one fragile leg and then the other. A police car sped past with its siren on. Clouds were hurrying over the buildings. Simpson felt something underfoot and looked down: a crushed orange cardboard box from one of the fried-chicken places. It was all going on. Everything was fucked but the broken machine of the world somehow kept working. It made Simpson feel light-hearted, even optimistic. He had enough coins in his pocket to pay for chips. Jerome would definitely let him stay for the night. He could think about tomorrow when it happened. ■

NOTICEBOARD

The Society of Authors

Next closing date: 30 September 2012

In addition to the Authors' Foundation grants and K Blundell Trust awards the following specific grants are also available within the Authors' Foundation:

The Great Britain Sasakawa Grant
(fiction or non-fiction about any aspect of Japanese culture or society)
Roger Deakin awards
(writing about the environment)
John Heygate Awards (travel writing)
John C Laurence awards
(promoting understanding between races)
Elizabeth Longford grants
(historical biography)
Michael Meyer awards (theatre)
Arthur Welton awards (poetry)

Full guidelines available from
www.societyofauthors.org | 020 7373 6642

FINANCIAL ASSISTANCE FOR WRITERS

The Royal Literary Fund

Grants and Pensions are available to published authors of several works who are in financial difficulties due to personal or professional setbacks.

Applications are considered in confidence by the General Committee every month.

For further details please contact:
Eileen Gunn, General Secretary
The Royal Literary Fund
3 Johnson's Court
London EC4A 3EA
Tel 020 7353 7159
email: egunnrlf@globalnet.co.uk
website: www.rlf.org.uk
Registered Charity No. 219952

Granta has editions in Spain, Italy and Brazil, and will soon be launching in China, Norway and Bulgaria.

Read the best new writing – from around the world.

'An overwhelmingly powerful force in English writing'
Spectator

CONTRIBUTORS

Simon Armitage's latest collection of poems is *Seeing Stars*. He lives in West Yorkshire and is Professor of Poetry at the University of Sheffield.

John Burnside teaches at the University of St Andrews. His most recent books are *Black Cat Bone*, a poetry collection, and *The Summer of Drowning*, a novel.

Sam Byers's 'Some Other Katherine' is an extract from his debut novel, *Idiopathy*, published by Fourth Estate in 2013. He lives in Norwich.

Jim Crace lives in Birmingham. His novels include *Quarantine* and *Being Dead*. 'Enclosure' is an extract from *Harvest*, published in 2013 by Picador in the UK and Nan A. Talese/Doubleday in the US.

Adam Foulds has written three books, including *The Quickening Maze*, a novel, and *The Broken Word*, a narrative poem. He lives in London.

Edith Grossman is the recipient, most recently, of the 2010 Queen Sofia Spanish Institute Translation Prize.

Mark Haddon was born in Northampton. His books include *The Curious Incident of the Dog in the Night-Time*, a best-seller. A new novel, *The Red House*, is published this year.

Tania James's story collection, *Aerogrammes*, is forthcoming from Alfred A. Knopf in May.

Cynan Jones was born in Wales. He is the author of *The Long Dry* and *Everything I Found on the Beach*. 'The Dig' is part of a novel in progress.

Yuri Kaliada is a political refugee from Belarus. He lives in the US.

Nikolai Khalezin and **Natalia Kaliada** are the founders of the Belarus Free Theatre.

Robert Macfarlane's books include *Mountains of the Mind* and *The Wild Places*. *The Old Ways*, from which 'Silt' is taken, is forthcoming this June from Penguin Books. He is a Fellow at Emmanuel College, Cambridge.

Jon McGregor's most recent book is *This Isn't the Sort of Thing That Happens to Someone Like You*, a story collection. He lives in Nottingham.

Jamie McKendrick was born in Liverpool. He has written five collections of poetry, including *Ink Stone* and *Crocodiles & Obelisks*.

Don Paterson's most recent collection of poetry is *Rain*. He teaches at the University of St Andrews.

Ross Raisin was born in Yorkshire. He has written two novels, *Waterline* and *God's Own Country*.

Robin Robertson is from the north-east coast of Scotland. His fifth collection of poems will be published in 2013.

Rachel Seiffert is the author of *The Dark Room*, *Field Study* and *Afterwards*. 'Hands Across the Water' is an extract from a novel in progress. She was born in Birmingham and now lives in London.

Tom Stoppard's plays include *Rosencrantz and Guildenstern Are Dead*, *Jumpers*, *Arcadia* and *Rock 'n' Roll*. He lives in London.

Andrea Stuart's *Sugar in the Blood* is forthcoming this June from Portobello Books. She was brought up in Barbados, Jamaica and the US and now lives in London.

Chris Thorpe is a writer, performer and translator from Manchester.

Mario Vargas Llosa was awarded the Nobel Prize for Literature in 2010. 'The Celt' is taken from *The Dream of the Celt*, forthcoming in English in June 2012, from Farrar, Straus and Giroux in the US and Faber & Faber in the UK.

Gary Younge was raised in Stevenage. He is a columnist for the *Guardian* and the *Nation*. His books include *No Place Like Home: A Black Briton's Journey Through the American South* and *Who Are We – and Should It Matter in the 21st Century?*

THIS MAY

GRANTA LAUNCHES
ISSUE 119: BRITAIN
WITH AN INTERNATIONAL
SERIES OF EVENTS

EVENTS

IN LONDON

Bloomsbury Institute
British Library, in association
  with *Writing Britain*
Paradise Row

AT WATERSTONES

Birmingham
Brighton
Cambridge
Edinburgh
Glasgow
Lancaster
Leeds
Liverpool
London – Gower Street
London – Hampstead
London – Piccadilly
Manchester
Norwich
Nottingham, in association
  with Writing East Midlands
Oxford
Sheffield
York

AROUND THE WORLD

Amsterdam
Berlin
Paris
Brussels
New York
Cambridge, MA
Chicago
Los Angeles
San Francisco
Washington, DC
Aberystwyth
Belfast
Dublin
Newcastle, in association
  with New Writing North
Plymouth, in association
  with Cyprus Well
Islamabad
Delhi

FESTIVALS

9 May
Brighton Festival
brightonfestival.org

17 May
Bristol Festival of Ideas
ideasfestival.co.uk

18 May
Yellow-Lighted Festival
yellow-lightedbookshop.co.uk

4 – 10 June
Dublin Writers Festival
dublinwritersfestival.com

22 June
Worlds Literature Festival
writerscentrenorwich.org.uk/
  worldsliteraturefestival.aspx

30 June – 14 July
London Literature Festival
londonlitfest.com

PLEASE VISIT
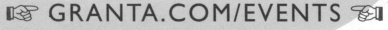
GRANTA.COM/EVENTS
FOR EVENT INFORMATION